高校专门用途英语（ESP）系列教材

BASIC ENGLISH for Economics and Finance
财经基础英语

主　编　周　茜　罗志高
副主编　陈丹杰　付　海
编　者　罗　敏　龙亚铉　静　张　轶
　　　　谢宗仙　董　茜　许杨阳　代　俊

清华大学出版社
北京

内 容 简 介

本教材是通识性财经英语教材，内容涵盖微观经济学、宏观经济学和金融学基础知识。教材旨在帮助学生熟悉并掌握与财经相关的词汇、术语、财经基本概念及基本原理的英文表达，为下一步学习财经专业英语打下基础；通过形式多样的练习帮助学生提升阅读、口语、翻译、写作等英语语言能力，学习如何用英语讲好中国财经故事。教材后附财经术语表，每个单元另有补充阅读材料，帮助学生理解和拓展财经知识。教材另配有练习参考答案、词汇表和PPT课件，读者可登录www.tsinghuaelt.com下载使用。

本教材可供普通本科院校财经类专业学生和对财经英语感兴趣的其他专业学生使用，也可供在工作中需使用财经英语的社会人士学习参考。

版权所有，侵权必究。举报：010-62782989，beiqinquan@tup.tsinghua.edu.cn。

图书在版编目（CIP）数据

财经基础英语/周茜，罗志高主编.—北京：清华大学出版社，2024.8
高校专门用途英语（ESP）系列教材
ISBN 978-7-302-66330-0

Ⅰ.①财… Ⅱ.①周…②罗… Ⅲ.①经济—英语—高等学校—教材 Ⅳ.①F

中国国家版本馆CIP数据核字（2024）第106460号

责任编辑：刘　艳
封面设计：平　原
责任校对：王荣静
责任印制：杨　艳

出版发行：清华大学出版社
　　　　网　　址：https://www.tup.com.cn，https://www.wqxuetang.com
　　　　地　　址：北京清华大学学研大厦A座　邮　编：100084
　　　　社 总 机：010-83470000　　　邮　购：010-62786544
　　　　投稿与读者服务：010-62776969，c-service@tup.tsinghua.edu.cn
　　　　质量反馈：010-62772015，zhiliang@tup.tsinghua.edu.cn
印 装 者：三河市龙大印装有限公司
经　　销：全国新华书店
开　　本：185mm×260mm　　印　张：16.5　　字　数：364千字
版　　次：2024年8月第1版　　　　　印　次：2024年8月第1次印刷
定　　价：72.00元

产品编号：104151-01

前言

进入新时代，我国坚定不移推进高水平对外开放，以此推动高质量发展。在此背景下，越来越多的国内企业参与到国际竞争及"一带一路"建设中。大量的跨国财经活动如国际贸易、跨国投资并购、外汇交易等需要具备"财经专业知识＋英语语言技能"的人才。

为支撑涉外财经人才培养，重庆工商大学外国语学院成立了财经英语教研团队，开设了财经英语相关课程。在教学实践中，老师们发现，学生特别需要熟悉并掌握与财经相关的词汇、术语、财经基本概念及基本原理的英文表达，为下一步学习财经专业英语打下基础。为满足教学需求，团队决定结合实践经验及学生反馈编写《财经基础英语》教材。

本教材的编写基于ESP（English for Specific Purposes）理论及CBI（Content-Based Instruction）理论。ESP是指与某个特定学科或职业相关的英语，如财经英语、商务英语、法律英语等。此类课程的教学旨在培养学生某个专业领域的英语运用能力。CBI理论强调将语言教学与某个学科内容的教学进行融合，在学生学习学科知识的同时促进其英语语言能力的提升。本教材围绕财经基础知识，通过课文学习及各种形式的练习，培养学生财经英语的运用能力。

本教材共14个单元，内容由两大板块组成。第一板块与经济学相关，包括中西方传统经济思想概述、需求与供给、消费与生产、市场竞争、要素市场、国民经济、经济增长与商业周期、宏观经济政策、国际经济等。第二板块与金融学相关，包括货币与利率、金融机构与金融市场、国际支付、金融风险、金融危机及金融监管等。

本教材具有如下特色：

通识性：教材内容涵盖经济学和金融学基础知识，旨在帮助学生熟悉并掌握与财经相关的词汇、术语、基本概念及基本原理的英文表达，为学习财经专业英语打下基础。

交叉性：本教材的编写体现经济学、金融学、语言学等学科的交叉。教材内容帮助学生了解财经学科基础知识；形式多样的习题有助于学生提升阅读、口语、翻译、写作等英语语言能力。

思政育人：教材通过翻译、项目等课后练习引导学生思考和了解中国社会经济发展的成就，练习用英语讲述中国财经故事，帮助学生树立民族自信心和自豪感。

为帮助学生进一步理解章节内容，编者为每个单元补充了阅读材料，学生可以通过扫码获得。本教材可供普通本科院校财经类专业学生和对财经英语感兴趣的其他专业学生使用，也可供在工作中需使用财经英语的社会人士学习参考。

本教材由重庆工商大学外国语学院财经英语教研团队编写，具体分工如下：第 1 单元由罗志高、周茜编写；第 2 单元由代俊编写；第 3 单元由罗敏编写；第 4、5 单元由陈丹杰编写；第 6 单元由周茜编写；第 7、10 单元由龙亚编写；第 8 单元由谢宗仙编写；第 9 单元由许杨阳（重庆邮电大学）编写；第 11 单元由张轶编写；第 12 单元由董茜编写；第 13、14 单元由铉静编写。付海［重庆市金融发展服务中心（重庆金融研究院）］负责全书专业知识的审定；Justin M. Thomas（中文名陶正，2015—2017 年作为美中友好志愿者在重庆工商大学教授英语）负责全书语言的审定。

本教材是重庆工商大学资助建设教材，也是重庆工商大学"讲好中国财经故事"系列英语教材之一。本教材的编写得到重庆工商大学经济学院、金融学院等学院专家的指导，重庆工商大学教务处及外国语学院的大力支持，在此致以诚挚感谢！由于编者水平有限，书中不当之处敬请广大读者批评指正。

编者
2024 年 7 月

Contents

Unit 1   What Is Economics?

    1.1 An Overview of Economics 2
        1.1.1 Branches of Economics 2
        1.1.2 Core Principles of Economics 4
        1.1.3 Types of Economic Systems 5
    1.2 An Overview of Microeconomics 6
        1.2.1 Key Concepts of Microeconomics 6
        1.2.2 Core Theories of Microeconomics 7
    1.3 An Overview of Macroeconomics 9
        1.3.1 Key Concepts of Macroeconomics 9
        1.3.2 Core Theories of Macroeconomics 10
    1.4 Positive Economics vs Normative Economics 11
        1.4.1 Positive Economics 11
        1.4.2 Normative Economics 12

Unit 2   An Overview of Traditional Economic Thought in the West and China

    2.1 An Overview of Traditional Economic Thought in the West 18
        2.1.1 Economic Thought in Ancient Greece and Rome 18
        2.1.2 Economic Thought in the Middle Ages 19
    2.2 An Overview of Traditional Economic Thought in China 22

2.2.1　Economic Thought Before the 6th Century 22

2.2.2　Economic Thought from the 7th to the 14th Century 24

Unit 3　Demand and Supply

3.1　The Law of Demand and Supply 30

    3.1.1　Definition of Demand 30

    3.1.2　Demand Curve 31

    3.1.3　Definition of Supply 34

    3.1.4　Supply Curve 35

3.2　Market Equilibrium 38

    3.2.1　Equilibrium and Equilibrium Price 38

    3.2.2　Change of Equilibrium 40

3.3　Elasticity of Demand and Supply 41

    3.3.1　The Elasticity of Demand 41

    3.3.2　The Elasticity of Supply 43

Unit 4　Consumption and Production

4.1　Utility and Consumer Surplus 48

    4.1.1　Total Utility and Marginal Utility 48

    4.1.2　Consumer Surplus 49

4.2　Consumer Behavior Theories 51

    4.2.1　Consumer Equilibrium 51

    4.2.2　Income Effect and Substitution Effect 53

4.3　Cost, Revenue and Profit 54

    4.3.1　Cost and Producer Surplus 54

    4.3.2　Revenue and Profit 57

4.4　Producers and Production Theory 58

    4.4.1　Producers and Production Functions 58

4.4.2 Productivity and Marginal Effects 59

Unit 5   Market Competition

5.1 Market and Market Structure 66

5.2 Competition and Monopoly 67

    5.2.1 Perfectly Competitive Market 67

    5.2.2 Monopolistic Market 71

5.3 Uncertainty and Game Theory 74

    5.3.1 Uncertainty and Its Impact on the Market 74

    5.3.2 Game Theory and the Prisoner's Dilemma 75

5.4 Market Failures and Public Goods 77

    5.4.1 Pareto Efficiency and Market Failures 77

    5.4.2 Externalities and Public Goods 78

Unit 6   Factor Market

6.1 Factor Market 86

    6.1.1 Factors of Production and Factor Market 86

    6.1.2 Perfectly Competitive and Imperfectly Competitive Factor Markets 88

6.2 Labor Market 89

    6.2.1 Demand and Supply of Labor 89

    6.2.2 The Price of Labor 92

6.3 Capital Market 94

    6.3.1 Demand and Supply of Capital 94

    6.3.2 The Price of Capital 95

6.4 Land Market 96

    6.4.1 Features of Land 96

    6.4.2 The Price of Land 97

Unit 7   National Economy

- 7.1 GDP and GNP 102
  - 7.1.1 Definitions of GDP and GNP 102
  - 7.1.2 Calculations of GDP and GNP 103
- 7.2 National Income 104
  - 7.2.1 Calculation of National Income 105
  - 7.2.2 Distribution of National Income 105
  - 7.2.3 Significance of National Income 106
- 7.3 Aggregate Demand and Aggregate Supply 107
  - 7.3.1 Aggregate Demand 107
  - 7.3.2 Aggregate Supply 109
  - 7.3.3 The Aggregate Demand-Aggregate Supply Model 111

Unit 8   Economic Growth and the Business Cycle

- 8.1 Inflation 118
  - 8.1.1 Inflation and Its Causes 118
  - 8.1.2 Impacts of Inflation 120
- 8.2 Unemployment 121
  - 8.2.1 Unemployment and Its Classification 121
  - 8.2.2 Impacts of Unemployment 122
- 8.3 Economic Growth 123
  - 8.3.1 Significance of Economic Growth 123
  - 8.3.2 Modern Economic Growth Theories 124
- 8.4 The Business Cycle 126
  - 8.4.1 The Business Cycle and Its Stages 126
  - 8.4.2 Causes of the Business Cycle 128

Unit 9 Macroeconomic Policy

- 9.1 The Role of Government in the Economy 134
  - 9.1.1 Market Regulation 134
  - 9.1.2 Provision of Public Goods and Services 135
  - 9.1.3 Economic Stabilization Through Macroeconomic Policies 137
- 9.2 Monetary Policy 138
  - 9.2.1 Monetary Policy and Its Functions 138
  - 9.2.2 Classification of Monetary Policy and Its Tools 139
  - 9.2.3 Challenges of Monetary Policy 141
- 9.3 Fiscal Policy 142
  - 9.3.1 Fiscal Policy and Its Functions 143
  - 9.3.2 Classification of Fiscal Policy and Its Tools 144
  - 9.3.3 Challenges of Fiscal Policy 145

Unit 10 International Economy

- 10.1 Absolute Advantage and Comparative Advantage 152
  - 10.1.1 Absolute Advantage 152
  - 10.1.2 Comparative Advantage 153
  - 10.1.3 Comparative Advantage and International Trade 154
- 10.2 International Economy and Globalization 155
  - 10.2.1 Economic Interdependence 155
  - 10.2.2 Evolution of Globalization 156
- 10.3 Tariffs 158
  - 10.3.1 Definition of Tariff 158
  - 10.3.2 The Economic Effects of Tariffs 159
  - 10.3.3 The Welfare Effects of Tariffs 160

Unit 11　Money and Interest Rates 165

11.1　Money 166
- 11.1.1　Definition of Money 166
- 11.1.2　Origins of Money 167
- 11.1.3　Function and Nature of Money 168
- 11.1.4　The Monetary System 170

11.2　Interest Rates 171
- 11.2.1　Definition of Interest Rates 171
- 11.2.2　Types of Interest Rates and Influential Factors 172

Unit 12　Financial Institutions and Financial Markets

12.1　Financial Institutions 180
- 12.1.1　Banking Institutions 180
- 12.1.2　Non-banking Financial Institutions 184

12.2　Financial Markets 186
- 12.2.1　Money Markets and Capital Markets 186
- 12.2.2　Primary Markets and Secondary Markets 187

Unit 13　International Payments

13.1　Foreign Exchange and Exchange Rate 194
- 13.1.1　Foreign Exchange 194
- 13.1.2　Exchange Rate 195

13.2　International Balance of Payments 199
- 13.2.1　Definition of International Balance of Payments 199
- 13.2.2　Imbalance of International Payments 200
- 13.2.3　Adjustment of the Imbalance of Payments 202

Unit 14 Financial Risk, Crisis, and Supervision 207

14.1 Financial Risk 208
14.1.1 Overview of Financial Risk 208
14.1.2 Management of Financial Risk 210

14.2 Financial Crisis 211
14.2.1 Overview of Financial Crisis 211
14.2.2 Impacts of Financial Crisis 213

14.3 Financial Supervision 215
14.3.1 Definition of Financial Supervision 215
14.3.2 Financial Regulation System 216

References 221
Glossary 225
Terms 241

Unit 1

What Is Economics?

Learning Objectives

After studying this unit, you should be able to:

1) have a general understanding of the subject of economics;
2) use the words and phrases in this unit;
3) illustrate the achievements of economic development since China's Reform and Opening-Up.

Economics, often referred to as the "**dismal**❶ science❷", is anything but dismal. It is a fascinating field of study that helps us understand how individuals, businesses, and societies make decisions on how to **allocate** resources to satisfy their wants and needs. Economics provides a framework for analyzing and understanding a wide range of issues, from personal finance to global trade, and examining the complexities of the production, distribution, and consumption of goods and services, as well as the factors influencing these processes. In other words, it involves issues of what to produce, how to produce, and for whom to produce. Economics analyzes the costs and benefits of different **alternatives** and how they affect human well-being. In this unit, we will explore the fundamental concepts, theories, and applications of economics, shedding light on its relevance and significance in our everyday lives.

1.1 An Overview of Economics

Economics has a long and varied history, with its roots arguably going back to ancient times. Early civilizations had to manage resources and trade, forming very basic economic systems. However, economics, as we know it today, began to emerge in the late 18th century. The **publication** of Adam Smith's❸ *An Inquiry into the Nature and Causes of the Wealth of Nations* in 1776 is often considered the starting point of modern economics. In the following centuries, other notable economists made significant contributions by addressing various economic aspects.

1.1.1 Branches of Economics

Economics can be broadly categorized into two main branches: microeconomics and macroeconomics.

Microeconomics studies the individual economic **agents**, such as consumers, producers, and single markets, by analyzing their behavior, decision-making processes, and interactions within specific markets. Key topics in microeconomics include supply and demand, consumer choice theory, production theory, and market structure (perfect competition, monopolies, etc.).

Macroeconomics, on the other hand, looks at the economy as a whole,

---

❶ 全书加粗的表示生词，在全书最后的 Glossary 中列出；灰底的为术语，在全书最后的 Terms 中列出。

❷ dismal science: a derogatory term coined by Scottish essayist, historian, and philosopher Thomas Carlyle to indicate that economics is a dreary, abject, and distressing discipline.

❸ Adam Smith (1723–1790): Scottish social philosopher and political economist.

focusing on **aggregate** measures such as national income, unemployment, inflation, and economic growth. It explores the interrelationships between various **sectors** such as households, businesses, and the government. Macroeconomic theories include Keynesian economics, monetarism[1], the neoclassical synthesis[2], and others.

There exists a large number of sub-disciplines in economics, such as development economics, international economics, monetary economics, environmental economics, etc. Each of these sub-disciplines applies economic principles or tools from microeconomics or macroeconomics to explain and deal with specific problems in their respective fields. Just to mention some of them:

Development economics: It examines the economic aspects of the development process in low-income countries. It looks at poverty, inequality, foreign aid, and strategies for sustainable development.

International economics: This sub-discipline focuses on economic interactions between countries, including trade, investment, and currency exchange. It analyzes the benefits of trade, exchange rates, balance of payments, and the impact of globalization on economic growth and development.

Monetary economics: It concerns the study of the functions and management of a country's money supply, interest rates, and credit conditions by a central bank to regulate inflation, stabilize the economy, and support economic growth. Central banks use tools such as open market operations, reserve requirements[3], and interest rate rediscounts to achieve their objectives.

Environmental economics: It is concerned with environmental issues, focusing on the economic effects of environmental policies and the impact of the economy on the environment. It seeks to understand how economic policies and market **mechanisms** can be employed to address environmental challenges such as pollution, climate change, and resource **depletion**.

Econometrics: This sub-discipline uses statistical and mathematical tools to test **hypotheses** and estimate the relationships between economic **variables**. It often serves as a basis for economic forecasting.

---

[1] monetarism: a school of economic thought which maintains that the money supply is the chief determinant on the demand side of short-run economic activity.

[2] neoclassical synthesis (also referred to as the neo-Keynesian theory): an economic theory which suggests that markets aren't self-regulating and can be below full employment for a considerable time.

[3] reserve requirements: the amount of funds that a bank holds in reserve to ensure that it can meet liabilities in case of sudden withdrawals.

Economics also **intersects** with other disciplines such as political science, psychology, sociology, and history, giving rise to interdisciplinary fields such as political economics, historical economics, and socioeconomics. Each offers a unique perspective and analytical **toolkit** for understanding various economic issues and phenomena.

1.1.2 Core Principles of Economics

In a world with limited resources but unlimited desires and needs, we are always faced with the question: How do we make decisions that will **optimize** our well-being? Economics provides, but is not limited to, the following core principles to answer the question above.

Principle 1. The foundation of economics lies in the concept of scarcity. Resources such as labor, land, capital, and time are limited in supply, while human desires are infinite. As a result, individuals and societies face the everlasting challenge of choosing how to best utilize their scarce resources to satisfy their needs and wants. For instance, in a drought-stricken area where water is drastically in short supply and cannot meet the needs of all residents, agriculture, and businesses, the community has to make tough choices: Do they **prioritize** drinking water, maintain crops, or support industries?

Principle 2. The benefits an individual could have received by taking an alternative action are the opportunity costs of the action he/she did take. In other words, by allocating resources to one particular use, individuals or firms must give up the next best alternative. If a person decides to go to a postgraduate program instead of working, his/her opportunity cost is the money he/she would have earned if he/she worked instead of taking a further education. Understanding opportunity cost helps evaluate the efficiency and effectiveness of decision-making.

Principle 3. People respond to **incentives**, and changes in incentives can influence people's behavior. For instance, offering tax incentives for **solar panel** installations may encourage homeowners to invest in renewable energy, reducing their reliance on fossil fuels.

Principle 4. Competitive markets tend to allocate resources efficiently, leading to lower prices and better products. As Adam Smith put it, firms and households' **interplay** in markets acts as if they are controlled by an "invisible hand" that guides them to desirable market outcomes. For instance, the smartphone market is highly competitive, leading to innovation, lower prices, and a wide range of choices for consumers.

Principle 5. Trade allows individuals and nations to specialize in producing what they are most efficient at and exchange goods and services, leading to mutual benefit. International trade allows countries to export products they can produce efficiently and import those they cannot, enhancing overall economic welfare. For example, Country A has a highly efficient **pharmaceutical** industry with advanced technology and skilled scientists, whereas Country B has a well-developed agricultural sector with a **surplus** of raw materials used in drug production. In exchange, Country A exports pharmaceutical products to Country B, which benefits the latter by improving healthcare. Country A's pharmaceutical industry grows, creating jobs and generating revenue, while Country B's agricultural sector flourishes, leading to economic growth as it exports raw materials and receives pharmaceuticals.

Principle 6. Households and firms make the best decisions through **marginal** analysis. Marginal analysis refers to the process of analyzing the additional benefits and costs of an action. It is used to determine whether the benefits of an action **outweigh** the costs and whether the action should be taken. For example, if a firm considers producing an additional unit of a product, it will use marginal analysis to determine whether the additional revenue generated by selling the unit will be greater than the additional cost of producing it.

Principle 7. Governments can influence economic outcomes through policies such as taxation, regulation, and **fiscal** stimuli. For example, during an economic **recession**, the government decides to increase its spending on various projects and programs. This could include investing in infrastructure projects like building roads and bridges, as well as funding education, healthcare, and research initiatives. Increased government spending injects money into the economy.

In summary, these principles are fundamental building blocks for understanding how individuals, businesses, and societies make decisions in the face of limited resources. The interplay between these principles influences economic outcomes and shapes policy recommendations.

1.1.3 Types of Economic Systems

Economic systems are the ways that societies organize the production, distribution, and consumption of goods and services. There are three main types of economic systems: the market economy, command economy, and mixed economy.

The essence of a market economy is that its resource allocation is determined by the market. In this market, prices and quantities of goods or factors of production are jointly determined by the forces of supply and demand, rather than excessive intervention by government administrative powers. The market economy is not confined to a single model; instead, it is intricately linked to the history, culture, and current national conditions of each country, therefore, different nations have developed distinct market economy systems. Currently, the majority of countries worldwide adopt some form of a market economy. Among them, developed countries such as the United States, Germany, France, and Japan, have relatively mature market economy models. China is actively developing towards a high-level socialist market economy system.

A command economy, also known as a planned or centrally planned economy, is based on public **ownership** of resources and centralized planning. In a command economy, prices are set by the government or a central authority, which also decides what, how, and for whom to produce. Command economies aim to achieve specific economic and social objectives. Historically, the Soviet Union and some Eastern European countries had this system.

A mixed economy differs from a mixed ownership economy in that it is not centered on a state or private ownership of resources but on **delineating** the boundaries between the market and the government. It combines the "invisible hand" of the market with the "visible hand" of the government, **leveraging** the market to **stimulate** economic **vitality** and optimize resource allocation, while the government **intervenes** to address market failures in public goods provision. Most countries have mixed economies, with varying degrees of market freedom and government intervention.

1.2 An Overview of Microeconomics

1.2.1 Key Concepts of Microeconomics

Microeconomics derives its name from the Greek **prefix** "micro-", meaning "small". As the name suggests, microeconomics studies the behavior of individual units within the economy. This could include understanding how a consumer makes decisions about what to buy within a limited budget, or how a firm decides the price and quantity of goods to produce given production **constraints**. The following are some key concepts in microeconomics.

Maximization: Maximization refers to the process in which individuals or firms make choices to achieve their goals or objectives while facing constraints. In microeconomics, there are two common types of maximization: profit maximization for firms, and utility maximization for consumers. A firm aims to maximize its profit, which is the difference between the total revenue and total cost. For example, a small bakery may decide how many pastries to produce each day to maximize its daily profit by considering factors like ingredient costs, labor costs, and the selling price of pastries. In the case of utility maximization, consumers aim to maximize their utility, which represents their satisfaction or well-being from consuming goods and services. Consider a consumer deciding how much of their income to spend on various goods, like food and clothing, to maximize their overall satisfaction.

Equilibrium: Equilibrium is a state in which there is no tendency for change because supply equals demand. In microeconomics, two types of equilibrium are commonly discussed: market equilibrium and firm equilibrium. In a competitive market, the equilibrium price and quantity occur where the supply and demand curves intersect. For example, in the market for smartphones, the equilibrium price and quantity are determined by the point at which consumers are willing to buy the same quantity that producers are willing to supply. For a firm, equilibrium occurs when it produces the quantity at which its marginal cost (the cost of producing one more unit) equals its marginal revenue (the additional revenue from selling one more unit). This ensures that the firm maximizes its profits.

Efficiency: Efficiency in microeconomics refers to the allocation of resources that maximizes overall well-being or benefits. There are two types of efficiency: allocative efficiency and productive efficiency. The former occurs when resources are allocated in a manner that maximizes the total consumer and producer surplus. In a perfectly competitive market, allocative efficiency is achieved because prices reflect the true value consumers place on goods and the true cost of production for firms. Productive efficiency occurs when goods are produced at their lowest possible cost. For instance, an automobile manufacturer achieves productive efficiency by minimizing the cost per car produced through efficient production techniques.

1.2.2 Core Theories of Microeconomics

In microeconomics, the following core theories reveal the operation of the world from a particular perspective:

Consumer choice theory: This theory explains how consumers make decisions to allocate their resources (income) among various goods and services to maximize their utility. The concepts of indifference curves and budget constraints are central to this theory.

Theory of production: This examines how firms **convert** inputs (such as labor and capital) into outputs. It involves concepts such as the production function❶, marginal product, and returns to scale.

Cost theory: It focuses on understanding how firms **incur** production costs and how these costs influence production levels. It introduces notions such as average cost, marginal cost, and economies of scale❷.

Theory of market structure: Market structure refers to the characteristics of a market that affect the behavior and performance of firms in that market. Different types of market structures exist, such as perfect competition, monopoly, monopolistic competition, and oligopoly. The market structure affects the price, output, profit, efficiency, and innovation of firms in a market.

Theory of market failure: Markets sometimes fail to produce efficient outcomes. The reasons can be externalities (when the actions of one party affect another), public goods (non-**excludable** and non-rival goods), and information asymmetry.

Microeconomics, far from purely theoretical, has many real-world applications. Firms use microeconomic principles to make crucial decisions about pricing, production levels, and capital investment; governments employ microeconomics when considering policies such as minimum wage, taxes, and **subsidies**; and by understanding how individuals make health-related decisions, policymakers and healthcare providers can **devise** effective strategies and policies. Thus, microeconomics provides invaluable insights into the **intricate** mechanisms driving individual decision-making processes within a larger economic framework. With deeper exploration into this discipline, people can find that seemingly abstract concepts often find very **tangible** manifestations in the world, making microeconomics not just a subject of academic interest but also a tool to interpret and shape economic realities.

---

❶ production function: an equation that expresses the relationship between the quantities of productive factors (such as labor and capital) used and the number of products obtained.

❷ economies of scale: the relationship between the size of a plant or factory and the lowest possible cost of a product. When a plant or factory increases output, a reduction in the average cost of a product is usually obtained.

1.3 An Overview of Macroeconomics

1.3.1 Key Concepts of Macroeconomics

Macroeconomics is the **counterpart** to microeconomics. Derived from the Greek prefix "macro-", meaning "large", macroeconomics investigates the behavior, decision-making, and performance of an economy as a whole.

Macroeconomics holds the following key concepts:

Gross domestic product (GDP): As one of the most critical indicators of macroeconomics, GDP represents the total value of all the goods and services produced in a country over a specific period. It is used to assess a nation's economic health and performance.

Inflation: It refers to a rise in price, leading to a decrease in the purchasing power of money. Moderate inflation is considered normal and healthy for an economy; however, high or hyperinflation can **erode** purchasing power and create economic instability.

Unemployment: As a key **metric** for any economy, this **denotes** the percentage of the labor force that is jobless but actively seeks employment. High levels of unemployment can lead to economic inefficiency and social problems.

Business cycle: The business cycle is the periodic fluctuation of economic activity around a long-term trend. The business cycle consists of four phases: expansion, peak, **contraction**, and **trough**, which refer to the different periods of economic activity in a cycle.

Fiscal policy: Fiscal policy relates to taxation and spending utilized by the government to influence macroeconomic conditions. It aims to achieve macroeconomic objectives such as economic growth, employment, and price stability.

Monetary policy: It refers to actions undertaken by a nation's central bank to control the supply of money, primarily through interest rates, to achieve macroeconomic objectives such as economic growth, employment, and price stability.

Aggregate demand and aggregate supply: Macroeconomists study the relationship between aggregate demand (total demand for goods and services in an economy) and aggregate supply (total production of goods and services in an economy). The equilibrium between these two factors determines the overall economic activity level.

Balance of payments: This refers to a record of all **transactions** between residents of a country and the rest of the world, showing how much a country is earning from its exports versus spending on its imports.

Economic growth: Economic growth indicates an increase in a country's real GDP over time. Sustained economic growth is essential for raising the standard of living and improving a nation's overall well-being.

1.3.2　Core Theories of Macroeconomics

Macroeconomics encompasses the following core theories:

Classical theory: Rooted in the idea of a self-regulating economy where markets automatically adjust to achieve equilibrium. It assumes that in the long run, the economy will naturally reach full employment without government intervention.

Keynesian economics: Proposed by John Maynard Keynes[1], this theory suggests that in the face of economic **downturns**, active government intervention can stabilize the economy. It emphasizes the importance of aggregate demand in driving economic activities.

Monetarism: Advocated by Milton Friedman[2], it emphasizes the importance of controlling the money supply to combat inflation. Monetarists believe that inflation is primarily a result of excessive growth in the money supply.

Supply-side economics: This theory **posits** that by reducing barriers to production (such as taxes and regulations), producers can produce more, leading to greater economic growth.

Macroeconomics has many applications in real-world **scenarios**. Governments and policymakers employ macroeconomic principles to design both short- and long-term economic policies; macroeconomics helps nations find the right way in the complex world of international trade, exchange rates, and global finance; businesses and governments alike use macroeconomic models and indicators to **anticipate** future economic conditions; in the case of economic crises, macroeconomic tools and theories will play a **pivotal** role in devising responses to major economic downturns.

---

[1] John Maynard Keynes (1883–1946): British economist, best known as founder of Keynesian economics and the father of modern macroeconomics.

[2] Milton Friedman (1912–2006): American economist and educator, one of the leading supporters of monetarism in the second half of the 20th century. He was awarded the Nobel Prize for Economics in 1976.

Macroeconomics offers a **panoramic** view of the economic landscape, striving to understand the broad forces that influence the collective prosperity and well-being of a nation. By understanding the **dynamics** of aggregate demand and supply, the intricate dance between inflation and unemployment, and the delicate balance of international trade, we gain a **holistic** comprehension of the economic forces that shape our world.

1.4 Positive Economics vs Normative Economics

In the study of economics, we need to understand two **paradigms** of research—positive economics and normative economics. The two answer different types of questions and play distinct roles in the analysis and **formulation** of economic policies.

1.4.1 Positive Economics

Positive economics, often referred to as "what is" economics, deals with objective explanations and the analysis of cause-and-effect relationships. It is based on facts and evidence and focuses on describing economic behaviors and explaining economic phenomena without offering judgments about whether the outcomes are desirable or not. Positive economics uses scientific methods such as observation, measurement, experimentation, and mathematical modeling to test hypotheses and theories. Essentially, positive economics seeks to describe and predict economic events using factual statements that can be tested and **validated** through **empirical** observations.

Thus, some key characteristics of positive economics can be summarized as follows:

Empirical: Statements in positive economics are based on real-world data and empirical evidence. They can be tested and **verified**.

Objective: Positive economics **refrains** from expressing value judgments. It strictly presents facts, relationships, and causation.

Descriptive and predictive: Positive economics describes how economic agents behave and predicts how they will respond under different circumstances.

Foundation for analysis: Positive economics provides the groundwork upon which economic theories and models are built.

Therefore, positive economics is applied to **justify** the following statements:

"An increase in the price of gasoline will reduce the quantity demanded." This statement can be tested by analyzing data on gasoline prices and consumption.

"A 10% increase in the minimum wage in City A led to a 2% decrease in employment among teenagers." This can be verified by examining the employment data before and after the wage hike.

"Higher interest rates reduce investment." We can study the correlation between interest rates and investment levels to validate this statement.

1.4.2 Normative Economics

Normative economics, on the other hand, deals with "what ought to be" in economic matters. It introduces subjective judgments, opinions, and value-based prescriptions regarding economic policies and outcomes. Instead of merely explaining phenomena, normative economics uses **ethical** principles, moral values, social preferences, and political ideologies to evaluate and recommend economic actions, suggesting how things should be rather than merely describing how they are.

Accordingly, normative economics has the following features:

It deals with subjective judgments. Normative statements often depend on personal beliefs, ethics, or values. They are rooted in opinions on what is right, fair, or desirable.

It is **prescriptive**. Instead of merely describing, normative economics often suggests a course of action or recommends policies.

It is not empirically testable. Normative statements cannot be proven or disproven solely through data or experimentation. They rely on ethical, moral, or subjective foundations.

It influences policy decisions. Though they are not based on empirical facts, normative views can significantly shape public policies and debates.

Thus, normative economics can help us understand the following statements:

"The government should increase taxes on the rich to redistribute wealth and reduce income inequality." This statement suggests a course of action based on value judgments about income distribution.

"Minimum wage should be raised so that all workers can have a living wage." This prescription is based on beliefs about fairness and the role of wages in society.

"Environmental **degradation** is a greater concern than economic growth, and hence policies should prioritize conservation over industrialization." This statement is grounded in specific values regarding environmental and economic growth.

The distinction between positive economics and normative economics is both fundamental and pivotal. In any **robust** economic analysis, it is essential to differentiate between what is empirically true and what is a matter of opinion or belief. By understanding the interplay between positive and normative economics, we can critically evaluate economic statements, proposals, and policies, and understand factual bases and underlying value judgments.

Exercises

❶ Short answer questions

Directions: *Answer the following questions in your own words or with sentences from the text.*

(1) What are the differences between microeconomics and macroeconomics?

(2) Can you list some core principles of economics?

(3) What is an economic system? Can you name the three main systems?

(4) What are the differences between positive economics and normative economics?

❷ Term explanation

Directions: *Explain the following terms in your own words or with sentences from the text.*

(1) international economics

(2) opportunity cost

(3) marginal analysis

(4) supply-side economics

财经基础英语
Basic English for Economics and Finance

❸ Banked cloze

Directions: *Fill in the blanks by selecting suitable words from the following box. You may not use any of the words more than once.*

A. applications	B. when	C. terms	D. subjective	E. economy
F. empirical	G. aggregate	H. what	I. individual	J. addition
K. issues	L. allocation	M. complex	N. scarcity	O. sub-disciplines

Economics is a charming field that studies resources (1) _____ to fulfill wants and needs. It analyzes production, distribution, consumption, and factors influencing them. Economics explores the issues of (2) _____, how, and for whom to produce, offering valuable insights into decision-making and human well-being.

Economics can be categorized into two main branches: microeconomics and macroeconomics. Microeconomics delves into (3) _____ decisions and market interactions. Elasticity measures responsiveness, whereas surplus quantifies the benefits for consumers and producers. Utility judges satisfaction and production costs influence firms. Market structures and game theory analyze strategic interactions. The theories of consumer choice, production, cost, and market structure are vital in microeconomics. It has real-world (4) _____, guiding business decisions, policy-making, and addressing challenges such as pollution.

Macroeconomics studies (5) _____ economy, involving GDP, inflation, unemployment, and business cycles. Fiscal and monetary policies influence outcomes, whereas supply and demand balances drive economic activity. Macroeconomic theories include classical, Keynesian, and supply-side theories.

Overall, microeconomics focuses on individual agents such as consumers and firms, and macroeconomics looks at the (6) _____ as a whole. In addition to these two, economics has other (7) _____ such as development economics, international economics, and environmental economics.

In the world of economics, normative economics and positive economics are two other important branches in (8) _____ of the content and analysis methods. Normative economics evaluates "what ought to be" by introducing value judgments and policy prescriptions. Positive economics focuses on (9) _____ explanations and cause-and-effect relationships.

Understanding these branches enables informed participation in economic discussions and decision-making, offering insights into the (10) _____ forces shaping our world.

4 Translation

Directions: *Translate the following paragraphs into Chinese or English.*

(1) Economics, often referred to as the "dismal science", is anything but dismal. It is a fascinating field of study that helps us understand how individuals, businesses, and societies make decisions on how to allocate resources to satisfy their wants and needs. Economics provides a framework for analyzing and understanding a wide range of issues, from personal finance to global trade, and examining the complexities of the production, distribution, and consumption of goods and services, as well as the factors influencing these processes. In other words, it involves issues of what to produce, how to produce, and for whom to produce.

(2) 改革开放以来，中国共产党将马克思主义政治经济学基本原理同改革开放实践相结合，形成了当代中国马克思主义政治经济学的许多重要理论成果，比如，关于社会主义本质的理论，关于社会主义初级阶段基本经济制度的理论等。这些理论成果，有力地指导了我国经济发展实践，开拓了马克思主义政治经济学新境界（a new realm）。

5 Project

Title: Introducing China's Economic Achievements Since the Reform and Opening-Up

Instructions: Initiated in 1978, China's Reform and Opening-Up transformed the country into an emerging economic powerhouse. Make some exploration and introduce economic achievements according to the following steps:

Step 1: Provide a brief history of China's Reform and Opening-Up, emphasizing the key milestones and the period it covers (the late 1970s onwards).

Step 2: Introduce essential macroeconomic indicators such as GDP growth, inflation, and unemployment. Present data illustrating China's economic performance over the years.

Step 3: Present your findings to the class.

Supplementary Reading

Scan the QR code to find out more about the unit.

Unit 2

An Overview of Traditional Economic Thought in the West and China

Learning Objectives

After studying this unit, you should be able to:

1) understand the traditional economic thought that emerged in different periods in the West and China;
2) use the words and phrases in this unit;
3) apply what you have learned from this unit to the discussion of the evolution process of traditional Chinese economic thought.

The economic thought of different eras reflects **socioeconomic** activities and **hinges on** the socioeconomic conditions of the given time. The vitality of various economic systems of thought or theories depends on whether they **cater to** the need for those activities. Once socioeconomic conditions change, so do the systems of thought or theories. In other words, economic thought would, adjusting itself to the **alteration** of socioeconomic conditions, bring the new from the old or establish the new and **eradicate** the old. This unit focuses on traditional Western economic thought in the period of ancient Rome, Greece, and the Middle Ages, and the important economic thought in ancient China from the Zhou Dynasty to the Yuan Dynasty.

2.1 An Overview of Traditional Economic Thought in the West

2.1.1 Economic Thought in Ancient Greece and Rome

The origins of Western economic thought can be traced back to the ancient civilizations of Greece and Rome, where thinkers and philosophers had already **contemplated** and explored various economic ideas and theories.

"Economics" first got its name from *Oeconomicus*（《家政论》）, a book discussing effective management and leadership by Xenophon (427 B.C.–355 B.C.), an **ideologist** in ancient Greece. Ideologists in ancient Greece, like Xenophon, often adopted the reasoning method in social sciences to discuss economic issues. In their eyes, the products did not share a unified form and were not exchanged in an organized manner. Therefore, they never had the idea of analyzing product exchanges concerning market regulation mechanisms. The interest of those ideologists centered on the effectiveness of the economy and the organization. Furthermore, they insisted on individual-centeredness rather than commercial-centeredness, and they prioritized the self-adjustment of individuals and emphasized the maximization of personal happiness through rational decision-making. Yet, they failed to discover the self-adjusting market.

One of the most notable figures in ancient Greece is Aristotle (384 B.C.–322 B.C.). In his work *Politics*, Aristotle discussed economic concepts within the context of his broader exploration of political systems. He emphasized the importance of natural wealth, such as land and its resources, and discussed issues such as the division of labor, exchange, and the role of money.

Aristotle's examination of the concept of "chrematistics" is an important aspect of his economic thought. Chrematistics refers to the **pursuit** of wealth. It **disregards** human needs and aims to accumulate money through speculation and **manipulation**. Unlike economics, which considers a broader perspective, chrematistics prioritizes monetary accumulation and personal benefits, while neglecting ethical and human welfare.

In Aristotle's view, economic activities should be guided by a broader ethical framework. He argued that wealth should serve as a means of promoting the well-being of individuals and the community as a whole. Aristotle highlighted the importance of distributive justice, advocating a fair distribution of resources and wealth among members of society. He believed that economic transactions should be conducted with honesty, **integrity**, and respect for the common good.

Roman statesman and philosopher Cicero (106 B.C.–43 B.C.) discussed economic concepts such as just prices and the morality of commerce. He explored the notion of "just prices", arguing that transactions should be conducted at fair and reasonable prices. He believed that both parties in a trade should benefit and transactions should be based on mutual **consent** and equity.

The influence of ancient Greek and Roman economic thought continued to **resonate** throughout history. It was during the Renaissance and the Enlightenment periods❶ that scholars and philosophers started to revisit and expand upon these ancient ideas. They sought to develop more robust economic theories and explore the relationships between economic activities, social structures, and political systems.

Overall, the ancient civilizations of Greece and Rome played a crucial role in shaping early economic ideas that would eventually form the basis of Western economic thought. The works of philosophers such as Aristotle and Cicero provided valuable insights into concepts such as wealth, exchange, justice, and ethics, laying the groundwork for the development of more elaborate economic theories in the centuries to come.

2.1.2 Economic Thought in the Middle Ages

From the 5th century to the 15th century, Western Europe saw the emergence, growth, and flourishing of **feudalism**, a time historically referred to as the

---

❶ The Renaissance, spanning the 14th to 17th centuries in Europe, marked a revival of art, science, and classical learning, while the Enlightenment of the 17th and 18th centuries was an intellectual movement that emphasized reasoning, individualism, and skepticism of traditional authority.

Middle Ages. Feudalism is a **regime** of production and distribution in which there is no **absolute** land ownership, and land ownership is never separated by obligations. The emperor was in charge of all the legal **property rights**, and he granted large areas of land to his favored **courtiers** and nobles, who later transferred the land to tenants of various kinds. The "ownership" in terms of production only referred to the right to use (profit **entitlement**).

The European Middle Ages lacked the social, economic, or political integration necessary for a powerful centralized regime. Every feudal lord was granted numerous government powers, which were valid in the domain of their lands. Production was also carried out in **manors** and farmlands. Moreover, the output was from small-scale production, utilizing rather **primitive** agricultural techniques. The majority of the workforce in agricultural production were peasants. Although both peasants and slaves were confined to a given land, they differed from each other in that the peasants were free men who did not have a personal bond with the landowner (manor owner). The aim of manor production was self-sufficiency. At that time, trade between regions and states was severely restricted.

There are two important factors distinguishing the Middle Ages from ancient Greece and Rome: The first is the uniformity of ideas and theories provided by the Roman Catholic Church, and the other is the spread of the market mechanism. The feudal society of Western Europe in the Middle Ages unconsciously bred the primary form of capitalism, which resulted from the increasing integration of the market (the product and production factor markets) into the daily **fabric** of people's economic lives.

The prominent figures among the economic ideologists in the Middle Ages include Albert the Great[1] (1206 A.D.–1280 A.D.), Thomas Aquinas[2] (1225 A.D.–1274 A.D.), Gerald Odonis[3] (1290 A.D.–1349 A.D.), etc.

---

[1] Albert the Great: medieval German Catholic theologian, philosopher, and natural scientist. He is also known by his Latin name, Albertus Magnus. He was widely recognized as an important thinker and scholar of his time and had a profound impact on the philosophy, theology, and science of the Middle Ages.

[2] Thomas Aquinas: also known as Saint Thomas Aquinas, prominent Italian Dominican friar, Catholic priest, and Doctor of the Church. He is considered one of the most influential theologians and philosophers in the history of the Catholic Church.

[3] Gerald Odonis: a prominent medieval philosopher and theologian. Odonis was a Franciscan friar and a leading figure in the Scholastic tradition of the Middle Ages.

Unit 2 An Overview of Traditional Economic Thought in the West and China

A common feature shared by the aforementioned ideologists is that they all adhered to the value theory proposed by Aristotle. Aristotle shed light on his **reciprocity** model in the 5th chapter of *Nicomachean Ethics*, which then became the very beginning of their economics. As enthusiastic **proponents** of the social moral principles of the Middle Ages, theologians' main concern was fairness, not exchange; fair exchange was merely a manifestation of fairness. In the process of accepting Aristotle's analysis of fair exchange, they also combined the concept of equilibrium with his original notion of value. They also conducted two unrelated economic **ratiocinations**: value determined by cost, and value determined by demand.

Albert Magnus was the first Latin scholar of Aristotelianism. His contributions to economics were mainly reflected in his **commentary** on the *Nicomachean Ethics* by Aristotle. In the commentary, he remodeled the economic thought of the ideologists in ancient Greece by combining them with the socioeconomic conditions of the Middle Ages, which served as a starting point for the **subsequent** idea of exchange and value. Moreover, it is notable that Albert once came up with the idea that the exchange value must comply with the production cost. He considered the pricing of goods from both the perspectives of natural order and economic order. He believed that according to the natural order, goods were valued differentially, whereas according to the economic order, goods were valued based on their association with labor. More generally speaking, he ascribed the price to "labor and **expenditure**". He also pointed out that production would come to a close if the production cost were not covered by the market price. This was a crucial leap forward in analysis: It demonstrated that the price could be viewed as an equilibrium price and a variable (cost) was established as a price regulator. It is certain that Albert did not illustrate and explain systematically the integrated determination of market prices, but his analysis still represented **momentous** progress in the 13th century.

In conclusion, the evolution of traditional Western economic thought reflects a continuous quest to understand and improve economic systems. From ancient philosophical inquiries to medieval theological debates, the exploration of economic principles has shaped modern economic theories and practices, emphasizing the importance of ethics, justice, and equilibrium in economic decision-making.

2.2　An Overview of Traditional Economic Thought in China

2.2.1　Economic Thought Before the 6th Century

Ancient China was a self-sufficient agricultural society, with most of its wealth coming from agricultural production. Agriculture was not only the most important source of living necessities but also a spring of privilege enjoyed by noble rulers. Therefore, the **emergence** of the ideology which stressed agriculture was closely related to the ruling system and the dominant role of agriculture in the national economy. Agriculture development in the Western Zhou Dynasty was rapid, and production techniques also saw a certain degree of advancement. The rulers of the Western Zhou Dynasty placed great importance on agricultural production, making the prioritization of agriculture a fundamental national policy.

As a fundamental production factor, labor played a particularly important role when production techniques were **immature**, and most work was done by hand. The ruling class of the Western Zhou Dynasty primarily recognized the wealth created by labor as "the result of success, which comes from persistence", meaning that painstaking efforts can ultimately bring wealth to people. They became fully aware of the importance of labor in creating material wealth.

The idea that labor creates wealth resulted in the protection of agricultural labor. This notion was primarily embodied in the Western Zhou Dynasty's concept of "respecting Heaven and protecting the people". This implies that the masses were born from Heaven, and Heaven would choose a wise emperor to govern the people and the territory on behalf of Heaven, with the duty of taking care of the people. Therefore, King Wen of Zhou claimed to have been designated by Heaven to take good care of the people and implemented policies that stressed agriculture, **frugality**, and the well-being of the people. The thought of kings in the Zhou Dynasty to protect the people on behalf of Heaven **mirrored** the priority and protection given to labor by the rulers under the system of **enfeoffment** in the Western Zhou Dynasty. By so doing, this new mode of production was covered by a veil of "caring for the people", which contributed to the development of productivity. The idea of maximizing the effects of labor in agriculture also emerged during the Western Zhou Dynasty. To bring manpower to full play in production, the simplest approach would be to extend the duration or increase the intensity of labor.

Unit 2 An Overview of Traditional Economic Thought in the West and China

In the Spring and Autumn Period (8th century B.C.–5th century B.C.) and the Warring States Period (5th century B.C.–3rd century B.C.), China witnessed the **disintegration** of the **feudal** economy and the transition to a landlord economy. This marked a historical **transformation** in the socioeconomic structure and nature, leading to a vibrant period of diverse economic ideologies with various schools of thought competing and **flourishing**. This laid the foundation for the fundamental framework of traditional Chinese economic thought.

During the Spring and Autumn Period, the development of feudal productivity brought about significant changes in the primary aspect of feudal production relations. The advancement of handicrafts, the development of towns, and commodity-money relations were the result of the changes in land ownership forms and causes that prompted these changes.

The theory of constant property is a unique economic concept of Mencius (372 B.C.–289 B.C.), a prominent figure of Confucianism, and it holds a crucial place in his ideological system. This was the first theory to explicitly support a private property system. According to him, "constant property" refers to the property that does not change, which people **invariably** possess and use. By taking advantage of the constant property, people could produce the basic means of subsistence required for the survival of their family. As social production at that time centered on agricultural production and most of the population were farmers, the constant property of Mencius **pertained** to the constant property of "tillers" or laborers. Meanwhile, Mencius proposed another term, "**persevering** heart", which means that farmers **embraced** the rule of their rulers instead of betraying them. Mencius concluded that a substantial amount of property owned by people was **indispensable** for maintaining the social order. Proceeding from maintaining social order, he advocated the establishment of a private property system. Given the socioeconomic conditions in the early Warring States Period, where the private property system enjoyed extensive development, this was a progressive idea.

Mencius recognized the necessity of the division of labor. He posited that a state, regardless of its size, must be comprised of both gentlemen and **commoners**. "Commoners" refers to the rural **populace**, including farmers, craftsmen, and other individuals engaged in physical labor; while "gentlemen" encompasses all those who are **detached** from physical labor including the emperor, and not only officials at all levels but also individuals involved in literature, arts, education, and those **valiant** warriors safeguarding national security. Mencius termed those engaged in agriculture and manual labor as "laborers of strength" and those involved in various state governance activities as "laborers of intellect". He believed that both laborers of intellect and strength existed in their respective social functions and societal needs.

From the 3rd century B.C. to the 6th century A.D., China went through the Qin, Han, Three Kingdoms, Jin, and Southern and Northern Dynasties. In addressing the question of governing the national economy, ancient China consistently harbored two ideologies: **interventionism** and non-interventionism. Confucianism, holding to the principle of conforming to the nature, advocated benefiting the people for their own welfare and promoting the equal importance of agriculture and commerce. Legalism, on the other hand, emphasized a prosperous country and strong military, advocating "a wealthy state and **impoverished** people", with a single focus on agriculture. The philosophical system of *Guanzi* presented a certain integration of "non-interventionism" and "interventionism". During the Western Han period, policy thought evolved from non-interventionism to state intervention. Sima Qian in the Western Han Dynasty was considered to **epitomize** the thought on the free economy of ancient China. He integrated the Taoist principle of harmonizing with nature into Confucianism, enriching and giving full play to the concept of a free economy. Sima Qian argued that the development of the social economy has an inherent **momentum**, and various aspects of social production and different regions would **spontaneously** participate in specialization and cooperation. Driven by the innate impulse to seek wealth and profit, human conditions would enable the operation and development of the social economy to be subject to spontaneous regulation.

2.2.2 Economic Thought from the 7th to the 14th Century

During the Tang, Song, and Yuan dynasties, commodity exchange and the commodity economy experienced unprecedented development. Notably, there was a surge in ideas promoting commerce and highlighting the importance of currency, with each era showcasing its own distinct characteristics in this regard.

Intellectuals, while criticizing the traditional taboo on discussing profits, put forth numerous viewpoints advocating the importance of commerce and the **veneration** of wealth. Liu Yan (716–780, Tang Dynasty) advocated the application of the principles of the commodity economy to handle national finances. He regarded significant fiscal measures such as transportation, salt

Unit 2 An Overview of Traditional Economic Thought in the West and China

production, and the constant pricing system as commercial operations. Liu Yan even spared no expense to establish a commercial intelligence network within various regional inspection offices, with the aim of staying informed about the dynamic trends in commerce. Lu Shirong, a scholar in the Yuan Dynasty, also emphasized the application of commercial principles, suggesting that the state should build ships and invest in overseas trade with merchants. Intellectuals like Han Yu (768–824, Tang Dynasty), Li Gu (1009–1059, Song Dynasty), and Sima Guang (1019–1086, Song Dynasty) defended the interests of the wealthy from different perspectives. The prevalence and development of the pro-commerce ideology during this period, breaking through the traditional "favoring agriculture, suppressing commerce" mindset, had profound reasons. It was not only a natural outcome of the development of the commodity economy to a certain stage but also an objective result of the gradual elevation of the political and social status of merchants during this period.

"Jiaozi" (交子), introduced during the Northern Song Dynasty, became the world's earliest form of paper currency. The emergence of paper currency resulted from the rapid development of the commodity economy and an insufficient supply of metallic currency. During this period, intellectuals engaged in discussions about the origin, functions, coinage rights, circulation speed, issuance, and circulation of currency. The scope of these discussions covered the framework of modern monetary systems. In particular, the renowned Northern Song scholar Shen Kuo (1031–1095), in his work *Dream Pool Essays*, first proposed an **inverse** relationship between the circulation speed of money and the necessary quantity of money in circulation. He believed that accelerating the circulation speed of money could compensate for the insufficient quantity of money in circulation, thereby addressing the contemporary issue of "currency shortage". This insight predated by 600 years the concept of currency circulation put forth in the 17th century by the English classical political economist William Petty—a splendid achievement in the history of Chinese monetary thought.

In general, traditional Chinese economic thought reflects a dynamic interplay among philosophical principles, socioeconomic conditions, and policy ideologies. The emphasis on agriculture, recognition of labor, and philosophical influences shaped economic policies and practices throughout China's history, contributing to its rich economic heritage and influence on global economic thought.

It is important to note that while these ancient thinkers laid the foundation for economic thought, their ideas were not as comprehensive or systematic as theories that would emerge in later centuries. However, their contributions provided a starting point for future generations to build upon and refine economic thinking.

Exercises

❶ Short answer questions

Directions: *Answer the following questions in your own words or with sentences from the text.*

(1) What is the focus of economic thought in ancient Greece and Rome?

(2) How did the economic ideas of ancient Greece and Rome influence the Renaissance and Enlightenment periods?

(3) Would you explain the concept of "constant property" and its significance in traditional Chinese economic thought, citing Mencius's ideas?

(4) Would you describe the development of commodity exchange and the commodity economy during the Tang, Song, and Yuan dynasties in China?

❷ Term explanation

Directions: *Explain the following terms in your own words or with sentences from the text.*

(1) chrematistics

(2) constant property

(3) commoners

(4) gentlemen

Unit 2 An Overview of Traditional Economic Thought in the West and China

❸ Banked cloze

Directions: *Fill in the blanks by selecting suitable words from the following box. You may not use any of the words more than once.*

A. introduced	B. effect	C. sustenance	D. means	E. resources
F. possessions	G. figure	H. significant	I. economic	J. stability
K. population	L. spending	M. loyalty	N. activities	O. groundwork

Mencius, a key (1) _____ in Confucianism during the period from 372 B.C. to 289 B.C., (2) _____ the concept of "constant property", a notion that held a pivotal role in his philosophical framework. "Constant property", as defined by Mencius, referred to (3) _____ that remained stable and unchanging, such as land, which people used for their (4) _____ and survival. He argued that this stable ownership allowed individuals, particularly farmers who constituted the majority of the (5) _____, to produce the necessities required for their families' well-being. Mencius emphasized the importance of farmers' (6) _____ to their rulers, attributing it to their ownership of constant property. He contended that widespread property ownership was essential for maintaining social order and (7) _____. Therefore, he advocated for the establishment of a private property system as a (8) _____ of preserving societal harmony. This perspective was notably progressive given the socioeconomic conditions prevalent during the early Warring States Period, where private property was experiencing significant development. Mencius's theory laid the (9) _____ for the eventual establishment and recognition of private property rights in ancient Chinese society, influencing subsequent philosophical and legal developments. His advocacy for property rights extended beyond (10) _____ benefits, suggesting a moral and ethical dimension to ownership. By ensuring that people had a stake in their land, Mencius believed it would lead to a more equitable and just society. He posited that when individuals had secure property rights, they were more likely to contribute positively to their communities and adhere to social norms, thereby fostering a more stable and prosperous state.

❹ Translation

Directions: *Translate the following paragraphs into Chinese or English.*

(1) There are two important factors distinguishing the Middle Ages from

ancient Greece and Rome: The first is the uniformity of ideas and theories provided by the Roman Catholic Church, and the other is the spread of the market mechanism. The feudal society of Western Europe in the Middle Ages unconsciously bred the primary form of capitalism, which resulted from the increasing integration of the market (the product and production factor markets) into the daily fabric of people's economic lives.

(2) 明初实行的工匠制度（artisan system）部分地解除了元朝以后手工业者的封建依附关系（feudal dependence），适当地解放了劳动力，手工业生产很快得到了恢复，技术水平也不断提高，其中纺织、造船、制盐、开矿等行业尤为突出。不仅官营手工业，就是民间手工业，明初都有了显著的发展。陶瓷器手工业（the ceramic handicraft industry）在永乐以后也进入了繁盛期，不但生产供宫廷使用的产品，也是对外贸易的主要商品。

5 Project

Title: An Inquiry into the Monetary Systems of Ancient Dynasties

Instructions: Students will investigate the currency systems of different dynasties, such as types of currency, minting techniques, and circulation scope.

Step 1: Selection of dynasty. Students will choose one dynasty among the Spring and Autumn Period, Tang, Song, and Yuan dynasties based on their interests and provide reasons for their selection, focusing primarily on economic development of the dynasty chosen.

Step 2: Presentation of results. Students will present their research findings to the class through oral presentations, posters, reports, etc. The presentation should include aspects such as the economic characteristics, significant events, and economic policies of the chosen dynasty.

Supplementary Reading

Scan the QR code to find out more about the unit.

Unit 3

Demand and Supply

Learning Objectives

After studying this unit, you should be able to:

1) understand the demand and supply model, the theories of equilibrium and elasticity;
2) use the words and phrases in this unit;
3) apply the theories of demand and supply to the analysis of real economic cases.

Demand and supply are at the very heart of economics. This model serves as a crucial guide in the intricate fabric of market dynamics, explaining the essence of consumer desires and producer offerings. Throughout this unit, we delve into the core elements of demand, supply, equilibrium, and elasticity, each playing a pivotal role in shaping the economic landscape. Understanding demand illuminates the driving forces behind consumer behavior while comprehending supply **unveils** the intricate mechanisms that steer producer decisions. The equilibrium point represents a state of balance in which demand and supply are in harmony. Moreover, elasticity sheds light on the responsiveness of these forces to price changes. As we explore these fundamental principles, we gain profound insights into the forces of scarcity and abundance, empowering us to **navigate** the complexities of economics using informed wisdom and strategic **expertise**.

3.1 The Law of Demand and Supply

3.1.1 Definition of Demand

In economics, demand represents the fundamental relationship between two economic variables: the price of a good or service, and the quantity of that good or service that consumers are willing and able to purchase at that price during a specific period, assuming all other conditions remain constant[1]. Economists universally consider price as the first variable and the quantity demanded as the second variable. Obviously, price is not the only determinant of the quantity consumers are willing to buy in a specific period, and a lot of other things will influence consumers' demand.

Demand consists of two factors: consumers' willingness and the ability to purchase a good at a specific time. Willingness is the desire for a good, determining the intention to buy the good at a specific price. The ability to buy means that, to buy a good at a specific price, an individual must possess sufficient wealth or income.

Both willingness and ability to buy are essential components of demand as they determine the actual quantity of goods or services that consumers demand in the market.

---

[1] This assumption is commonly used in economic analysis, allowing economists to analyze the relationship between two variables in a simplified manner.

3.1.2 Demand Curve

The law of demand states that as the price of a good decreases, the quantity demanded increases if all other factors remain constant, and vice versa. In other words, the law of demand states that the price and quantity demanded are **negatively** related, with all other things held constant. Let us consider the quantity of chicken demanded in some country as an example of the relationship between the price and demand. If the price of chicken is very high, consumers will find ways to get along with less chicken and buy beef or pork. If the price of chicken drops, people will tend to consume more. They may serve more dishes with chicken and switch away from beef.

The relationship between price and demand can be represented by a **numerical** table or a graph. In either case, demand describes the relationship between price and quantity bought. Table 3-1 shows the demand schedule, showing the quantity of chicken that will be demanded in one year at each possible price ranging from $4.80 to $5.40 per pound in a particular area. Of course, there are many different kinds of chicken—organic chicken, free-range chicken, pasture-raised chicken, conventional chicken, and **antibiotic** chicken, and here we simplify and think about this table as describing demand for average, or typical chicken.

Table 3-1 Demand Schedule for Chicken

Price ($ Per Pound)	Demand (Million Pounds)	Point on Demand Curve
5.40	20	A
5.30	25	B
5.20	30	C
5.10	35	D
5.00	40	E
4.90	45	F
4.80	50	G

At the price of $5.20, 30 million pounds of chicken are consumed. As the price rises to $5.40, the consumption of chicken declines to 20 million pounds. On the other hand, if the price of chicken decreases from $5.00 to $4.80, the quantity of chicken demanded increases from 40 to 50 million pounds. It is safe to conclude that the higher the price of chicken, the lower the quantity demanded in the market, and the lower the price, the higher the quantity demanded.

The relationship between the price and quantity of chicken demanded can also be represented in a graph like Figure 3-1, which is called the demand curve. In a typical demand curve, the price of a good or service is plotted on the **vertical** axis (y-axis), whereas the quantity demanded is shown on the **horizontal** axis (x-axis). Each point in the graph corresponds to a row in the table. For example, if the price is $5.00, the amount of chicken sold is 40 million pounds for a year. This relationship is shown in point E. While the demand for chicken is 45 million pounds for a year, the price must decline to $4.90 (point F). All these points together form a curve that slopes downward from left to right, indicating an inverse relationship between price and quantity demanded. This means that as the price of a product increases, the quantity demanded by consumers tends to decrease and vice versa.

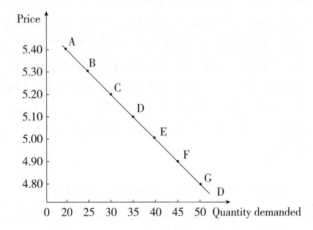

Figure 3-1　Demand Curve of Chicken

With the help of the demand curve, it is easy to differentiate between the two concepts of quantity demanded and demand.

A movement along the demand curve occurs when there is a change in the quantity demanded due to a change in the price of the product or service, assuming that all other factors remain constant. In other words, it reflects how consumers respond to changes in the price of a good while holding everything else constant. If the price of a product decreases, the quantity demanded typically increases, resulting in movement along the demand curve from left to right (from point A to point G in Figure 3-1). **Conversely**, if the price of a product increases, the quantity demanded usually decreases, leading to movement along the demand curve from right to left (from point G to point A in Figure 3-1). This movement shows a change in the quantity demanded.

On the other hand, a shift in the entire demand curve occurs when there is a change in any factor other than the price that influences the quantity demanded. This movement reflects a change in demand. For example, because of an economic crisis, people earn less income and cannot afford chicken. It turns out that the demand for chicken decreases, and the entire demand curve moves from right to left. These factors include changes in consumers' income, consumers' preferences, prices of related goods (**substitutes** and **complements**), and consumers' expectations.

When the economy is booming, people's income increases and the quantity of products and services they buy at each price level also rises. For example, with an increase in income, people are likely to adjust the room temperature higher during winter than when their incomes are lower. Most products are considered normal goods, in which demand increases as consumers' income rises. However, for some products, demand decreases as income increases. High-income individuals, for instance, are less likely to use public transportation than low-income individuals. Products that experience a decrease in demand as income increases are known as inferior goods. When people can afford them, they stop buying inferior goods and shift to higher-priced items. Therefore, when a product is an inferior good, an increase in income leads to a leftward shift in the demand curve, whereas a decrease in income causes the demand curve to shift to the right.

As people's income rises, the demand for McDonald's, a fast-food chain, might decrease while the demand for dining at fancy restaurants with higher-quality offerings might increase. McDonald's becomes an inferior good, as its demand decreases with increasing income.

For some consumers with higher income, they might still frequent McDonald's, since they prefer the fried food sold there. Therefore, consumers' preferences or tastes can influence demand for certain goods.

Why do people desire certain things? We do not need to seek an answer to this question; we only need to acknowledge that people indeed have certain preferences or tastes that determine their consumption choices, and these tastes are not static. In the eyes of economists, changes in fashion, beliefs, culture, and other aspects are considered changes in one's taste.

The prices of related goods will cause the movement of the demand curve. While coffee prices have increased, consumers may choose to buy more tea as a substitute for coffee. If the price of one product in a group (such as coffee) rises, consumers are likely to buy more of another product (tea), and these two products become substitutes. Substitutes typically have similar functions in some aspects, such as airplanes and trains, natural gas and gasoline, cornflakes and oatmeal, etc..

However, the demand for one product can drive the demand for another product. This group of products are known as complements or complementary goods. Complements are products that consumers need to consume together in some sense, such as computers and software, cars and gasoline, e-book readers and e-books. etc. Consumers prefer to consume one product along with its complementary goods. Changes in the price of a product can affect demand for its complementary goods. Specifically, when the price of one product rises, demand for its complementary goods decreases, leading to a leftward shift in the demand curve of complementary goods. Therefore, when the price of gasoline rises, the demand for **gas-guzzling** cars decreases.

Generally, when consumers choose a product, they will make a rough prediction of the price trend of that product before deciding whether to make a purchase. For example, when buying a house, consumers usually pay close attention to housing price trends. When there is a high possibility of a future price increase, consumers tend to make timely purchases, leading to an increase in demand. However, when the predicted future price increases are small or there is a downward trend, consumers often choose to wait and observe, resulting in a decrease in demand. Therefore, the expectation of product prices is also an important factor that affects consumer demand.

3.1.3 Definition of Supply

While demand refers to the behavior of consumers, supply refers to the behavior of firms. Supply represents the relationship between two economic variables: the price of a good or service and the quantity of that good or service that firms are willing and able to supply at that price during a specific period, assuming all other conditions remain constant. Economists universally consider price as the first variable and the quantity supplied as the second variable. Here, we also hold other factors equal while examining the relationship between price and quantity supplied.

Supply consists of two factors: willingness and ability to supply goods at a given price in a specific period. Willingness is the intention to provide the good at a specific price. The ability to supply means that to provide a good at a specific price, a firm must possess sufficient wealth or assets. Both willingness and ability to provide are essential components of supply, as they determine the actual quantity of goods or services firms supply in the market.

3.1.4 Supply Curve

The law of supply states that the higher the price of the good, the higher the quantity supplied; the lower the price of the good, the lower the quantity supplied. In other words, the law of supply states that the price and quantity supplied are positively related, with all other factors being held constant. Let us consider the quantity of chicken supplied in some countries as an example of the relationship between price and supply. If the price of chicken is very high, the profits from selling chicken will be huge. Firms and farms will find ways to raise more chickens and produce more meat. If the price of chicken drops, selling chicken will no longer be profitable, and firms and farms will decrease the production of chicken.

The relationship between the price and quantity of chicken supplied can be represented by a numerical table or a graph. In either case, supply describes how much firms will supply a good at each price. Table 3-2 shows the supply schedule of the quantity of chicken that will be supplied in one year at each possible price in a particular area.

Table 3-2 Supply Schedule for Chicken

Price ($ Per Pound)	Supply (Million Pounds)	Point on Supply Curve
5.40	50	A
5.30	45	B
5.20	40	C
5.10	35	D
5.00	30	E
4.90	25	F
4.80	20	G

At the price of $5.20, the quantity of chicken supplied is 40 million pounds. As the price rises to $5.40, the quantity increases to 50 million pounds. On the other hand, if the price of chicken decreases from $5.10 to $4.90, the quantity of chicken supplied decreases from 35 million to 25 million pounds. It is safe to conclude that as the price of chicken rises, the firms supply more chicken, while when the price drops, the firms decrease their supply. Table 3-2 presents a typical example of the law of supply.

The relationship between the price and quantity of chicken supplied can also be represented in a graph like Figure 3-2, which is called the supply curve. In a typical supply curve, the price of a good or service is plotted on the vertical axis (y-axis), whereas the quantity demanded is shown on the horizontal axis (x-axis). Each point in the graph corresponds to a row in the table. For example, if the price is $5.00, the chicken supply is 30 million pounds for a year. This relationship is shown in point E. While the price rises to $5.40 (point A), the supply of chicken is 50 million pounds for a year. All these points together form a curve that slopes upward from left to right, indicating a positive relationship between price and quantity supplied. This means that as the price of a product increases, the quantity supplied by firms tends to increase and vice versa.

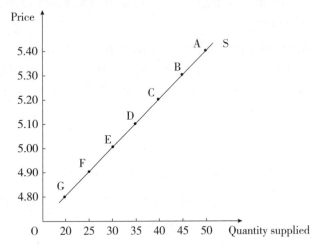

Figure 3-2 Supply Curve of Chicken

With the help of the supply curve, it is easy to differentiate the two concepts of quantity supplied and supply.

A movement along the supply curve occurs when there is a change in the quantity supplied due to a change in the price of the product or service, assuming that all other factors remain constant. In other words, it reflects how firms respond to changes in the price of a good while holding everything else constant. If the price of a product decreases, the quantity supplied typically decreases, resulting in movement along the supply curve from right to left (from point A to point G in Figure 3-2). Conversely, if the price of a product increases, the quantity supplied usually increases, leading to movement along the supply curve from left to right (from point G to point A in Figure 3-2). This movement along the supply curve shows a change in the quantity supplied.

On the other hand, a shift in the entire supply curve occurs when there is a change in any factor other than price that influences the quantity supplied. This movement indicates a change in supply. For example, owing to advancements in technology, the feeding system for chickens is simplified and fewer workers are needed. The cost of meat production has reduced significantly. Firms supply more meat, although the price of chicken remains unchanged. The entire supply curve moves from left to right. This is the change in supply.

Various factors affect the movement of supply curves. These factors include technological advances, input prices, weather conditions, consumers' expectations, etc.

Advancements in automation, robotics, and artificial intelligence have revolutionized production processes, enabling greater efficiency and higher output rates. With the implementation of advanced supply chain management systems, companies can **streamline** logistics, reduce **lead times**, and optimize **inventory** levels. Consequently, technology-driven improvements in the supply chain and production capabilities have led to increased availability of goods and overall improved the supply of goods.

Under unchanged product prices, an increase in production costs leads to a reduction in the supply of goods. This may be attributable to a decrease in the prices of production factors. When production costs (such as raw materials, labor, and capital) decrease, the same input of factors will yield more goods, resulting in a relatively increased supply quantity.

Weather plays a significant role in influencing the supply of goods across various industries. Extreme weather events, such as hurricanes, floods, droughts, and snowstorms, can **disrupt** transportation networks, damage crops, and disrupt production processes, leading to decreased supply. For instance, severe droughts can reduce agricultural yields, leading to a scarcity of crops and higher food prices. Similarly, harsh winters can disrupt shipping and logistics, causing delays in the delivery of goods and affecting supply chain operations. However, favorable weather conditions can boost supply, as a large harvest in agriculture or **optimal** wind conditions for renewable energy generation can lead to an abundance of goods available in the market.

Firms' expectations regarding the price of a good affect their supply. For instance, if they anticipate that the price of a particular commodity will rise, the producers will increase the future supply of that commodity while making production plans. This allows them to gain higher profits if the price rises in the future. Consequently, the current supply of goods may decrease as a result of their decisions.

3.2 Market Equilibrium

3.2.1 Equilibrium and Equilibrium Price

So far, we have separately explained the behavior of buyers and sellers, but we have not yet brought these two parties together in the market. How do buyers and sellers interact? What determines the market prices at which they trade? What determines the quantity of goods bought and sold by the buyers and sellers? We use demand and supply curves to answer these questions.

These two curves are placed on the same **coordinate** system (with the horizontal axis representing quantity and the vertical axis representing price). For the demand curve, price and quantity are negatively related, while for the supply curve, price and quantity are positively related. Therefore, within the same coordinate system, two opposing forces act on the price. When these two forces are equal or in equilibrium, a state of balance is formed. In Figure 3-3, point E is the equilibrium point, P_E is the equilibrium price, and Q_E is the equilibrium quantity.

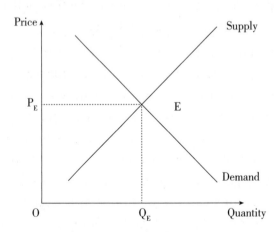

Figure 3-3 Equilibrium Price and Equilibrium Quantity

In economics, equilibrium refers to a state in which economic decision-makers (buyers or sellers) realize that by readjusting resource allocation or purchasing methods, they cannot gain any further benefits, and thus they no longer change their economic behavior. Therefore, equilibrium is a state reached by relevant variables in economic affairs under certain interaction conditions and is formed when the demand curve intersects the supply curve.

However, this state is not the norm. Generally, there are more situations in the market that **deviate** from equilibrium. As shown in Figure 3-4, the demand and supply curves intersect at point E. The equilibrium price is P_E and the equilibrium quantity is Q_E. When the price is above the equilibrium price P_E, such as P_1, the quantity supplied is Q_1 and the quantity demanded is Q_2. Evidently the quantity supplied exceeds the quantity demanded. In other words, when the price is higher than the equilibrium price, there is an excess supply, known as surplus. On the other hand, when the price is below the equilibrium price P_E, such as P_2, the quantity supplied is Q_4, and the quantity demanded is Q_3. Evidently the quantity demanded exceeds the quantity supplied. In this case, when the price is lower than the equilibrium price, there is excess demand, known as a shortage.

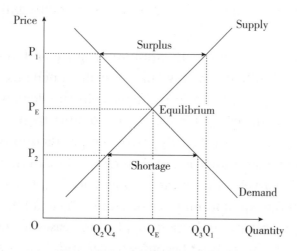

Figure 3-4 Surplus and Shortage

When the market price deviates from equilibrium, the goods are in a non-equilibrium state, where supply and demand are not equal. However, through the interaction of the supply and demand forces in the market, the deviated market price can automatically return to the equilibrium price level. The specific mechanisms involved are as follows:

When the market price P_1 is higher than the equilibrium price P_E, there is a surplus of products, leading to competition among producers to offer lower prices. This, in turn, lowers the price, increases the quantity demanded, decreases the quantity supplied, and eventually brings the quantity demanded and supplied into equilibrium, with the market price being equal to the equilibrium price.

When the market price P_2 is lower than the equilibrium price P_E, causing a shortage of goods, there is competition among producers to offer higher prices. This leads to an increase in price, resulting in a decrease in the quantity demanded and an increase in quantity supplied. Eventually, the quantity demanded equals the quantity supplied, and the market price reaches the equilibrium price.

It can be seen that when the actual price deviates, there are always forces of change in the market, ultimately leading to market equilibrium.

3.2.2 Change of Equilibrium

The demand and supply curves jointly determine the market equilibrium, which determines the equilibrium price and quantity of a good. If, for some reason, the demand or supply curve shifts, the market equilibrium changes accordingly.

First, we analyze the changes in equilibrium price and quantity when the demand curve shifts while the supply curve remains unchanged. Let us assume that during a hot summer, there is an increase in the demand for ice cream. This causes the demand curve for ice cream to shift to the right. However, because the weather does not directly affect the production of ice cream, the supply of ice cream remains unchanged. As a result, the intersection point of the demand and supply curves for ice cream changes, leading to a change in market equilibrium. When the equilibrium price increases, the equilibrium quantity will also increase. The quantity of ice cream supplied increases to equal the demand. On the other hand, if the weather becomes cooler and there is a decrease in the demand for ice cream, the demand curve shifts to the left, resulting in a decrease in the price and quantity of ice cream.

Second, let us examine the equilibrium change when the supply curve shifts while the demand curve remains unchanged. Now consider the situation in which a major oil-exporting country experiences a production **halt**, leading to a decrease in the supply of oil. This causes the supply curve for oil to shift to the left, while the demand curve remains unchanged. As a result, the equilibrium price of oil increases, and the equilibrium quantity decreases to match the reduced supply with demand. In fact, price increases due to oil scarcity are quite common. Conversely, if there is a significant technological breakthrough that increases oil supply, the supply curve shifts to the right. With an abundant supply of oil, its price decreases from its original level to equate supply with demand. This leads to a decrease in equilibrium price and an increase in equilibrium quantity.

Third, when both the demand and supply curves shift simultaneously, the changes in the equilibrium price and quantity are uncertain.

3.3 Elasticity of Demand and Supply

According to the law of demand and the law of supply, when the price of a good changes, it will lead to changes in the quantity demanded and supplied. Therefore, when the price of a good changes by 1%, how much will the quantity demanded and supplied of this good change as a percentage? The basic meaning of elasticity is the sensitivity of the dependent variable to the changes in the independent variable. In other words, when the independent variable changes by 1%, the dependent variable will change by a certain percentage.

3.3.1 The Elasticity of Demand

Demand elasticity refers to the sensitivity of demand to changes in its influencing factors. Here, we discuss the price elasticity of demand, income elasticity of demand, and the cross elasticity of demand.

Price elasticity of demand refers to the sensitivity of the quantity demanded for a certain good to changes in its price, with other conditions remaining constant. This is the percentage change in the quantity demanded divided by the percentage change in price. This means for every 1% change in price, the quantity demanded will change by a certain percentage. The formula for calculating it is as follows:

$$\text{Price Elasticity of Demand} = \frac{\text{Percentage Change in the Quantity Demanded}}{\text{Percentage Change in Price}}$$

Goods with a price elasticity of demand greater than 1 are considered to have elastic demand. When the price elasticity of demand is greater than 1, the percentage change in the quantity demanded is greater than the percentage change in price. For example, peanuts and olive oil often have elastic demand.

Demand can be perfectly elastic, meaning that the quantity demanded is highly sensitive to price changes. Even the slightest increase in price can completely stop consumers from purchasing the product.

Goods with a price elasticity of demand equal to 1 are said to have a **unitary** elastic demand. For such goods, a 1% price change results in a 1% change in the quantity demanded. In this case, an increase in price does not affect the total expenditure on the product.

Goods with a price elasticity of demand less than 1 are considered to have inelastic demand. When the price elasticity of demand is less than 1, the percentage change in the quantity demanded is less than the percentage change in price. For example, cigarettes and potato chips have an inelastic demand, meaning that the quantity demanded is not very responsive to price changes.

Demand can also be perfectly inelastic, indicating that it is not influenced by price at all. An example is the insulin needed by patients with **diabetes**, where even if the price increases, the demand remains unchanged.

For example, if the price of a good changes by 2% and the quantity demanded changes by 5%, then the elasticity is 5% divided by 2%, which is greater than 1. This means that a slight change in price leads to a significant change in the quantity demanded. Luxury goods are an example of such commodities. After a slight increase in price, people can choose to buy them or not, which leads to a considerable change in the quantity demanded.

On the same demand curve, the elasticity can differ. In the higher price range, elasticity is greater than 1, indicating an elastic demand, which means that the commodity is a luxury good. In the lower price range, elasticity is less than 1, and the commodity is considered a necessity. Whether a commodity is a luxury good or a necessity depends on its price level.

The income elasticity of demand, with other conditions remaining constant, measures the percentage change in the quantity demanded of a certain commodity in response to a change in consumer income. In other words, it represents the percentage change in the quantity demanded of a commodity, resulting from a 1% change in consumer income.

The cross elasticity of demand, with other conditions remaining constant, measures the sensitivity of the quantity demanded for a certain commodity to changes in the price of a related commodity. In other words, it represents the percentage change in the quantity demanded of a related commodity resulting from a 1% change in the price of another commodity.

3.3.2 The Elasticity of Supply

Supply elasticity refers to the sensitivity of supply to changes in its influencing factors. Here, we discuss the price elasticity of supply. Price elasticity of supply refers to the sensitivity of the quantity supplied of a certain good to changes in its price, with other conditions remaining constant. It is the percentage change in the quantity supplied divided by the percentage change in price. This means that for every 1% change in price, the quantity supplied will change by a certain percentage. The formula for calculating it is as follows:

$$\text{Price Elasticity of Supply} = \frac{\text{Percentage Change in Quantity Supplied}}{\text{Percentage Change in Price}}$$

If the percentage change in the quantity supplied is greater than the percentage change in price (i.e., the absolute value of elasticity is greater than 1), the supply is considered elastic. This means that producers are relatively responsive to price changes, and the quantity supplied can change significantly in response to price changes.

If the percentage change in the quantity supplied is less than the percentage change in price (i.e., the absolute value of elasticity is less than 1), the supply is considered inelastic. In this case, producers are not very responsive to price changes, and the quantity supplied changes **proportionally** less than the price change.

If the percentage change in the quantity supplied is exactly equal to the percentage change in price, the supply is unitary elastic. This implies that the quantity supplied changes in proportion to the price change.

In theory, if the quantity supplied can change by an infinite percentage in response to any change in price, the supply is considered perfectly elastic. This is rare in real-world scenarios.

If the quantity supplied remains constant, regardless of price changes, the supply is perfectly inelastic. This is also a theoretical extreme and uncommon in practice.

Understanding the price elasticity of supply is crucial for both producers and policymakers as it helps predict how changes in market conditions, particularly price changes, will impact the quantity of goods or services supplied to the market.

Exercises

❶ Short answer questions

Directions: *Answer the following questions in your own words or with sentences from the text.*

(1) What's the difference between demand and quantity demanded?

(2) What factors besides price will cause the shift of the supply curve? Give examples in your life.

(3) What is equilibrium?

(4) What are normal goods and inferior goods? Give some examples in your life.

❷ Term explanation

Directions: *Explain the following terms in your own words or with sentences from the text.*

(1) law of demand

(2) supply

(3) substitute

(4) price elasticity

❸ Banked cloze

Directions: *Fill in the blanks by selecting suitable words from the following box. You may not use any of the words more than once.*

A. surpasses	B. neglect	C. pivotal	D. external	E. stem
F. responsiveness	G. intersects	H. allocation	I. pressure	J. enterprises
K. Conversely	L. denoting	M. common	N. confuse	O. cornerstone

In economics, the intricate dance between supply and demand emerges as a(n) (1) _____ of market dynamics. These two forces, similar to the ebb and flow of a tide, exert a profound influence on pricing and (2) _____ of resources. Supply, (3) _____ the quantity of goods or services that producers are willing to offer at various price levels, represents the essence of production capabilities.

Conversely, demand, reflecting consumers' willingness and ability to purchase a particular product, signifies the market's desire for these offerings.

The equilibrium point, where supply (4) _____ with demand, is a state of balance. When demand (5) _____ supply, scarcity appears, leading to an increase in prices—a fundamental principle captured by the law of demand. (6) _____, an oversupply scenario leads to a surplus, triggering a price decline in accordance with the law of supply. This delicate equilibrium generalizes the intricate interplay that defines the market equilibrium, where neither shortage nor excess prevails.

Price elasticity, a(n) (7) _____ concept in this economic domain, states the sensitivity of quantity demanded or supplied concerning price fluctuations. Elastic goods exhibit substantial (8) _____ to price shifts, while inelastic goods manifest a more moderate reaction. This subtle understanding is important for businesses and policymakers navigating the labyrinth（迷宫）of market forces.

Moreover, (9) _____ factors such as technological advancements, government interventions, and global economic trends can alter equilibrium, reshaping the frame of supply and demand. In this intricate economic ecosystem, businesses good at gauging and adapting to these fluctuations often thrive, while those who (10) _____ the subtle differences may face challenges in a changing marketplace.

In conclusion, the symbiotic（共生的）relationship between supply and demand forms the fundamental principles of economic theory, dictating market dynamics and influencing the track of prices. A comprehensive grasp of these forces, coupled with an awareness of external variables, empowers stakeholders to navigate the ever-changing currents of the economic landscape.

❹ Translation

Directions: *Translate the following paragraphs into Chinese or English.*

(1) According to the law of demand and the law of supply, when the price of a good changes, it will lead to changes in the quantity demanded and supplied. Therefore, when the price of a good changes by 1%, how much will the quantity demanded and supplied of this good change as a percentage? The basic meaning of elasticity is the sensitivity of the dependent variable to the changes in the independent variable. In other words, when the independent variable changes by 1%, the dependent variable will change by a certain percentage. Demand

elasticity refers to the sensitivity of demand to changes in its influencing factors.

(2) 猪肉收储机制（pork storage mechanism）是平衡猪肉供求矛盾，稳定猪肉价格的有效手段，通过政策保障合理引导生产，改善供需矛盾，避免猪价过度下跌或过度上涨，从而稳定市场。我国猪肉收储机制自实施以来已经在产业和市场中产生了重要影响，对稳定市场主体信心，减少市场恐慌情绪，发挥了稳定器作用。

5 Project

Title: Understanding the Supply and Demand Model in Daily Life

Instructions: Imagine in a small city, the demand for rental apartments has surged due to an influx of new residents attracted by employment opportunities. However, the supply of rental properties has not kept pace with the growing demand, leading to soaring rental prices that are becoming unaffordable for many residents. In response to the housing affordability issue, the government has decided to implement rent control measures. They set a price ceiling, stating that landlords cannot charge more than a certain amount as rent for their apartments. For example, they might establish a price ceiling of $1,500 per month for a one-bedroom apartment.

Step 1: Analyze the scenario with the demand and supply model.

Step 2: Discuss the effects of the government rent control measures.

Step 3: Give another example of government price control in your real life and analyze the effects of this control.

Step 4: Present your findings to the class.

Supplementary Reading

Scan the QR code to find out more about the unit.

Unit 4

Consumption and Production

Learning Objectives

After studying this unit, you should be able to:

1) comprehend the concepts of utility, consumer surplus, cost, revenue and profit, and the theories of consumer behaviors and production decision-making;
2) use the words and phrases in this unit;
3) establish a rational and healthy perspective on consumption, and understand the manifestation of values such as innovation and social responsibility in the production sector of contemporary China.

Consumption and production are pivotal economic activities that shape the functioning of markets and economies. Consumption is defined as the process by which goods and services are put to final use by people, whereas production involves transforming inputs into goods or services. In some sense, consumption means **extracting** utilities from goods and services, and production means putting utility into them. This unit aims to examine concepts related to consumption and production such as utility, consumer surplus, cost, revenue, and profit, and explore consumer behaviors and production decision-making in more detail.

4.1 Utility and Consumer Surplus

4.1.1 Total Utility and Marginal Utility

Utility refers to the subjective value or level of satisfaction that individuals derive from the consumption of goods and services. It is assumed that people choose goods and services based on their highest **perceived** value. In other words, the objective of consumer behavior is to pursue maximum utility within certain constraints. Under this **premise**, utility theory seeks to understand and analyze individuals' preferences and decision-making under conditions of uncertainty. It provides a framework for analyzing how individuals allocate their resources and make decisions based on their preferences and the constraints they face.

The overall satisfaction or usefulness that a person derives from consuming a certain quantity of a good or service is called the total utility. It represents the **cumulative** sum of the marginal utilities obtained from each unit consumed. Marginal utility, on the other hand, refers to the additional utility gained by consuming one additional unit of a good or service. It measures the change in total utility resulting from the consumption of an extra unit.

The total utility and marginal utility can be understood in the scenario of drinking soda. When you drink soda, the first sip may provide significant enjoyment and satisfaction, leading to an increase in the total utility. The second sip adds to the total utility, **albeit** to a slightly lesser extent. With each subsequent sip, the marginal utility gradually diminishes. Eventually, additional drinking will no longer add to your satisfaction or utility.

Hence, we have the law of diminishing marginal utility, which states that as the quantity consumed increases, the additional utility or satisfaction derived from each unit decreases gradually. This holds great importance in economics, providing guidance for decision-making and resource allocation. According to this law, individuals tend to consume more of a particular good or service during the early stages of fulfilling their most pressing needs and subsequently reduce their consumption to maximize overall satisfaction.

4.1.2 Consumer Surplus

As a result of the law of diminishing marginal utility, consumers may receive more than they pay for. The gap between the total utility of a good or service and its total market value is called consumer surplus, which is the difference between the highest price a consumer is willing to pay and the actual price the consumer pays.

Suppose you see a handicraft you like when browsing a night market. You ask the vendor for the price, thinking that $50 is the highest price you would be willing to pay. The vendor asks for $30. In this case, the consumer surplus is $20: the difference between the $50 you would be willing to pay and the $30 you actually pay. Consumer surplus arises from the fact that we pay the same amount for each unit of the commodity we buy. According to the law of diminishing marginal utility, earlier units provide more satisfaction or utility than the subsequent ones. Therefore, we have a utility surplus in earlier units.

The concept of consumer surplus is not limited to a single consumer but can also be applied to the market as a whole. To simplify the case, we suppose there are only four possible consumers in the market for the handicraft, namely, Zhang, Li, Wang and Chen. The highest price that each of them is willing to pay varies (Table 4-1).

Table 4-1 The Highest Price Four Possible Consumers Are Willing to Pay

Consumer	Highest Price Each Consumer Is Willing to Pay ($)
Zhang	60
Li	50
Wang	40
Chen	30

Accordingly, the demand curve shows consumers' willingness to buy a product at different prices (Figure 4-1). If the price is set above $60, no item is sold, because $60 is the highest price that the consumers are willing to pay. At prices of $30 and below, four handicrafts are sold because all four consumers are willing to buy.

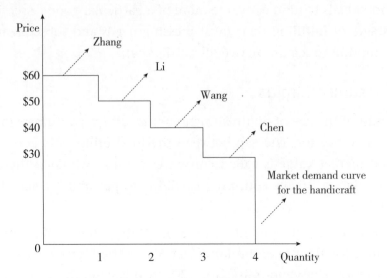

Figure 4-1　The Demand Curve for the Handicraft

The demand curve also measures the total consumer surplus in the market. In Figure 4-2, if the market price is $35, the quantity demanded is 3, and the total consumer surplus is $45 ($25 + $15 + $5), represented by the area above the market price and below the demand curve.

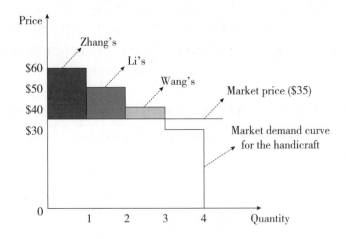

Figure 4-2　Consumer Surplus with a Market Price of $35

With a large number of consumers, the market demand curve becomes smooth. The total consumer surplus is represented by the shaded triangle below the demand curve and above the market price (Figure 4-3).

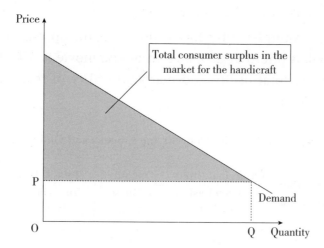

Figure 4-3　Total Consumer Surplus in the Market for the Handicraft

4.2　Consumer Behavior Theories

4.2.1　Consumer Equilibrium

In this section, we further examine how consumers make their purchasing decisions based on the economic assumption that people act in a rational and **self-interested** way. The purpose of consumption is to obtain utility and maximize satisfaction under certain constraints. Generally, factors such as personal preferences, income, and the prices of goods and services are taken into account. Economists refer to the limited amount of income available to consumers to spend on goods and services as budget constraints.

In economics, consumer equilibrium occurs when individuals allocate their resources in a manner that best suits their needs and preferences within budget constraints. At the equilibrium point, consumers distribute their income in such a way that the marginal utility per dollar spent is equal across all goods and services they choose to purchase. The marginal utility per dollar spent can be figured out as follows:

Marginal Utility per Dollar Spent = Marginal Utility (MU) / Price (P)

Consumer equilibrium is achieved when individuals cannot further increase their overall satisfaction by reallocating their budgets to different goods and services. The key to making optimal consumption decisions lies in maximizing utility by following the rule of equal marginal utility per dollar, which ensures that the additional satisfaction gained from spending one more dollar is the same across all goods and services chosen for purchase.

Look at this example: Amy has $100 to spend on e-books and online movies. An e-book is priced at $20, and an online movie is $10. Table 4-2 gives information on the total utility and marginal utility of reading e-books and watching online movies.

Table 4-2 Amy's Utility from Buying E-books and Online Movies

Quantity of E-books	Total Utility from E-books	Marginal Utility from Last E-book	Quantity of Online Movies	Total Utility from Online Movies	Marginal Utility from Last Online Movie
1	60	60	1	50	50
2	105	45	2	85	35
3	145	40	3	110	25
4	175	30	4	130	20
5	195	20	5	140	10
6	185	−10	6	135	−5

If Amy did not have a budget constraint, she would buy 5 e-books and 5 online movies to achieve a maximum utility of 335 (= 195 + 140). Unfortunately, this combination costs $150, exceeding her budget. With the information from Table 4-2 we can calculate the marginal utility per dollar, as shown in Table 4-3.

Table 4-3 Amy's Marginal Utility per Dollar from Buying E-books and Online Movies

Quantity of E-books	Marginal Utility from Last E-book	Marginal Utility per Dollar (E-books)	Quantity of Online Movies	Marginal Utility from Last Online Movie	Marginal Utility per Dollar (Online Movies)
1	60	3	1	50	5
2	45	2.25	2	35	3.5
3	40	2	3	25	2.5
4	30	1.5	4	20	2
5	20	1	5	10	1
6	−10	−0.5	6	−5	−0.5

Amy's marginal utility per dollar remains constant for a combination of

3 e-books and 4 online movies, where the marginal utility per dollar is 2. In this case, the total spending is $100 (= $20*3 + $10*4) and the total utility is 275 (= 145 + 130). Given her budget constraints, this combination provides maximum **attainable** utility.

To put it simply, by adhering to the rule of equal marginal utility per dollar, consumers can effectively manage their budgets by allocating limited resources to goods and services that provide the greatest satisfaction. Achieving consumer equilibrium not only enhances individual welfare but also contributes to the efficient functioning of market economies.

4.2.2 Income Effect and Substitution Effect

When market prices change, consumers tend to adjust their purchasing decisions. Let us consider the aforementioned example. Amy finds that e-books are now on sale, with the unit price falling to $15. This change has two effects on the quantity of e-books Amy purchases: income effect and substitution effect.

The income effect refers to the change in consumption levels resulting from variations in income due to price changes. When the price of a good decreases, consumers perceive an increase in their purchasing power, which allows them to buy more goods and leads to an increase in consumption. In this example, the combination of 3 e-books and 4 online movies costs only $85 now, less than the previous $100. Conversely, when the price of a good increases, consumers experience a decrease in their purchasing power, which leads to a reduction in consumption. The income effect reflects the overall impact of price changes on consumption levels.

The substitution effect explains how consumers adjust their consumption patterns in response to changes in their relative prices. When the price of a good decreases, consumers are **incentivized** to purchase more of that good and reduce their demand for relatively more expensive substitute goods. In the above case, the substitution effect from the fall in the price of e-books relative to the price of online movies may cause consumers to buy more e-books.

The income effect and substitution effect often **coexist**. These two concepts explain how consumers react to price changes, providing insights into consumer responses and changes in consumption decisions when prices **fluctuate**. Understanding these factors enables businesses to anticipate and adapt to ever-changing consumer demand and policymakers to strategize and implement effective economic decisions.

4.3　Cost, Revenue and Profit

4.3.1　Cost and Producer Surplus

Now, let us shift to the other side of the market to consider the perspective of sellers and examine the benefits they derive from engaging in market activities. Imagine that a father is looking for a piano teacher to help his son with his musical performance. Four teachers, namely Zhang, Li, Wang, and Chen, are willing to provide service if the price offered exceeds the cost of doing the work. The term "cost" in economics refers to the value or sacrifice associated with the production of goods or services. This should be interpreted as the teacher's opportunity cost. Here, the teachers' cost includes out-of-pocket expenses (for transportation, teaching material, etc.) and the value that the teachers place on their own time (the opportunity cost of time). Table 4-4 shows the costs incurred by each teacher.

Table 4-4　The Costs of Four Possible Sellers

Seller	Cost ($)
Zhang	200
Li	180
Wang	170
Chen	150

A teacher's cost is the lowest price he or she would accept for work, which is the measure of his or her willingness to sell the services. Teachers would be motivated to offer services at a price that exceeds the cost, show no interest in selling at a price equal to the cost, and be reluctant to sell at a price lower than the cost. As the buyer **solicits** bids from the sellers, initially the price may be high, but it gradually decreases as the sellers compete for the job. When Chen places a bid of $170 or slightly lower, he becomes the only remaining bidder. The seller who can provide the services at the lowest cost is ultimately chosen for the job.

In this case, Chen's cost is $150, but he gets $170 for doing the job, so we can say that he receives a benefit of $20. This benefit is referred to as producer surplus, which is the difference between the price that producers are willing to supply a good or service for and the price they actually receive in the market. Producer surplus represents the additional benefit or surplus that producers gain from participating in a market transaction and is calculated by **subtracting** the cost of production from the revenue received by producers.

Unit 4 Consumption and Production

Suppose the father wants to hire an additional teacher to tutor his other child. Now, he needs two teachers instead of one. This time, the price falls until only two teachers, Wang and Chen, are willing to sell their services at a price of $180 (or slightly less). At this price, Wang and Chen receive a producer surplus of $10 and $30 respectively. If we assume these are all market participants, the total producer surplus in the market is $40, as shown by the shaded area below the price and above the supply line in Figure 4-4.

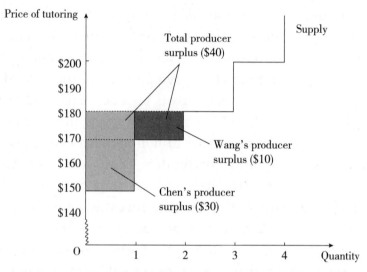

Figure 4-4 Producer Surplus with a Market Price of $180

Graphically, as the number of market participants increases, the supply curve becomes smoother. The total producer surplus at a specific price and quantity is illustrated by the shaded triangle in Figure 4-5.

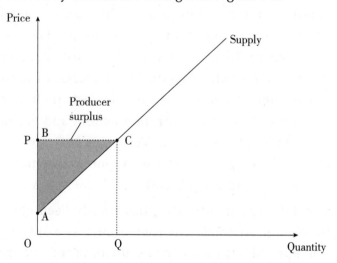

Figure 4-5 Total Producer Surplus at Price P

Producer surplus influences the willingness of producers to sell and is directly determined by costs. Examining the full **array** of economic costs will lay the foundation for understanding the supply decisions of producers. Economic cost involves total cost, **explicit** cost, and **implicit** cost. In economics, these are all opportunity costs borne by **entrepreneurs**.

Total cost (TC) refers to the overall expense incurred by a firm in producing a given quantity of output, including both explicit costs and implicit costs. Explicit costs are direct and measurable out-of-pocket expenses incurred by a firm during the production process. These costs involve the actual payments made to purchase or hire resources or services. Since explicit costs can be displayed in a company's **financial statements**, they are also referred to as accounting costs. Examples of explicit costs include wages paid to employees, costs of raw materials, **rent** for office or factory space, utility bills, marketing expenses, and taxes. Implicit costs refer to non-monetary costs associated with the use of resources or **forgone** opportunities. These costs represent the value of resources that could be alternatively utilized. Implicit costs do not involve actual monetary payments but reflect the forgone benefits and revenues. Examples of implicit costs include the forgone income from using self-owned capital or property, the time and effort of the business owner, and the potential opportunities that are given up to pursue the current business venture.

The total cost can also be divided into **fixed cost** (FC) and **variable cost** (VC). The fixed cost is the portion of the total cost that remains constant regardless of the level of output produced. These costs do not vary in the short run even if production increases or decreases. Examples of fixed costs include rent, salaries for permanent employees, and certain types of capital investments. They are called "fixed" because they remain fixed irrespective of the production level. Variable cost refers to the portion of the total cost that changes in direct proportion to the level of output. As production increases or decreases, variable costs fluctuate accordingly. Examples of variable costs include raw materials, direct labor wages, utilities that vary with production, and expenses related to packaging or transportation. By definition, VC begins at zero when the output is zero, and it is part of TC that grows with the output. **Mathematically**, the total cost is the sum of the fixed and variable costs, i.e., TC = FC + VC.

Another concept, marginal cost (MC), has already been covered in Unit 1. It represents the change in total cost that occurs as a result of increasing production by one unit. MC is calculated by dividing the change in total cost

(ΔTC) by the change in quantity (ΔQ), that is, MC = ΔTC / ΔQ. MC helps firms determine their optimal level of production by comparing the additional cost of producing an extra unit with the revenue generated from selling that unit.

The principle behind profit maximization is to produce at a level where marginal cost equals marginal revenue. Marginal revenue refers to the additional revenue earned by selling one more unit of output. When the marginal cost is less than the marginal revenue, producing an additional unit increases profitability. In contrast, if the marginal cost exceeds the marginal revenue, producing another unit would lead to a decrease in overall profitability.

4.3.2 Revenue and Profit

To assess the profitability, growth, and overall success of a business, two terms are often employed: revenue and profit. Revenue refers to the total income or sales generated by a business from its operations. This represents the **inflow** of funds or assets resulting from the sale of goods, services, or other revenue-generating activities. We can calculate revenue by **multiplying** the price of a product or service by the quantity sold, that is, R = P * Q. In this **equation**, R stands for revenue, P for the price of a product or service, and Q for the quantity of products or services sold. This is a fundamental equation used to determine the overall revenue or sales generated from a particular product or service.

Profit refers to the excess revenue from costs and expenses, the amount of money or financial gain that remains after all relevant costs are **deducted** from revenue, including both explicit and implicit costs. The equation π = TR − TC represents the calculation of profit (π), where TR stands for the total revenue, and TC represents the total cost.

Due to different interpretations of costs by economists and accountants, there are two different methods to measure profits: economic profit and accounting profit. Economic profit is calculated by subtracting all costs, including both explicit and implicit costs, from total revenue. Economic profit reflects the true financial gain or loss generated by an activity considering the alternative uses of resources. Accounting profit refers to the profit reported in a company's financial statements, which is calculated by deducting only explicit costs from total revenue. Figure 4-6 demonstrates the relationship between economic profit and accounting profit.

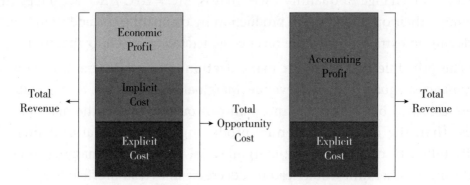

Figure 4-6　Economic Profit and Accounting Profit

Accounting profit is always greater than economic profit because accountants overlook implicit costs. However, from an economic perspective, it is necessary to account for all opportunity costs in order to measure profitability accurately.

Normal profit is viewed in **conjunction** with economic profit as a measure that considers both explicit and implicit costs. Normal profit occurs when the difference between a company's total revenue and combined explicit and implicit costs equals zero. This is the return to the entrepreneur or business owner for their time, skills, and capital investment. It can be seen as the minimum operating goal for a business, ensuring that it generates the necessary profit to sustain its operations. It reflects the efficiency of a business's operations and is associated with the long-run equilibrium in industries under perfect competition.

4.4　Producers and Production Theory

4.4.1　Producers and Production Functions

The term "producers", in the context of economics, refers to **entities** or individuals involved in the process of creating and supplying goods or services in the market. They are responsible for transforming raw materials, labor, and capital into finished products or services that can satisfy consumer needs and wants. They decide what and how to produce according to their costs and market conditions. In reality, the majority of production is carried out by specialized organizations, including small, medium, and large firms, which **dominate** the landscape of the modern economy.

Let us examine the concepts of production theory and understand how firms transform their inputs into desirable outputs. For instance, a bakery utilizes inputs such as flour, additives, energy, machinery, and labor to produce cakes. In this context, raw materials, machinery, and labor serve as inputs, while cakes constitute the output. The relationship between the inputs used in the production process and the output or quantity of goods or services produced is described as the production **function**, which specifies the maximum output that can be produced with a given quantity of input in the given state of engineering and technical knowledge. In general, a production function takes the form $Q = f(K, L, T, \ldots)$, where Q represents the quantity or output of production, K denotes the quantity of capital, L stands for labor, T refers to other factors of production such as technology or raw materials, and f is a function that describes the relationship between the input and output.

In the simplified analytical framework, the discussion typically revolves around labor (L) and capital (K). This simplification assumes the exclusion of other potential production factors to **facilitate** a clearer study of the impact of labor and capital on production. Therefore, the corresponding mathematical representation is $Q = f(L, K)$.

By studying production functions, businesses can gain a better understanding of the factors that influence their output levels and make informed decisions regarding resource allocation. They can identify areas in which resources can be optimized or reallocated to enhance productivity and maximize output. This optimization process involves evaluating the marginal effects of each input factor, such as labor or capital, and determining the point at which diminishing returns are set.

Furthermore, production functions aid in setting **benchmarks** and evaluating performance. By comparing the actual output with the expected output based on the production function, businesses can assess their efficiency and identify areas for improvement. This analysis enables them to make informed decisions regarding investments in new technologies, business process reengineering, or other strategies that positively impact production capabilities.

4.4.2 Productivity and Marginal Effects

By utilizing the production function of a firm, we can calculate three crucial **metrics**: the total product (TP), average product (AP), and marginal product (MP). Total product refers to the overall quantity of output that a firm generates by employing a certain combination of inputs (such as labor and capital) in the production process. This represents the cumulative amount of output produced at a particular level of input utilization. The average product is calculated by dividing the total product by the amount of input used. It represents the average output generated per unit of input. For example, the average product of labor (APL) is obtained by dividing the total product by the quantity of labor used. Marginal product is the additional output generated by utilizing one additional unit of input while keeping the other inputs constant. It measures the rate of change in the total product resulting from a small change in input. The marginal product helps determine the **incremental** contribution of each additional unit of input to the overall output. For instance, the marginal product of labor (MPL) is calculated by determining the change in the total product due to an additional unit of labor.

Take the bakery as an example. Table 4-5 shows the total product (cakes) that can be produced for different inputs of labor (bakers) when other inputs and the state of technical knowledge are unchanged. The total product starts at zero for zero bakers, and then increases as additional bakers participate in the production process. It reaches a maximum of 390 cakes with the presence of 5 bakers. In addition, we can calculate the marginal product of labor, as shown in the third column. The marginal product of labor starts at 200 cakes for the first baker and drops to 10 for the fifth one. The fourth column shows the average product of labor. In this example, the average product of labor declines consistently as the number of bakers increases from 1 to 5.

Table 4-5 Total, Marginal, and Average Product of a Bakery

Quantity of Bakers	Total Product of Labor	Marginal Product of Labor	Average Product of Labor
0	0	0	0
1	200	200	200
2	300	100	150
3	350	50	117
4	380	30	95
5	390	10	78

The production function helps us understand one of the most frequently mentioned laws in economics—the law of diminishing returns, also known as the law of diminishing marginal productivity. It states that, as the quantity of one input is increased while other inputs are kept constant, there will be a point beyond which the additional output or productivity gained from each additional unit of the input will start to decrease.

This relationship is not difficult to understand. When increasing a specific input (such as labor) while holding other inputs constant, the firm may encounter a situation in which the available resources to work with this input become scarcer. The workshop is overcrowded, and the machinery is overworked. Therefore, the marginal product of labor declines. Table 4-5 illustrates the law of diminishing returns. It is notable that what holds for labor is equally applicable to any other input.

The law of diminishing returns suggests that there is an optimal level of input utilization, beyond which further increases may lead to smaller incremental gains in output. It is an important concept in production theory as it helps explain the relationship between inputs and outputs and guides decision-making regarding the optimal allocation of resources in production processes.

Many factors influence the production process. Regarding new production methods, the **dictum** "science and technology constitute a primary productive force" is widely known, highlighting the crucial role of technological change in driving productivity and economic output.

From an economic perspective, we distinguish between process and product innovations. Process innovation refers to the creation or implementation of new or improved methods, techniques, or systems to produce existing goods or services, resulting in an upward shift in the production function. On the other hand, product innovation involves the development, creation, or enhancement of new or improved products, services, or features that provide added value to customers or fulfill unmet market needs. Product innovation has a significant impact on the quality of life. To illustrate this, think about some products that have emerged in recent years and greatly improved your daily life.

Exercises

❶ Short answer questions

Directions: *Answer the following questions in your own words or with sentences from the text.*

(1) What is consumer surplus?

(2) What are the conditions for a consumer equilibrium?

(3) What is the difference between revenue and profit?

(4) What is the law of diminishing returns?

❷ Term explanation

Directions: *Explain the following terms in your own words or with sentences from the text.*

(1) utility

(2) income effect

(3) total cost

(4) production function

❸ Banked cloze

Directions: *Fill in the blanks by selecting suitable words from the following box. You may not use any of the words more than once.*

A. innovation	B. strive	C. conversely	D. competitive	E. motivate
F. optimize	G. effect	H. fostering	I. assume	J. utilizing
K. output	L. degradation	M. restrict	N. pivotal	O. interplay

Consumption and production are two (1) _____ components of an economy, working hand in hand to drive economic growth. Consumers play a crucial role by (2) _____ goods and services based on their needs, preferences, and available resources. Their choices are influenced by factors such as income, price levels, advertising, and cultural forces.

Meanwhile, producers (3) _____ to meet consumer demand by organizing resources efficiently and manufacturing goods and services. Their goal is to

(4) _____ production processes, allocate resources effectively, and maintain product quality. This may involve implementing various strategies to streamline (使效率更高) operations and reduce costs.

Technological advancements upgrade production processes, resulting in higher efficiency. Automation systems, machinery, and software solutions simplify operations, increase (5) _____, and decrease the need for manual labor. Besides, producers work for better (6) _____ edge in various other ways as well, such as through effective supply chain management, quality control measures, and strategic resource allocation.

Moreover, the (7) _____ between consumers and producers creates a dynamic market economy. Consumer demand stimulates production, leading to income generation, employment opportunities, and overall economic growth. Increasing consumption levels often prompt producers to expand their operations and invest in new technologies to meet market demands. This, in turn, boosts (8) _____, productivity, and economic development.

It is worth noting that achieving a balance between consumption and production is crucial for sustainability. Excessive consumption can lead to resource depletion (耗竭) and environmental (9) _____. Thus, promoting responsible and sustainable consumption practices is essential for long-term economic and environmental well-being.

In conclusion, the relationship between consumption and production is at the core of a thriving economy. Consumers drive the demand for goods and services, while producers aim to meet that demand efficiently. Achieving a sustainable balance between consumption and production is key to (10) _____ a vibrant and resilient economy.

❹ Translation

Directions: *Translate the following paragraphs into Chinese or English.*

(1) As a measure that takes into consideration both explicit and implicit costs, normal profit is often viewed in conjunction with economic profit. Normal profit occurs when the difference between a company's total revenue and combined explicit and implicit costs equals zero. This is the return to the entrepreneur or business owner for their time, skills, and capital investment. If a business earns normal profit, it is considered economically efficient as it covers its opportunity costs without making any additional return. An industry is expected

to experience normal profit under the circumstances of perfect competition.

(2) 国家发展改革委（the National Development and Reform Commission, NDRC）就恢复和扩大消费提出了多项措施。坚持有效市场（efficient market）和有为政府（effective government）更好结合，坚持优化供给和扩大需求更好结合，坚持提质升级（quality upgrading）和创新发展更好结合。包括稳定大宗消费（spending on big-ticket items），扩大服务消费，促进农村消费，拓展新型消费，完善消费设施，优化消费环境。这些措施已得到国务院批准，旨在更好地实施扩大内需的战略，充分发挥消费在刺激经济增长中的基础性作用，支持国家的高质量发展（high-quality development）。

5 Project

Title: Green Consumption

Instructions:

Step 1: Research the concept and significance of green consumption, share your perspectives on environmental issues and sustainable development, and explore the individual and collective impact on the environment.

Step 2: Select several common consumer products and research their production processes, materials, and environmental standards. You can analyze and compare the eco-friendly features of different products and identify examples of green consumption.

Step 3: Analyze consumer behaviors and develop a personal or group green consumption plan that includes purchasing eco-friendly products, reducing waste, and practicing energy conservation. You can also share your experiences and challenges.

Step 4: Reflect on your learning experiences and personal growth throughout the project. Report your findings and practices to the class, and promote an exchange of ideas.

Supplementary Reading

Scan the QR code to find out more about the unit.

Unit 5

Market Competition

Learning Objectives

After studying this unit, you should be able to:

1) comprehend the concepts of markets and competition, game theory, and market failure;
2) use the words and phrases in this unit;
3) use the knowledge in this unit to investigate the use of a public good.

This unit focuses on the dynamics of market competition and monopoly, and examines their impact on economic outcomes. It begins with the concept and **categorization** of the market, and then examines the equilibrium conditions under which firms maximize profits in various markets. Additionally, the role of uncertainty and game theory in understanding strategic decision-making in markets is discussed. Finally, it analyzes market failures and the provision of public goods.

5.1 Market and Market Structure

A market is a system in which buyers and sellers come together to exchange goods, services, or resources. It is a mechanism through which individuals, businesses, and organizations interact to buy and sell goods and services to fulfill their needs and wants. It can be physical, such as a traditional marketplace or a shopping mall, or **virtual**, such as an online platform or an electronic trading system. It can also refer to a specific industry or sector, in which the buying and selling of particular goods or services take place. Markets play a crucial role in the functioning of the market economy. The study of markets serves as the foundation for analyzing supply and demand dynamics, price determination, competition, and allocation of resources, and is therefore essential for understanding how individuals and businesses make economic decisions and how these decisions shape the overall economy.

Based on the characteristics that influence the behavior and outcomes of firms working in a specific market, we define various market structures. Market structure refers to the classification and **differentiation** of different industries based on the degree and nature of the competition for goods and services. Some of the factors that determine market structure include the following: number of firms in the market, degree of product differentiation, degree of price control, and barriers to market entry. These factors collectively determine the characteristics and functions of the different market types. The four popular types are perfect competition, monopolistic competition, oligopoly, and monopoly (see Table 5-1).

Table 5-1 Types of Market Structure

Structure	Number of Firms	Degree of Product Differentiation	Degree of Price Control	Barriers to Market Entry	Examples of Industries
Perfect competition	Many firms	Identical products	None	Very low	Agricultural products
Monopolistic competition	Many firms	Many real or perceived differences in products	Some	Low	Clothing stores, restaurants
Oligopoly	Few firms	Identical or differentiated products	Significant	High	Steel, cars, petroleum
Monopoly	Single firm	Product without substitutes	Considerable	Entry blocked	Franchise monopolies (electricity, tap water…)

The focus of market theory is to analyze the behavior of firms pursuing profit maximization in various markets as well as the equilibrium prices and quantities in these markets. In this book, we briefly examine two extreme market structures, perfect competition and monopoly, in the following section. However, we must acknowledge that real markets are more intricate than simplified models. To gain a deeper understanding, factors such as imperfect competition, industry differentiation, and the interplay of diverse market forces need to be explored.

5.2 Competition and Monopoly

5.2.1 Perfectly Competitive Market

A perfectly competitive market is characterized by full and unrestricted competition without any **hindrance** or interference. Allocative, productive, and perfect competition promotes efficiency, leading to consumer welfare and economic growth.

A perfectly competitive market must fulfill four conditions: a large number of buyers and sellers, **homogeneous** products, perfect information, and freedom of entry and exit. It is a non-individualized market where traders' personalities are absent. It can be said that meaningful competition, as experienced in real economic life, does not exist in a perfectly competitive market. Certain agricultural product markets such as the rice market, wheat market, etc., are often regarded as being relatively close to perfectly competitive markets. Nevertheless, analyzing perfect competition market models helps us derive fundamental principles about market mechanisms and resource allocation, and provides a benchmark for assessing real-world market structures and their efficiency.

Based on the aforementioned conditions, a perfectly competitive market is the world of price-takers. Consumers, as do firms, generally accept the market prices. If a producer attempts to raise its price, it will not sell anything at all because consumers will switch to buying the product from its competitors. In a perfectly competitive market, once demand and supply reach equilibrium, firms can sell any quantity of goods at the equilibrium price without affecting market equilibrium. Whether a firm chooses to sell all of its products or not, the market equilibrium price remains unchanged.

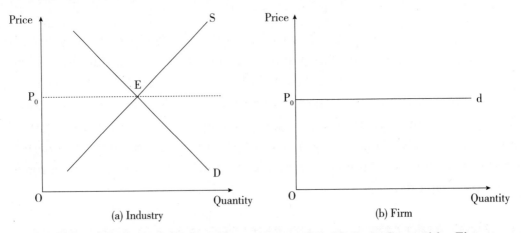

Figure 5-1 The Demand Curve for the Output of a Perfectly Competitive Firm

Look at Figure 5-1. Panel (a) shows that in a perfectly competitive market, the industry demand curve (D) slopes downward to the right, similar to the demand curves in other market types. The demand curve intersects the supply curve (S) at point E, the equilibrium price being P_0. In contrast to the industry demand curve, a single firm's demand curve (d), shown in Panel (b), appears completely horizontal. At the market equilibrium price, the market demand for a product from a firm is infinite. A firm can sell any quantity of its product at the market equilibrium price without facing a demand limit.

In Unit 4, we learned some concepts regarding cost, revenue, and profit.

Note that for any level of output, a firm's average revenue (AR) is always equal to the market price, because total revenue (TR) is calculated by multiplying the price (P) of a good or service by the quantity (Q) sold, that is, TR = P*Q. Additionally, the average revenue equals the total revenue divided by the quantity (AR = TR/Q); therefore, AR = (P*Q)/Q = P. The firm's marginal revenue (MR) is the change in total revenue from selling one more unit:

$$MR = \frac{\Delta TR}{\Delta Q}$$

In a perfectly competitive market, the firm faces a **predetermined** price (P). Therefore,

$$MR = \frac{\Delta TR}{\Delta Q} = \frac{P*\Delta Q}{\Delta Q} = P$$

Here is an important equation: AR = MR = P. For a firm in a perfectly competitive market, the price is equal to both the average revenue and marginal revenue.

Then let us examine how a firm maximizes its profit in a perfectly competitive market. The principle of profit maximization requires firms to compare marginal costs (MC) with marginal revenue (MR) in order to determine the level of output. The firm achieves the profit-maximizing level of output when MR equals MC, i.e., MR = MC. As long as the MR **surpasses** the MC, the firm experiences increasing profits, prompting it to expand its production. The firm continues producing until the MR it receives equals the MC of production. At this output level, selling an additional unit does not generate any extra profit. Thus, the firm achieves profit maximization.

In Figure 5-2, the equilibrium price determined by the market supply and demand is represented as P_0. The horizontal line starting from this price represents the demand curve, which is the marginal revenue (MR) curve and average revenue (AR) curve for the firm. The marginal cost (MC) curve for the firm is a U-shaped curve that initially decreases and then increases. Point E represents the intersection between the firm's marginal revenue curve and demand curve. At this point, the firm's marginal revenue equals its marginal cost, indicating that it reaches the level of output that maximizes its profits.

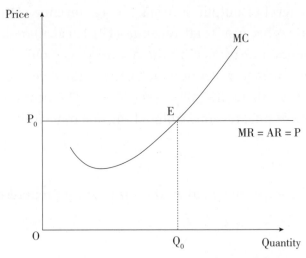

Figure 5-2　The Profit-Maximizing Level of Output

The conclusion that the level of output that maximizes profits occurs when marginal revenue equals marginal cost (MR = MC) applies to all firms, regardless of whether they operate in a perfectly competitive industry. Achieving profit maximization does not necessarily guarantee profitability, as losses can still occur. For a firm operating at a loss, adhering to the profit maximization principle in organizing production is essential. Failure to do so could **exacerbate** the losses even further.

Break-even point (BEP) is a financial term that refers to the level of sales at which a firm's total revenue is equal to its total costs (TR = TC). When a firm determines its output level according to the principle of profit maximization and exceeds the production level represented by the BEP, it leads to profitability. Conversely, if a firm's output falls below this level, it incurs losses. The shutdown point represents the output level at which the revenues are only able to cover the variable costs (VC) or where the losses are equal to the fixed costs (FC). Below the shutdown point, it is more economically **viable** for the firm to suspend operations and minimize losses.

In the short run, firms cannot enter or exit the market. Their equilibrium output is determined based on the profit-maximizing principle, that is, whether they make profits, incur losses, or achieve a state of profit-loss balance. In the long run, firms can modify their production factors. Existing firms may exit the market, whereas new firms may enter. Consequently, the profits and losses are **eliminated**. In a perfectly competitive market, the long-run equilibrium is marked by zero profit, indicating that firms neither generate profits nor suffer losses.

5.2.2 Monopolistic Market

At one end of the market **spectrum** is perfect competition, while at the other end stands monopoly. In economics, monopoly refers to a situation where the market is controlled and dominated by a single seller (producer or supplier).

In a monopolistic market, a single seller produces or supplies a unique product or service with no close substitutes and faces no direct competition. Barriers to entry prevent other firms from entering the market, giving the monopolist significant market power and the ability to **exert** control over the market by influencing market prices, output levels, or other market conditions. As a result, the monopolist becomes a price maker, setting prices at levels that maximize profits. Consumers have limited choices and are often **compelled** to purchase a monopolist's product even at a higher price.

Every firm would like a monopoly to benefit from the absence of competition. To establish a monopoly, barriers to entry must be set at a sufficiently high level to **deter** other firms from entering the market. Barriers may emerge for the following reasons:

1. A firm has exclusive ownership or access to scarce resources that are crucial to its production process.

2. Government regulations, **patents**, copyrights, or intellectual property rights can create legal barriers.

3. In certain industries, network effects occur when the value of a product or service increases as more people use it, creating a natural advantage for early **entrants**.

4. A firm can develop a natural monopoly when economies of scale are substantial.

5. High entry costs, including investments in infrastructure, R&D, and establishing distribution networks, can deter potential competitors from entering the market.

Firms in a perfectly competitive market are considered price takers, whereas monopolistic firms are price makers. When price makers raise their prices, they experience a decrease in the number of customers. Graphically, a monopolistic firm faces both a downward-sloping demand curve (D = AR) and a downward-sloping marginal revenue (MR) curve (Figure 5-3).

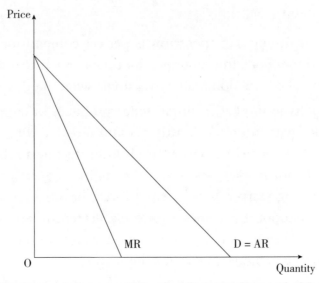

Figure 5-3 The Demand Curve and Marginal Revenue Curve of a Monopolistic Firm

From Figure 5-3, it can be observed that the MR curve of a monopolistic firm intersects its demand curve and average revenue curve (D = AR) on the vertical axis. This is because a monopolistic firm sets its price equal to its marginal revenue when selling the first unit of output, but from the second unit onwards, the marginal revenue becomes less than the price. Whenever there is an inverse relationship between price and quantity demanded, marginal revenue will necessarily be lower than price, causing the MR curve to lie below the demand curve (D = AR).

Like any other firms, a monopolist aims to maximize its profit. The condition for profit maximization remains consistent, producing at the point where marginal revenue (MR) equals marginal cost (MC).

According to Figure 5-4, the intersection of the MR and MC curves at point A indicates the level of output that maximizes the firm's profit. This optimal output quantity, denoted as Q_1, ensures that the firm achieves maximum profitability. Q_1 represents a monopolistic firm's equilibrium output.

Point B on the demand curve corresponds to profit-maximizing quantity Q_1, where the monopolistic firm sells its products at price P_1. The total revenue of the firm is shown as the area of rectangle OP_1BQ_1 under the demand curve. The quantity Q_1 corresponds to Point C on the average total cost (ATC) curve, with the average total cost P_C marked on the vertical axis at this level. Hence, the total cost is depicted by the rectangle OP_CCQ_1. At this point, the monopolistic firm generates economic profits, which can be calculated by subtracting total costs from total revenue, represented by the area of the rectangle P_CP_1BC. The area in the graph represents the monopolistic firm's economic profits.

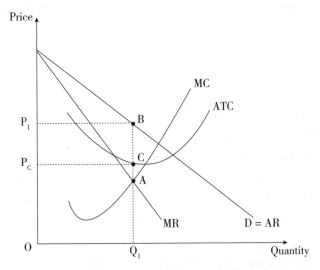

Figure 5-4 Profit Maximization for a Monopolistic Firm

In the short run, a monopolistic firm may make profit, suffer losses, or break even. In the long run, it reaches a specific equilibrium, as shown in Figure 5-4. Other firms may seek to enter the industry, but the presence of significant barriers to entry prevents them from doing so. Consequently, the monopolistic firm can maintain its monopolistic profits in the industry.

Monopolistic firms determine their output based on the profit-maximizing principle (MR = MC), and then set the price based on this output and market demand. Therefore, there is no single supply curve for a monopolistic firm because it is not a passive price taker but has an influence on the price.

Monopolistic firms possess market power, measured by the difference between the price and marginal cost, whereas in a competitive market equilibrium, the price **aligns** with the firm's marginal cost, **signifying** zero market power.

When firms have market power, they may increase their profits through price discrimination. Price discrimination is a practice in which a company sets different prices for the same product or service for different consumers or markets. For example, airlines implement price discrimination by charging different prices based on factors such as advance purchases, time of travel, and seat class. This allows them to cater to the preferences and budgets of different travelers while optimizing their profitability.

Public policies regarding monopolistic markets have been developed to promote market competition, protect consumer rights, and ensure fair and effective market operation. Governments combat monopolistic practices through anti-monopoly laws and enforcement agencies, monitor the market, and examine mergers and pricing behaviors. They also promote competition and utilize price controls to safeguard consumers' interests. For example, China has implemented anti-monopoly laws and established the State Administration for Market Regulation (SAMR) to enforce these laws. The SAMR investigates various sectors such as telecommunications, banking, and the Internet, to ensure fair competition. Violating companies can face fines, be required to provide fair treatment to competitors, and be compelled to take corrective measures. The ultimate aim of these public policies is to maintain a level playing field in the market while protecting the interests of consumers and society.

5.3 Uncertainty and Game Theory

5.3.1 Uncertainty and Its Impact on the Market

In market analysis, we assume that the costs and demands are fully known and certain. However, in reality, the business environment is characterized by a **multitude** of uncertainties. For instance, the emergence of new energy vehicles (NEV) has brought significant uncertainty to the product markets. Factors such as government regulations, advancements in battery technology, and consumer acceptance contribute to the uncertainty for automakers, suppliers, and consumers. This uncertainty impacts automakers' investment decisions and consumer behaviors, thereby influencing market competition and pricing strategies. Engaging in economic activities inherently involves both risks and uncertainties.

When analyzing the behaviors of businesses and households, risks and uncertainties should be considered. Markets can spread risks over time and space. Let us now examine the role of speculation as an example. Speculation involves engaging in financial transactions with the intention of profiting from predicted price fluctuations in assets, such as stocks, commodities, or currencies. Speculators make investment decisions based on their expectations of future market conditions and asset prices, rather than relying solely on **intrinsic** values. They are willing to assume greater risks in pursuit of potentially higher returns.

Consider the involvement of speculators in the rice markets. They enter the market before harvest time, creating demand to **offset** potential price decreases due to increased supply. As the harvest season progresses and the rice supply reduces, speculators sell their holdings. This selling activity adds to market supply, preventing any potential upward pressure on prices that may arise due to reduced availability.

The presence of speculators may enhance liquidity and efficiency in the market, helping market participants reduce their exposure to price **volatility** and effectively manage price risks through risk assumptions and **proactive** trading strategies. However, we should also be cautious that excessive speculation or speculative bubbles can lead to market volatility and potential financial instability.

5.3.2 Game Theory and the Prisoner's Dilemma

Game theory provides a framework for analyzing strategic decision-making in situations of uncertainty, where the outcome of one's actions depends on the actions taken by others. The game theory offers insights into how rational actors make decisions under uncertainty by studying how individuals or entities interact in competitive or cooperative settings.

One of the most well-known examples is the prisoner's dilemma. In the given scenario, two suspects are arrested and held separately, unable to communicate with each other. The **prosecutor** lacks sufficient evidence for **conviction**, so the prisoners face a choice: to **conspire** with each other (refuse to confess) or to betray each other (confess).

If both prisoners choose to conspire, due to a lack of evidence, the prosecutor can only convict them of a lesser crime, and each faces a 1-year sentence. If one prisoner remains silent while the other confesses, the confessor will receive **leniency** and be **exempt** from punishment, whereas the silent one will receive a 10-year imprisonment. If both confess, each is subject to an 8-year prison term.

We often use a two-way payoff table, also known as a payoff matrix, to analyze the interaction. It is a **tabular** representation that illustrates the rewards or payoffs associated with the different strategies chosen by players involved in a game theory scenario. The rows of the table represent the possible actions or decisions of one player, whereas the columns represent the possible actions or decisions of the other player. The entries in the table indicate the rewards or payoffs for each player, based on the combination of actions chosen.

In Table 5-2, prisoner A can choose between the two rows, while prisoner B can choose between the two columns. Both have two options: conspire or betray, resulting in four possible outcomes indicated in the four cells in the matrix. In each cell, the number in the left triangle represents the prison sentence for prisoner A and the number in the right triangle represents the prison sentence for prisoner B.

Table 5-2 The Two-Way Payoff Table for the Prisoner's Dilemma

Prisoner A	Prisoner B	
	Conspire	Betray
Conspire	1 yr / 1 yr	10 yrs / 0 yr
Betray	0 yr / 10 yrs	8 yrs / 8 yrs

Let us focus on prisoner A. As A is unaware of B's decision, A must consider the consequences based on various assumptions of what B might choose. Assume that B chooses to conspire. If A also chooses to conspire, the sentence is 1 year. However, if A chooses to betray, A is exempt. It is clear that betraying is advantageous for A. Now, suppose that B chooses to betray. If A refuses to confess, the sentence is 10 years, but if A also betrays, the sentence is 8 years. Again, betraying proves to be advantageous for A. In other words, whether B chooses to conspire or betray, betraying is more favorable for A. This optimal choice, regardless of the potential strategies of the other **opponents**, is the dominant strategy.

The situation is the same for prisoner B. Therefore, as rational individuals, both prisoners **ultimately** choose to betray to benefit themselves. However, in terms of the overall outcome, this self-interested decision-making leads to the worst possible result: a combined sentence of 16 years. Thus, the prisoner's dilemma illustrates that individuals acting in their own interests can result in the poorest overall efficiency.

We can apply the principle of game theory to a duopoly, in which two firms compete in the market. Suppose there are only two bookstores, Acme and Bookworm, operating in the same region, with similar customer bases. Both bookstores have the option to lower their prices to attract more customers, but the price-cutting strategy may result in reduced profits. The payoffs associated with different strategies are illustrated in Table 5-3.

Table 5-3 A Payoff Table for a Price War

		Bookworm			
		Normal price		Price-cutting	
Acme	Normal price	$10	$10	−$10	−$100
	Price-cutting	−$100	−$10	−$50	−$50

Consider the options for Acme. If Bookworm keeps its normal price, Acme will gain $10 of profit if it also maintains the normal price and will lose $100 if it cuts the price. On the other hand, if Bookworm launches a price war, Acme will lose $10 if it maintains the normal price but incur a loss of $50 if it also cuts the price. The same logic applies to Bookworm. Hence, charging the normal price is their dominant strategy in this scenario. When both firms play dominant strategies, the outcome is a dominant equilibrium.

5.4 Market Failures and Public Goods

5.4.1 Pareto Efficiency and Market Failures

Adam Smith's concept of the invisible hand suggests that in economies characterized by perfect competition, markets will naturally allocate resources efficiently and produce goods and services that align with consumers' needs and preferences. In achieving equilibrium, consumers and producers can maximize their own interests without negatively impacting anyone else's interests, thereby achieving Pareto optimality or Pareto efficiency. Named after Italian economist Vilfredo Pareto, it refers to an economic state in which resources cannot be reallocated to make one individual better off without making at least one individual worse off. Pareto efficiency implies that the resources are allocated in the most economically efficient manner. When there is a possibility of redistributing resources or changing the allocation in a way that benefits at least one individual without harming others, Pareto improvement occurs. Pareto optimality, along with the concept of perfect competition, is used as a benchmark to judge the efficiency of real markets. However, it is important to note that both are primarily theoretical constructs in economics. In reality, there are various ways in which markets may deviate from the ideal conditions of perfect competition and Pareto optimality, leading to market failure. This is **aptly** named because in these situations the market fails to allocate goods optimally or efficiently.

Market failures are primarily attributed to imperfect competition, externalities, and public goods. Imperfect competition prevails in a market where perfect competition does not hold because individual sellers can affect the market price. The major kinds of imperfect competition are monopolistic competition, oligopoly, and monopoly, as shown in Table 5-1. In the following section, we focus on the other two factors, externalities and public goods.

5.4.2 Externalities and Public Goods

Externalities (or spillover effects) are a type of market failure that occurs when one party's actions in a transaction have an impact, either positive or negative, on a third party outside the marketplace without adequate compensation. For example, vaccine development provides a positive externality. When pharmaceutical companies invest in the research and development of vaccines, healthcare providers can share knowledge and breakthroughs, leading to improved health situations for a broader population. This positive impact extends beyond individuals directly vaccinated, benefiting society as a whole. In contrast, the **emission** of harmful pollutants into the environment conveys negative externalities, posing health risks to nearby residents, and causing environmental degradation. However, these costs are not factored into the production costs of the factory responsible for the pollution.

In both examples, externalities demonstrate **divergence** between private and social costs or benefits. Private cost refers to the cost incurred by an individual or firm in the production or consumption of a good or service, including explicit and implicit costs. Social cost captures the total cost of an economic activity, including both private and any external costs imposed on society. External costs are borne by third parties who are not directly involved in the transaction. Negative externalities such as environmental pollution or health impacts exemplify these external costs.

Negative externalities occur when private costs are lower than social costs. One solution to address this market failure is to impose taxes on sellers, with the tax amount being equal to the difference between social and private costs, thus aligning private costs with social costs. This solution, first proposed by British economist Arthur Cecil Pigou (1877–1959), is known as Pigouvian taxation. The strategy of internalizing externalities through taxation aims to integrate external costs into prices, thereby incentivizing market participants to adjust their decisions and produce or consume quantities closer to the socially optimal level.

This approach helps **rectify** the efficiency gap caused by externalities.

Market failure caused by positive externalities can be addressed in a similar way. Instead of **internalizing** costs, the goal is to internalize benefits. One approach is to provide subsidies to consumers that are equal to external benefits, thus promoting Pareto optimality and ensuring the efficient allocation of resources.

Public goods can also lead to market failure. To define public goods, we can group various goods based on two characteristics: Is the good excludable? (Can people be restricted or prevented from using the good?) Is the good rival? (Does one person's use of the good diminish another person's use of it?) The four types are displayed in Table 5-4.

Table 5-4 Four Types of Goods

		Rival?	
		Yes	No
Excludable?	Yes	Private goods · Food · Clothing · Personal vehicles	Natural monopolies · Cable TV · Railways · Telecommunications infrastructure
	No	Common resources · Fish in the ocean · **Grazing** land for livestock · Water in a common reservoir	Public goods · Street lighting · National defense · Public parks

Public goods are non-excludable and non-rivalrous, such as street lighting. It is difficult or impossible to prevent anyone from benefiting from street lighting, and consumption by an individual does not diminish its availability to others. It provides positive externalities, such as enhanced safety and easier navigation, benefiting both direct users and wider communities. However, these benefits are not fully captured by the market, which leads to market failure. The **free-rider** problem arises because individuals can benefit from street lighting without contributing to its provision. The private market may lack an incentive to adequately provide and maintain it, as social benefits are not monetarily rewarded. As a result, government intervention or collective action is often necessary for society's overall well-being.

Public goods often require government intervention. However, governments face challenges in deciding what and how much to produce, as public goods lack price mechanisms. Cost-benefit analysis (CBA)[1] is commonly used by governments, despite the difficulty in accurately quantifying costs and benefits in monetary terms. It facilitates the efficient allocation of resources and maximization of social welfare. Continuous monitoring and evaluation are crucial to the provision of public goods.

Exercises

1 Short answer questions

Directions: *Answer the following questions in your own words or with sentences from the text.*

(1) What are the characteristics of a perfectly competitive market?

(2) What is monopoly?

(3) What is the dominant strategy in the game theory?

(4) Why is national defense considered a public good?

2 Term explanation

Directions: *Explain the following terms in your own words or with sentences from the text.*

(1) break-even point (BEP)

(2) market power

(3) Pareto efficiency

(4) externality

---

[1] cost-benefit analysis (CBA): a systematic approach used to evaluate the costs and benefits of a project, policy, or decision. It involves comparing the expected costs and benefits associated with different options and determining whether the benefits outweigh the costs.

Unit 5 Market Competition

3 Banked cloze

Directions: *Fill in the blanks by selecting suitable words from the following box. You may not use any of the words more than once.*

A. absence	B. continuously	C. intersect	D. manipulative	E. substantial
F. exempt	G. sectors	H. exclusively	I. hinder	J. dominates
K. contrasting	L. construct	M. privileges	N. variety	O. incentive

Competition and monopoly are two (1) _____ concepts in the market. Competition refers to the presence of multiple firms vying for (争夺) customers and market share, while monopoly implies a situation where a single firm (2) _____ the market.

Competition is widely regarded as a key driver of market efficiency. It fosters innovation, as firms strive to develop better products, enhance efficiency, and attract customers. In a competitive market, companies must (3) _____ improve to stay ahead and meet customer demands effectively. This leads to lower prices, increased product (4) _____, and better quality, thus benefiting consumers.

On the other hand, monopolies can distort market dynamics and pose potential threats to consumer welfare. A firm enjoying a monopoly has the market power to set higher prices, restrict output, and limit consumer choices. The (5) _____ of competitive pressure can lead to lower levels of innovation, as the monopolistic firm lacks the (6) _____ to upgrade or introduce new products. Additionally, monopolies can (7) _____ market entry for potential competitors, stifling competition and preventing new ideas from flourishing.

While competition is generally desirable, some industries may benefit from temporary monopolies or limited market power. In certain cases, firms need (8) _____ resources, investment, and time to develop breakthrough technologies or undertake risky ventures. Granting temporary monopoly rights in the form of patents or copyrights can encourage such investments by providing exclusive market (9) _____ for a limited period. However, striking the right balance is crucial to ensure that monopoly power is not abused and that barriers to entry are not insurmountable.

To maintain a healthy market environment, governments often regulate and monitor markets, particularly in (10) _____ prone to monopolistic tendencies. Antitrust laws, competition commissions, and regulatory bodies operate to thwart anticompetitive behavior and promote fair competition. These measures aim to protect consumer interests, stimulate innovation, and ensure market efficiency.

4 Translation

Directions: *Translate the following paragraphs into Chinese or English.*

(1) Adam Smith's concept of the invisible hand suggests that in economies characterized by perfect competition, markets will naturally allocate resources efficiently and produce goods and services that align with consumers' needs and preferences. In achieving equilibrium, consumers and producers can maximize their own interests without negatively impacting anyone else's interests, thereby achieving Pareto optimality, which refers to an economic state in which resources cannot be reallocated to make one individual better off without making at least one individual worse off. Pareto efficiency implies that resources are allocated in the most economically efficient manner.

(2) 公平竞争是市场经济的核心。党的二十大就"构建高水平社会主义市场经济体制（socialist market economy）"做出专门部署，要求"加强反垄断和反不正当竞争，破除地方保护（local protection）和行政性垄断（administrative monopolies），依法规范和引导资本健康发展"。强化反垄断、深入推进公平竞争政策实施，是完善社会主义市场经济体制的内在要求（an intrinsic requirement）。

5 Project

Title: Survey on the Use of a Public Good

Instructions: In this project, you are supposed to explore the public's needs, usage, and opinions regarding a specific public good (a library, a park, street lighting...) in order to assess its provision and management effectiveness and make suggestions based on feedback.

Step 1: Select individuals who use the public good, including residents, users, and relevant staff members.

Step 2: Conduct face-to-face, phone, or online surveys, or employ other methods to collect data.

Step 3: Analyze the collected data to generate a report.

Step 4: Report the findings to the class, and propose measures for improvement.

Unit 5 Market Competition

Supplementary Reading

Scan the QR code to find out more about the unit.

Unit 6

Factor Market

Learning Objectives

After studying this unit, you should be able to:

1) understand the theories of factor market, demand and supply, and the prices of production factors of labor, capital, and land;
2) use the words and phrases in this unit;
3) use the knowledge in this unit to discuss and analyze the reform and development achievements and status quo of production factors in key industries of China.

The factor market is a fundamental component of an economy. The dynamics of the production factor market provide insights into the allocation of resources, income distribution, and the overall functioning of the economy. This unit introduces the factor market and explains how the price of each factor (labor, capital, and land) is determined and the equilibrium of demand and supply is achieved.

6.1 Factor Market

6.1.1 Factors of Production and Factor Market

Production factors, also known as inputs, are the various resources utilized in the production process. In other words, they are not consumed by households, but by firms to produce final outputs—services and goods. For instance, it is not possible to produce a car without the necessary machinery (capital), the expertise of automobile IT professionals (labor), or space for production (land) where capital and labor are engaged through a company employer (entrepreneur). Therefore, labor, capital (machinery, buildings, and equipment), land (natural resources), and **entrepreneurship** (innovation, organization, and risk-taking ability) are required and combined in an economy for production to take place. The first three factors are traded in the factor market and are the focus of this unit.

Being traded in the market, the factors of production bring income to their owners—the income of the laborer or the price of labor is the wages; that of the owner of capital or the price of capital is interests; and the income earned by landowners (the price of land) is rent. Therefore, it can be said that the issue of determining the prices of factors of production is the issue of income distribution of factor owners.

The factor market and the product market are two distinct markets within the economy. An important differentiation between the demand for factors and demand for products concerns utility. Consumers demand products as they derive utility from their consumption; on the other hand, firms demand factors with the view of conducting production operations with the intent to attain **maximal** revenue and profits out of production. The factor market is where the production factors are bought and sold. Buyers are firms or individuals seeking to acquire production factors for use in their production processes, while sellers are individuals or entities that own and supply the factors of production. In contrast, the product market is where final goods and services are exchanged between producers and consumers.

Thus, the demand for factors of production has the following two characteristics. First, it is a derived or induced demand from the demand for the goods and services that the factors help produce. When the demand and price for final goods and services increase, producers require more input to expand production and meet consumer demand. Consequently, the demand for production factors of labor, capital, and land increases and vice versa. However, like the demand for a good or service, there is an inverse relationship between the price of the factor and the quantity of the factor demand, that is, a downward-sloping demand curve. Second, it is a joint demand. The production of any product requires more than one production factor; therefore, the firm's demand for production factors is often a comprehensive demand for two or more factors. And then there is a relationship of substitution or **complementarity** between various production factors. Therefore, the firm's demand for a certain production factor depends on the price of all the factors involved.

In addition to the market demand for the product, the following elements also affect the demand for production factors:

Factor intensity type of production: If the production is capital-intensive, then the demand for capital will be large. If it is labor-intensive, then labor will be in high demand. In the fast-developing age of artificial intelligence, automation, and virtual markets, production processes employing the above technologies are likely to become more capital-intensive (and less labor-intensive).

Elasticity of demand for production factors: The more elastic the demand for goods is, the greater the elasticity of demand for that production factor, because when the demand for goods is elastic, the ratio of changes in the quantity demanded of goods is greater than that in the price of goods. If the price of goods decreases, the quantity demanded of goods will increase by a substantial proportion, and the quantity demanded of production factors for producing such goods will also increase in proportion to the increase in goods.

Substitutability of production factors: The lower the price and better the quality of a substitute for a certain production factor, the greater the elasticity of demand for the substitute, and the quantity demanded of that production factor will decrease significantly. For example, when a firm produces a certain product, it can use more machinery and equipment or more labor. If the wage level is low and the technical level of workers is high, labor will be used to replace machinery and equipment in production, thereby increasing the demand for labor.

6.1.2 Perfectly Competitive and Imperfectly Competitive Factor Markets

Similar to product markets, factor markets are divided into perfectly competitive and imperfectly competitive factor markets.

In a perfectly competitive market where there are numerous buyers and sellers, the demand for production factors is influenced by the marginal product of each factor, which refers to the additional output generated by employing one more unit of the factor while holding other factors constant. In such a case, firms demand a production factor up to the point where the marginal product equals the factor price to maximize their profits.

In imperfectly competitive markets such as monopolistic or oligopolistic markets, firms have some degree of market power and can influence prices. They may demand production factors to maximize their profits by considering not only the marginal product but also the market price of the final goods or services they produce. The demand for production factors depends on the elasticity of demand for the final product, the pricing strategy employed by the firm, and the level of competition in the market.

Consider the pharmaceutical market, an imperfectly competitive market. Firms such as Pfizer and Moderna not only consider the marginal product of their production factors but also the market price of the drugs they produce.

Suppose that Pfizer produces a new patented drug. The price Pfizer can charge for this drug is not purely a function of the production costs. Instead, it is influenced by a variety of factors, including patent protection, drug effectiveness, competition from other drugs, and demand elasticity from patients and insurers. If the new drug can be sold at a high price owing to its effectiveness and lack of substitutes, Pfizer may be willing to pay more for production factors (e.g., highly skilled researchers) because the marginal revenue from the sale of the drug is high.

Meanwhile, Pfizer must consider the bargaining power of its suppliers. If a particular raw material is supplied by only a few companies, these suppliers may be able to charge a high price. Hence, even though the raw material's marginal product may be high, Pfizer might look for alternatives or invest in research to reduce the need for that raw material to avoid over-dependence on its suppliers.

The supply of production factors refers to the numbers of factors available in the market, which can be influenced by factors such as population size, education and training, availability of resources, technological advancements, and government policies. The supply of labor and capital also depends on their mobility, because the two factors can be mobile, allowing them to move across sectors or regions in response to changes in demand or opportunities.

In perfectly competitive factor markets, equilibrium is achieved when the demand and supply of each factor intersect. The price of each factor settles at a level where the quantity demanded equals the quantity supplied.

In the presence of a monopoly, a single firm dominates the market and can exert control over the factor prices. A monopolistic firm may exploit its market power by demanding production factors at lower prices than in a perfectly competitive market. This can lead to a reduction in factor income and potential inequalities in income distribution within the factor market.

6.2 Labor Market

6.2.1 Demand and Supply of Labor

The labor market encompasses the entire range of interactions between employers seeking to hire workers and individuals actively seeking employment. There is a different market for each type of labor that differs by the type of work (e.g., tailor vs engineer), skill level (beginner's level or proficiency), and geographic location (the market for administrative assistants is more local or regional than the market for university professors). Wages are income derived from human labor; they technically cover all compensation made to workers for either physical or mental work. The wage rate is the amount of base wage paid to a worker per unit of time (as per hour or day) or per unit of output if on **piecework**.

Demand for labor represents the quantity of labor that employers are willing and able to hire at a given wage rate and time, all other things being equal. This is an inverse relationship, represented by a downward-sloping curve on a graph where the wage rate is on the y-axis and the quantity of labor is on the x-axis (Figure 6-1).

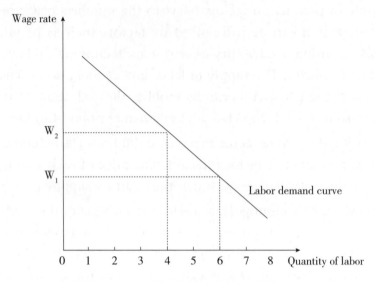

Figure 6-1　The Labor Demand Curve

When making decisions about how many workers to hire, firms also use marginal analysis. The concept of the marginal revenue product (MRP) of labor is an indispensable tool for understanding labor economics. The MRP of labor is the additional revenue generated by employing an additional unit of labor. This represents the contribution of each worker to a firm's output and profitability. The MRP of labor is derived from the marginal product of labor (MPL) and the marginal revenue (MR) of the firm. Mathematically, MRP = MPL × MR. Firms tend to hire workers up to the point where MRP equals the wage rate.

Consider Starbucks as an example. Suppose that each additional **barista** hired by Starbucks generates an extra $5,000 of revenue per month by serving additional customers. If Starbucks pays the new barista a wage of $3,000 per month, the firm's gain from employing the additional barista is greater than the cost (wage). This situation motivates Starbucks to hire more baristas.

Now Starbucks keeps hiring until it has 50 baristas. If the company hires an additional barista and the additional revenue generated is still $5,000, but due to overtime payments and the decreased efficiency of an overcrowded workspace, the wage for this worker is now also $5,000. At this point, the wage rate equals the MRP. This is the equilibrium point in hiring for Starbucks—where the cost of employing an additional barista equals the additional revenue that the barista brings in.

As businesses expand and demand for their products or services increases, the demand for labor also increases. However, technological advancements, such as automation and artificial intelligence, can reduce the demand for certain types of labor while increasing the demand for skilled workers. Government policies, **demographic** shifts, changes in consumer preferences, and market conditions also influence labor demand.

Conversely, the supply of labor symbolizes the total hours that workers or employees are willing to work at a given wage rate, considering that all other conditions are constant. The higher the wage rate, the greater the quantity of labor supplied. It should be noted that the labor supply curve can be divided into the market supply curve and the individual supply curve of workers. The former is a straight line sloping to the upper right (Figure 6-2), and is the sum of the individual labor supply curves of all workers in that market.

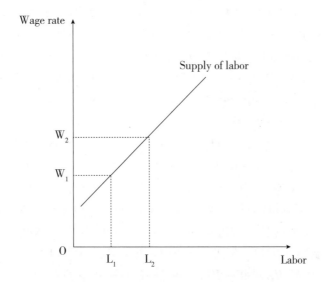

Figure 6-2　The Labor Market Supply Curve

The labor supply curves of individual laborers can be derived through the process of the optimal choice of individual work and leisure. The time available to individuals in a day is a fixed amount, that is, 24 hours. No one can supply 24 hours of labor every day; they always need to spend a certain amount of time on resting, entertainment, housework, and so on. In economics, it is common to refer to all this time used for various purposes outside the labor market as leisure. People often allocate their time between work and leisure activities. The allocation decision follows the principle of utility maximization. Once an individual decides how much time to devote to the firm, he also decides how much leisure time to devote to himself.

In real life, changes in demographics, including age distribution and migration patterns, can alter labor supply. Educational attainment and training programs impact the supply of skilled labor. Additionally, government policies, such as changes in minimum wage **legislation** or labor market regulations, can affect labor supply dynamics.

6.2.2 The Price of Labor

In the labor market, the price of labor is wages, which are determined by the supply and demand of workers. If there is a shortage of workers with a particular skill set, the price of labor for those workers will increase. This, in turn, incentivizes more workers to acquire those skills and more employers to hire those workers. This allocation of labor resources ensures that they are being used efficiently.

Labor becomes a source of utility because workers are **remunerated** for their labor to purchase goods and services to meet their needs. Leisure can also bring utility to workers because rest, recreation, family activities, etc., can meet workers' needs for enjoyment. Thus, the first factor that workers consider when deciding whether to devote their **disposable** time to labor or leisure is the opportunity cost of leisure—the hourly wage rate.

The hourly wage rate is the price of leisure enjoyed by workers and represents the amount of goods and services that can be bought at the expense of an hour's wage to enjoy an hour of leisure. A higher wage rate means that leisure becomes expensive relative to other goods and services that individuals may purchase; that is, the cost or opportunity cost of leisure increases, so workers are willing to increase the labor supply and reduce leisure time. However, when the wage rate and the living standard of workers rise to a certain level, workers feel that they can maintain a high living standard even if they reduce the number of working hours, and at the same time, they feel that leisure is more important. Therefore, people reduce their labor and income in exchange for more leisure. Thus, the individual labor supply curve is a backward-bending curve (Figure 6-3).

Equilibrium in the labor market occurs when the quantity of labor demanded by employers equals the quantity of labor supplied by workers at a particular wage rate. This point of equilibrium ensures a balance between the demand and supply of labor, leading to a stable labor market. If there is a shortage of labor, wages tend to rise, encouraging more workers to enter the labor market. Conversely, an excess supply of labor leads to downward pressure on wages, prompting workers to seek alternative employment opportunities.

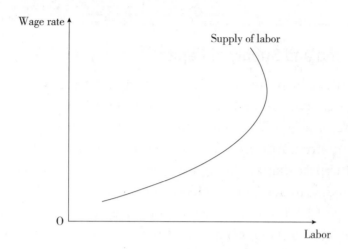

Figure 6-3 The Individual Labor Supply Curve

Again, Starbucks reaches labor equilibrium when its demand for baristas aligns with the number willing to work at an agreed wage rate. Suppose that Starbucks plans to open a new branch in San Francisco. The firm determines that 30 baristas are required to operate efficiently. This number represents labor demand. In the local job market, there are 100 individuals interested and qualified in barista roles. However, the wages and conditions offered by Starbucks attract only 50 individuals to apply for positions. This group represents the initial labor supply.

To achieve labor equilibrium, Starbucks might need to adjust its conditions—either by raising wages, modifying working hours, or offering additional benefits—to attract the exact number of baristas required. Alternatively, the firm might decide to operate with a larger staff than initially planned, spreading the workload more broadly. In this hypothetical case, if Starbucks successfully hires 30 of the 50 applicants, labor equilibrium will be achieved at the new Starbucks branch. If the firm raises the conditions (wages, hours, etc.) and attracts five more workers, the labor equilibrium will shift to 35 baristas.

In a competitive labor market, the interaction between labor demand and supply determines the equilibrium wage rate and the employment level. At equilibrium, the wage rate ensures that the quantity of labor demanded matches the quantity of labor supplied. However, in the real world, labor markets may face imperfections such as **monopsony** power, which can **distort** wage levels and employment outcomes.

6.3　Capital Market

6.3.1　Demand and Supply of Capital

In the context of production factors, capital generally refers to physical assets (or physical goods), including buildings, physical tools, and equipment needed to increase work productivity. In other words, it is the stock of equipment and structures used for production or the accumulation of goods produced in the past that are being used in the present to produce new goods and services. Today, in addition to physical goods such as tools, equipment, and buildings, intellectual discoveries such as computer software and patents are also capital. Unlike labor or land, capital is artificial and must be created by people's hands and can be used to produce other goods and services. Please note that money is not considered capital, because a firm cannot use money directly to produce other goods. However, firms can use money to acquire capital.

Physical capital may be purchased or rented by firms in the market, or produced by the firms themselves. So, there are the purchase price and the rental price. The former is the price a firm pays to own those physical goods for an unlimited period of time, whereas the latter is the price a firm pays to use those physical goods for a limited period of time.

The demand for capital is similar to the demand for labor. A firm increases the quantity of capital hired until the value of its marginal product equals the capital price.

Demand for capital arises from individuals, businesses, and governments seeking funds for investment and expansion. Firms often need to make investments in order to maximize profits, that is, buying more equipment, tools, etc., generating demand for capital. Firm demand depends on the price of capital goods—interest rates and the expected return on investment projects. If interest rates rise, the cost of firms' investments will increase and returns will decrease, leading to a reduction in investment. Consequently, capital demand decreases, interest rates decline, and investment costs are reduced, prompting firms to expand their investments. In addition to interest rates, economic conditions and investment opportunities affect the demand for capital. Higher interest rates tend to **dampen** the demand for capital, while favorable economic conditions and promising investment prospects stimulate it.

The supply of capital comes from savers who have surplus funds to invest. In the capital market, households create a capital supply primarily through bank deposits (savings) or bond purchases. These funds originate from the remaining portion of total household income after deducting household consumption. Firms also have their own savings, formed from depreciation funds❶ before purchasing new machinery and equipment. In addition, cash reserves, temporarily **idle** funds, and undistributed profits contribute to firm savings. Government fiscal surpluses are also a source of social capital.

6.3.2 The Price of Capital

In economics, interest is the price of capital, and the percentage of interest to the total capital over a certain period is called the interest rate. Economic theory suggests that savings lead to an increase in the quantity of capital. When the demand for capital exceeds its supply, interest rates tend to rise, signaling a higher borrowing cost. Conversely, when the supply of capital exceeds demand, interest rates decline, making borrowing affordable. That is, interest and interest rates regulate the balance between capital supply and demand. In Figure 6-4, the vertical axis represents the interest rate and the horizontal axis represents the investment volume of capital. The S curve represents the capital supply curve, indicating that as the interest rate rises, investors are willing to supply more capital. The D curve represents the capital demand curve, indicating that as the interest rate decreases, companies or investors have increased demand for capital. The intersection point K* represents the market equilibrium point where the supply of capital equals the demand for capital.

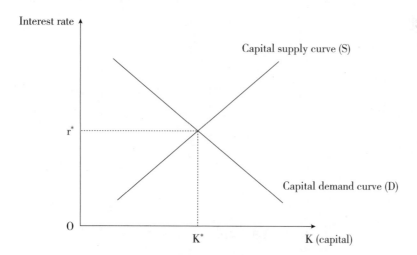

Figure 6-4　The Equilibrium in Capital Market

---

❶　depreciation funds: an amount of money that a company has to buy new assets.

In addition, interest rates affect consumer behavior. Higher interest rates make savings more attractive, as they offer a higher return, while lower interest rates encourage spending and borrowing. The interplay between savings, investment, and consumption is crucial for maintaining a balanced and sustainable economy.

Moreover, the existence of interest can make capital most effectively utilized. If the interest rate in society is predetermined, then people will use capital in the sector with the highest profit rate. The sector with the highest profit rate is also the sector in which capital can best play its role.

6.4 Land Market

6.4.1 Features of Land

In economics, land refers to the natural resources provided by the earth, including the surface area of the earth, minerals, water bodies, forests, and other resources contained within it.

Land possesses several unique features that distinguish it from other economic resources. First, land is fixed in supply, which means that its quantity is limited. Regardless of the amount of human effort exerted, the amount of land available for use remains constant. Therefore, the supply curve of land is vertical, indicating a fixed quantity supplied at various price levels (Figure 6-5).

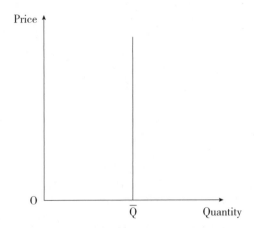

Figure 6-5   Supply Curve of Land

Additionally, land is immobile, meaning that it cannot be moved from one location to another. The location of a piece of land plays a significant role in its value and potential uses. The land also exhibits **heterogeneity**, as different pieces of land possess varying qualities, natural features, and fertility levels. This heterogeneity influences land prices because the value of land is determined by its location, **accessibility**, **proximity** to **amenities**, and potential for development or productive use.

6.4.2 The Price of Land

In economics, rent is the income derived from ownership of land and other gifts of nature (e.g., fertility of the soil). Land rent is generated by the scarcity and desirability of land. The concept of land rent is rooted in the economic principle of opportunity cost. As land is limited, individuals or businesses must pay rent to secure its use, as they forgo alternative uses or opportunities that could have been pursued.

Rental price represents the cost of leasing or renting land for a specific period. It is determined by factors such as demand for land, productivity, potential uses, and location. Rental prices may vary based on the duration of the lease, with longer leases typically commanding lower rental prices because of reduced uncertainty and transaction costs. In highly sought-after locations such as New York, the scarcity of land and its prime urban setting contribute to overly high land prices. Limited supply and high demand result in significant land rent, driving up rental prices.

In the land market, when demand for land exceeds its supply, land rent tends to increase, signaling a higher price to secure limited available land. Conversely, if the supply of land exceeds the demand, land rent may decrease, reflecting a lower price to attract potential users. The demand for land is derived from its potential uses and economic activities that can be undertaken. The supply of land, as discussed, is fixed in the short run. Equilibrium land rent is the price at which the quantity of land demanded equals the quantity supplied.

Exercises

1 Short answer questions

Directions: *Answer the following questions in your own words or with sentences from the text.*

(1) What are the differences between the factor market and the product market? Please give an example.

(2) What principles will firms follow when hiring workers?

(3) What are the sources of the production factor of capital?

(4) What are the features of the production factor of land?

2 Term explanation

Directions: *Explain the following terms in your own words or with sentences from the text.*

(1) factor market

(2) wage rate

(3) capital

(4) rent

3 Banked cloze

Directions: *Fill in the blanks by selecting suitable words from the following box. You may not use any of the words more than once.*

A. anything	B. households	C. purchase	D. contribute	E. surpasses
F. income	G. separately	H. derived	I. upward	J. equals
K. downward	L. respectively	M. common	N. blocks	O. profit

The factors of production are resources that are the building (1) _____ of the economy; they are what people use to produce goods and services. The three important types of factors in economics are labor, capital, and land, and their prices are wages, interest, and rent, (2) _____. The demand for production factors is a(n) (3) _____ demand, and firms follow the principle of profit maximization when demanding production factors. The demand curve for the production factors slopes (4) _____ to the right owing to diminishing marginal output. Suppliers of production factors are individuals or (5) _____ who provide them in exchange for income. The supply curve of the production factors slopes upward to the right, indicating a positive correlation between supply and factor prices. In factor markets, the equilibrium principle for firms is that the marginal revenue product (6) _____ the marginal factor cost.

Labor is the effort that people (7) _____ to the production of goods and services. If you have ever been paid for a job, you have contributed labor resources to the production of goods or services. The income earned by labor resources is called wages and is the largest source of (8) _____ for most people. As a factor of production, capital refers to all the tools and equipment used in the process of making other goods, like buildings, office equipment, machinery, and software programs. Money is used to (9) _____ those things, but it is not used directly to make products. The income earned by owners of capital resources is interest. The third factor of production is land. It includes not just land, but (10) _____ that comes from the land such as water, oil, copper, natural gas, coal, and forests. The income that resource owners earn in return for land resources is referred to as rent.

4 Translation

Directions: *Translate the following paragraphs into Chinese or English.*

(1) The demand for factors of production is a derived or induced demand from the demand for the goods and services that the factors help produce. When the demand and price for final goods and services increase, producers require more input to expand production and meet consumer demand. Consequently, the demand for production factors, such as labor, capital, and land, increases, and vice versa. However, like the demand for a good or service, there is an inverse relationship between the price of the factor and the quantity of the factor demand, that is, a downward-sloping demand curve.

(2) 中国政府将完善产权制度（property right system）和生产要素市场化配置（market-oriented allocation）作为经济体制改革的重点。近年来，党中央、国务院制定了相关政策，对推进生产要素市场化配置改革的目标和举措进行了系统设计。政策实施以来，多项实质性（substantial）改革举措相继落实，激发了市场主体（market entities）活力，增强了发展内生动力（endogenous driving force），为促进经济高质量发展发挥了重要作用。

5 Project

Title: Understanding the Factor Markets in the Chinese Service Industry

Instructions:

Step 1: Select a sector of the service industry (tourism, catering, healthcare, etc.) in China and briefly describe each sector's role and development in the economy.

Step 2: Explore the factors influencing the demand for different services and investigate how changing demographics and consumer preferences influence the demand for different services, how technological advancements (e.g., mobile apps, online platforms) shape service delivery and customer experience, and examine how government policies, regulations, and trade agreements impact the service industry's growth and competition. Take detailed notes on your research, making sure to record key facts and concepts.

Step 3: Explore how labor markets in the specific sector are influenced by factors such as education, skills, and wage trends. Discuss how capital investment and access to funding affect service businesses.

Step 4: Present your findings to the class. Explain the basic concepts of factor markets and how they apply to the sector. Use examples from your research to illustrate your points.

Supplementary Reading

Scan the QR code to find out more about the unit.

Unit 7

National Economy

Learning Objectives

After studying this unit, you should be able to:

1) understand the concepts of GDP and GNP, national income theory, and model of aggregate demand (AD) and aggregate supply (AS);
2) use the words and phrases in this unit;
3) apply what you have learned in this unit to discuss China's GDP growth and economic achievements.

National economy refers to the total production, consumption, and distribution of goods and services in a country. It is an **integral** part of the larger global economy and has a significant impact on the economic growth and development of a nation. This unit provides a brief introduction to the key concepts in the national economy—GDP and GNP, national income theory, and aggregate supply and demand, and explains how the AD-AS model works.

7.1 GDP and GNP

Gross domestic product (GDP) and gross national product (GNP) are two important metrics used to measure the economic performance of a country or global economy.

7.1.1 Definitions of GDP and GNP

GDP is the market value of all final goods and services produced within a country in a given period of time. It measures the total economic output of a country, including both domestic production and imports. One way of calculating GDP involves summing up all expenditures made by households, businesses, and governments in a particular year and subtracting the taxes paid by these entities. It is also expressed as GDP per capita, which indicates the average GDP generated per person in a country.

Real GDP and **nominal** GDP are the most referenced metrics to measure economic growth and development.

Real GDP is a measure of a country's economic output that is adjusted for changes in price levels, typically the effects of inflation or deflation. It represents the value of all final goods and services produced within a nation during a given period, but it is adjusted to reflect the purchasing power of money at a specific base year[1]. This means that real GDP removes the impact of price changes, giving a more accurate picture of economic growth and allowing for comparisons across different periods without the distortion of inflation or deflation.

In essence, real GDP shows whether the economy is genuinely expanding by producing more goods and services or merely experiencing increases in prices. It is calculated by applying a price index, such as the consumer price index or the GDP deflator, which adjusts current year prices to match those of the base year,

---

[1] base year: the first of a series of years in an economic or financial index.

thereby reflecting the real changes in production output.

Nominal GDP, on the other hand, is the gross domestic product measured at current market prices. It reflects the total market value of all final goods and services produced within a country during a specified period without adjusting for inflation or deflation. Nominal GDP is influenced by the current price levels, so it can be inflated or deflated by changes in prices rather than actual changes in the quantity of goods and services produced.

While nominal GDP is straightforward and does not require adjustments for inflation, it can give a distorted view of economic growth if there are significant fluctuations in prices. For example, an increase in nominal GDP might just be due to higher prices (inflation) rather than an increase in production or improvements in living standards. Nonetheless, nominal GDP is important for assessing the absolute size of the economy, government budgeting, and understanding international economic transactions at current market values.

GNP represents the gross national product, which includes the production of goods and services within and outside the country's borders. It is calculated by taking the sum of personal consumption expenditure, private domestic investment, government expenditure, net exports, and any income earned by residents from overseas investments, then subtracting income earned by foreign residents. Similar to GDP, GNP can be expressed as GNP per capita.

Generally, GDP and GNP are measures of a country's output level over a certain time period. Understanding the relationship between GDP and GNP will help us better interpret economic data and provide a basis for formulating economic policies.

7.1.2 Calculations of GDP and GNP

GDP measures the economic activity within a country's borders. It includes all the goods and services produced within the country, whether by domestic or foreign companies. GDP also takes into account changes in the value of money over time, as well as the distribution of income between households and firms. Therefore, when calculating GDP, data on production, sales, and employment are collected from businesses and governments across the country.

There are primarily three methods for calculating GDP: the production approach, the income approach, and the expenditure approach.

The production approach is calculated as follows:

Gross Domestic Product = Total Output − Intermediate Consumption (Material Product Input + Service Input).

The income approach is calculated as:

Gross Domestic Product = Compensation of Employees + Depreciation of Fixed Assets + Net Production Taxes + Operating Surplus.

The expenditure approach is calculated as:

Gross Domestic Product = Total Consumption (Household Consumption + Government Consumption) + Total Investment (Gross Fixed Capital Formation + Change in Inventories) + Net Exports of Goods and Services (Exports of Goods and Services − Imports of Goods and Services).

On the other hand, GNP is the value of all goods and services made by a country's residents and businesses, regardless of production location. The formula for calculating the GNP is as follows:

$GNP = C + I + G + X + Z$

Where:

C represents consumption, that is, spending by households on goods and services, with the exception of purchases of new housing.

I represents investment, that is, spending on capital equipment, inventories, and structures, including household purchases of new housing.

G represents government purchases, or spending on goods and services by local and state government.

X represents net exports (value of imports minus that of exports).

Z represents net income earned by domestic residents from overseas investments minus net income earned by foreign residents from domestic investments.

7.2 National Income

National income refers to the money value created in the material production sector during a certain time period. It is the sum of wages, interest, rent, and profits that owners of a country's production factors (including land, labor, capital, entrepreneurial talent, etc.) receive during a certain period of time.

7.2.1 Calculation of National Income

National income is the sum of wages, interest, rent, and profits earned by a country's residents and businesses. The profits obtained solely from the changes in asset prices are not included. Residents refer to all individuals and institutions whose economic interests are centered around the country or region, regardless of their nationality or source of funds. Therefore, they also include foreign workers and subsidiaries who have been working and operating in the region for a long time.

Thus, the increase in national income depends on an increase in the amount of labor invested in material production. Provided that labor productivity remains constant, national income is directly **proportional** to the amount of labor invested. The greater the amount of labor invested, the greater the national income, and vice versa.

The increase in national income also rests on the improvement in labor productivity. The higher the labor productivity, the faster the growth in national income. When social labor resources have been fully utilized and economic development has reached a higher level, developing science and technology to improve social labor productivity is the major way to increase national income, and the fundamental way to increase national income calculated based on the population average.

Furthermore, savings on production factors contribute to an increase in national income. Saving production enables more total social products with the same resource input, consequently raising the relative proportion of national income within the equivalent sum of total societal products.

Among these three factors, the improvement in social labor productivity is the most important in the growth of national income.

7.2.2 Distribution of National Income

National income needs to be distributed. The distribution process is divided into the initial distribution and redistribution of national income.

The initial distribution of national income is conducted among the various parties involved in the production sector, which creates national income. The national income distribution system adopted by most countries is the functional value distribution system which is considered to hold a balanced link between production and consumption. The functional distribution of income refers to the income paid to individuals or households. A single individual may receive income from more than one production factor or source. A person may earn income by offering his labor service, renting his property (land or building), and from his holdings of company shares or government bonds.

Redistribution is carried out based on initial distribution between the material and non-material production sectors, among various departments of the national economy, and different parts of the population. For those people who are engaged in activities in the field of **intangible** production, such as national administrative personnel, military personnel, cultural and artistic workers, teachers, and medical workers, their income is formed through the redistribution of national income. Generally, the redistribution of national income is carried out through economic **levers** such as taxes, prices, insurance premiums[1], and national budgets.

After the initial distribution and redistribution, national income is divided into accumulation and consumption funds according to its ultimate use, which are used for accumulation and consumption respectively.

7.2.3 Significance of National Income

The calculation of national income is valuable for the economy. It serves as an indicator of a nation's economic performance, shedding light on its level of social productivity and overall growth and development. With the help of national income figures, governments can formulate economic policies, including decisions concerning taxation, trade, and expenditures. National income **assessments** provide the foundation for comparing economic achievements among different countries, demonstrating their relative strengths and weaknesses. National income statistics also help allocate resources in an efficient fashion, enabling the identification of sectors that require increased investment and promote economic development. By analyzing data on national income, governments can inquire into employment trends to carry out targeted interventions to create more job opportunities. National income data also act as a basis for economic **projections**, enabling anticipation of forthcoming economic patterns and challenges. In addition, national income metrics can help measure the living standard of people, which promotes the exploration of strategies to enhance it by stimulating economic progress. For international organizations that offer aid and support to countries confronting economic

---

[1] insurance premium: the amount of money an individual or business pays for an insurance policy.

difficulties, national income data are the most important indicator.

However, price volatility has an impact on national income in the same region, over time. Therefore, comparisons of national income across different periods within the same region are typically conducted indirectly. Fixed prices or actual national income are calculated after deducting price changes before making the comparison. As for national income without deducting price changes, it is called nominal national income at that time. National income serves as an indicator of regional residents' prosperity; however, it is limited in that it solely mirrors current earnings and fails to account for accumulated wealth.

7.3 Aggregate Demand and Aggregate Supply

Aggregate demand (AD) and aggregate supply (AS) are fundamental concepts in macroeconomics that help explain how economic activity is driven by changes in both consumer and producer behavior.

7.3.1 Aggregate Demand

Aggregate demand refers to the amount of total spending on domestic goods and services in an economy. Strictly speaking, aggregate demand is what economists call total planned expenditure.

Aggregate demand includes the following four components: consumption, investment, government spending, and net exports—exports minus imports.

Aggregate demand is determined by a number of factors, one of which is price level.

An aggregate demand curve shows the quantity of goods and services that households, firms, governments, and customers abroad want to buy at each price level. Here is an example of the aggregate demand curve.

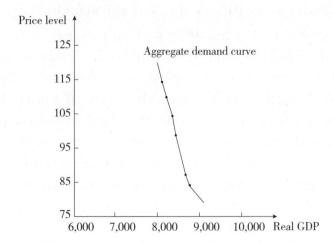

Figure 7-1 An Example of Aggregate Demand Curve

The horizontal axis shows real GDP, and the vertical axis represents the price level. This downward aggregate demand curve indicates that increases in the price level of outputs lead to lower total spending.

To fully understand why price level increases lead to lower spending, we need to understand how changes in price level affect the different components of aggregate demand. Remember that the following components make up aggregate demand: consumption spending, investment spending, government spending, and spending on exports minus imports.

Aggregate demand = C + I + G + X − M

Where C represents consumption; I represents investment; G is government spending; X is exports, and M is imports.

Economic theory identifies three key effects of price level changes on the economy: the wealth effect, the interest rate effect, and the exchange rate effect.

The wealth effect poses impact on C, holding that as the price level increases, the buying power of savings that people have stored in bank accounts and other assets will diminish, eaten away to some extent by inflation. Because a rise in the price level reduces people's wealth, consumption spending falls as the price level rises.

The interest rate effect explains that as outputs rise, the same purchases will take more money or credit to accomplish. This additional demand for money and credit increases the interest rates. In turn, higher interest rates will reduce borrowing by businesses for investment purposes and reduce borrowing by households for homes and cars, thus reducing both consumption and investment spending.

The exchange rate effect points out that, if prices rise in a home country while remaining fixed in other countries, then goods in the home country will be relatively more expensive than goods in the rest of the world. Exports in the home country will be relatively more expensive, and thus the quantity of exports sold will decrease. Imports from abroad are relatively cheaper; therefore the quantity of imports will increase. Thus, a higher domestic price level relative to price levels in other countries reduces net export expenditures.

Due to the above three effects, the aggregate demand curve in the above example slopes fairly steeply downward. The steep slope indicates that a higher price level for final outputs does reduce aggregate demand for all three reasons, but the change in the quantity of aggregate demand as a result of changes in price level is not very large.

7.3.2 Aggregate Supply

Aggregate supply refers to the total amount of goods and services produced by companies at a certain price level for a specific period.

An aggregate supply curve shows the quantity of goods and services that firms choose to produce and sell at each price level. Figure 7-2 shows an aggregate supply curve.

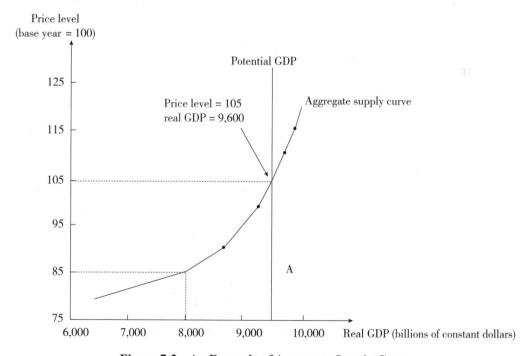

Figure 7-2 An Example of Aggregate Supply Curve

The horizontal axis of the Figure shows real GDP, that is, the level of GDP adjusted for inflation. The vertical axis shows price levels. The price level is the average price of all goods and services produced in the economy. It is an index number, such as the GDP deflator (a price index measuring the average prices of all goods and services included in the economy).

Please note that as the price level rises, the aggregate supply—the quantity of goods and services supplied—rises as well.

The price level shown on the vertical axis represents the prices for final goods or outputs bought in the economy, not the price level for **intermediate** goods and services that are inputs to production. The aggregate supply curve in Figure 7-2 describes how suppliers react to a higher price level for the final outputs of goods and services, while the prices of inputs such as labor and energy remain constant.

If firms across the economy face a situation where the price level of what they produce and sell is rising but their costs of production are not, then the lure of higher profits will induce them to expand production.

The classical aggregate supply curve is vertical at the full employment level of real production, indicating that the quantity of aggregate production is independent of price level. The graph below illustrates a classical aggregate supply curve.

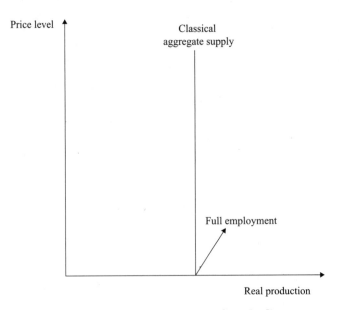

Figure 7-3 Classical Aggregate Supply Curve

The aggregate supply curve is vertical at the full employment level in real production. If the price level rises or falls, the economy moves up and down along the curve and real production remains unchanged.

7.3.3 The Aggregate Demand-Aggregate Supply Model

The aggregate demand-aggregate supply (AD-AS) model (Figure 7-4) shows what determines total supply or total demand for the economy and how total demand and total supply interact at the macroeconomic level. Economists use this model to analyze economic fluctuations.

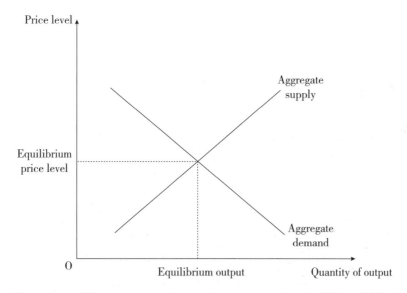

Figure 7-4　The Aggregate Demand-Aggregate Supply (AD-AS) Model

The vertical axis represents the overall price level of the economy. The horizontal axis is the total quantity of goods and services produced in the economy, that is, the real GDP. The aggregate demand curve shows the quantity of goods and services that households, firms, governments, and customers abroad want to buy at each price level. The aggregate supply curve shows the quantity of goods and services that firms produce and sell at each price level. According to this model, the price level and quantity of output adjust to balance aggregate demand and aggregate supply.

The upward-sloping aggregate supply curve, also known as the short-run aggregate supply curve, shows a positive relationship between price levels and real GDP in the short run. The aggregate supply curve slopes up because when the price level for outputs increases while the price level of inputs remains fixed, the opportunity for additional profits encourages more production. The downward-sloping aggregate demand curve shows the relationship between the price level of outputs and the quantity of total spending in the economy.

The point at which the aggregate supply and aggregate demand curves intersect is the equilibrium, meaning that aggregate supply equals aggregate demand. Figure 7-4 shows the equilibrium output level (real GDP) and equilibrium price level in the economy. At a relatively low output price level, firms have little incentive to produce, although consumers are willing to purchase a high quantity. As the price level for outputs rises, aggregate supply rises, and aggregate demand falls until the equilibrium point is reached.

Exercises

❶ Short answer questions

Directions: *Answer the following questions in your own words or with sentences from the text.*

(1) What are the differences between GDP and GNP?

(2) What factors lead to an increase in national income?

(3) Why is the calculation of national income valuable for the economy?

(4) What is the AD-AS model? How does the model differ from the analysis of demand and supply in microeconomics?

❷ Term explanation

Directions: *Explain the following terms in your own words or with sentences from the text.*

(1) GDP

(2) GNP

(3) aggregate demand curve

(4) aggregate supply curve

3 Banked cloze

Directions: *Fill in the blanks by selecting suitable words from the following box. You may not use any of the words more than once.*

A. domestic	B. distinction	C. other	D. another	E. increases
F. higher	G. lower	H. graphical	I. distinct	J. combined
K. decreases	L. less	M. in turn	N. uncertainty	O. stability

The aggregate demand curve is a(n) (1) _____ representation of the relationship between the total quantity of goods and services demanded by consumers and the price level in an economy. The curve is downward sloping because of three (2) _____ but related reasons: the wealth effect, the interest rate effect, and the exchange rate effect.

The wealth effect refers to the impact of changes in consumer wealth on aggregate demand. When the price level decreases, consumers' wealth (3) _____ as they have more money left over after paying for necessities. This increase in wealth leads to an increase in consumer spending, which (4) _____ drives up aggregate demand.

The interest rate effect is (5) _____ factor that affects aggregate demand. A decrease in interest rates makes borrowing cheaper, which encourages businesses to invest more in production and expansion. As a result, there is an increase in investment, leading to (6) _____ levels of economic growth and increased aggregate demand.

Finally, the exchange rate effect refers to the impact of changes in exchange rates on aggregate demand. When the value of a country's currency decreases relative to other currencies, its exports become more expensive, making them (7) _____ attractive to foreign buyers. This can lead to a decrease in (8) _____ consumption as consumers are willing to spend less on imported goods.

In summary, the downward slope of the aggregate demand curve is a result of the (9) _____ effects of these three factors: an increase in consumer spending due to a decrease in prices, increased investment due to lower borrowing costs, and decreased domestic consumption due to the rise in the cost of imports. Understanding these effects is crucial for policymakers and economists in determining how to manage the economy during periods of economic (10) _____ or change.

4 Translation

Directions: *Translate the following paragraphs into Chinese or English.*

(1) National income needs to be distributed. The distribution process is divided into the initial distribution and redistribution of national income. The initial distribution of national income is conducted among the various parties involved in the production sector, which creates national income. Redistribution is carried out based on initial distribution between the material and non-material production sectors, among various departments of the national economy, and different parts of the population. After the initial distribution and redistribution, national income is divided into accumulation and consumption funds according to its ultimate use, which are used for accumulation and consumption respectively.

(2) 中国政府提出并贯彻新发展理念（philosophy），着力推进高质量发展，推动构建新发展格局（pattern），实施供给侧结构性改革（supply-side structural reform），制定一系列具有全局性意义的区域重大战略，我国经济实力实现历史性跃升。近十年来，国内生产总值从五十四万亿元增长到一百一十四万亿元，我国经济总量占世界经济的比重达百分之十八点五，提高七点二个百分点，稳居世界第二位；人均国内生产总值从三万九千八百元增加到八万一千元。

5 Project

Topic: China's GDP Growth in the Past Decade

Instructions:

Step 1: Define the scope and objectives. Clearly define what aspects of China's GDP growth you want to explore in the past decade, such as the overall trend, fluctuations, and major contributing factors. Also, establish your research goal: Is it to understand the impact of policies, to analyze the economic situation during specific years, or anything else?

Step 2: Gather data. Start by gathering all relevant data on China's GDP growth over the past decade. This could include official statistics from the National Bureau of Statistics of China, the World Bank, the International Monetary Fund (IMF), and so on. You may also need to gather other types of data such as inflation rates, exchange rates, and population growth, which can affect GDP growth.

Step 3: Organize and analyze the data. Once you have collected all the necessary data, organize it in a way that allows for easy analysis. This might involve creating graphs and charts to visualize trends and patterns. You will then need to analyze the data to answer your research questions.

Step 4: Write up your findings. After analyzing the data, write up your findings in a clear and concise manner. Make sure to explain what you have found and how it relates to your research objective. In addition, be sure to include any limitations of your study.

Step 5: Give a presentation. Share your research findings by giving a presentation in class.

Supplementary Reading

Scan the QR code to find out more about the unit.

Unit 8
Economic Growth and the Business Cycle

Learning Objectives

After studying this unit, you should be able to:

1) understand the implication and driving force of economic growth, the four phases, and the causes of the business cycle;
2) use the words and phrases in this unit;
3) use the knowledge in this unit to discuss and analyze cases of economic growth and business cycles.

Sustainable and stable economic growth can provide greater well-being to the residents of an economy. However, economic growth rates differ significantly across countries, and the living standards of the average people in some countries can, therefore, increase quickly, while in some other countries, they are barely higher or even lower than they were in the past. Some economies have experienced alternating periods of expansion and recession, influencing average people's lives. Why do some countries grow much faster than others do? Why do economies fluctuate during the growth process? To answer these questions, this unit begins with inflation and unemployment, because the state of the economy is usually measured by the inflation and unemployment rates.

8.1 Inflation

8.1.1 Inflation and Its Causes

Inflation is a primary indicator of an economy's operations. It occurs when the prices of most goods and services in an economy rise continuously over time. Considering the **complexity** of the real-world economy with thousands of different goods and their prices, some prices rising while others falling, and the extent of price changes varying, the concept of price index is therefore employed to explain inflation. The price index, also known as the price level, represents the overall average price of various goods and services in the entire economy. The main price indices include the GDP deflator, consumer price index (CPI), and producer price index (PPI). The CPI measures the expenditure of an average household on a representative set of goods and indicates how much more it costs to buy this set of goods today compared with a specific base year in the past. For example, in the base year 2020, an average household spent $964 per month on a set of goods, and in 2023, the cost of buying the same set of goods is $1,285. Then the CPI for 2023 would be $CPI_{2023} = (1,285/964) * 100 \approx 133$. With the concept of price level (price index), inflation can be accurately described as a sustained and significant increase in the price level of an economy over a certain period. The degree of inflation is usually measured by the inflation rate, which is the percentage change in the price level over a period of time. For example, if an economy's CPI increases from 100 in the previous year to 129 in the current year, then the inflation rate for this period is $(129 - 100) / 100 = 29\%$.

Inflation rates up to 10% are considered moderate inflation, and many countries are currently experiencing this kind of mild and gradual increase in prices, which some people believe can have a positive effect on the economy and income growth. Inflation rates between 10% and 100% are classified as **galloping** inflation. If galloping inflation occurs, the public will expect further price increases, taking various measures to protect themselves from the harm of inflation, which will exacerbate inflationary pressure. Inflation rates above 100% are considered hyperinflation. When hyperinflation occurs, prices soar and people rush to get rid of currency as quickly as possible, leading to a significant increase in the **velocity** of money circulation. Consequently, people lose trust in the currency as its purchasing power **plunges**. Normal economic activities are disturbed, and in severe cases, social **unrest** occurs.

Economists have tried to understand inflation from various perspectives. The quantity theory of money asserts that the price level rises with a rapid increase in the quantity of money in circulation. The demand-pull inflation theory claims that an increase in aggregate demand is the source of inflation. When the value of aggregate demand exceeds that of aggregate supply, the price level increases. Factors that contribute to demand-pull inflation include fiscal policy, monetary policy, sudden changes in consumer habits, and shifts in international market demand. Cost-push inflation theory states that in the absence of excessive demand, the price level will increase if the cost of production of goods and services rises.

Some Western scholars attribute cost-push inflation primarily to wage increases. In a perfectly competitive labor market, wages are solely determined by the supply and demand for labor, and wage increases alone do not cause inflation. However, in an imperfectly competitive labor market of some countries, labor unions press employers to grant wage increases considerably, thereby raising the cost of production of goods and services. Employers, in turn, raise the prices of their products. An increase in prices induces unions to demand higher wages. Thus, cost-push or wage-push inflation occurs. Some Western economists also argue that inflation may occur when there are changes in the economic structure, termed structural inflation. This type of inflation is attributed to the inherent characteristics of the structure of an economy. In terms of the speed of productivity improvement, certain sectors of the economy may experience rapid productivity growth, whereas others may grow slowly. As for the process of economic development, some sectors are expanding, while others are declining. In terms of international market relations, some sectors are closely connected to the world market, whereas others are less integrated. Structural inflation is typically explained by two sectors with different productivity growth rates. As the rates of productivity growth differ, the wage growth in these two sectors is expected to differ as well. However, workers in the slow-productivity sector demand the same wage growth as that in the fast-productivity sector; hence, the rate of wage growth in the entire society exceeds the rate of productivity growth, and inflation occurs in a **spiral** of rising wages and prices.

8.1.2 Impacts of Inflation

To a certain extent, all individuals are affected by inflation. Inflation is **detrimental** to those who rely on fixed incomes to sustain their lives. With their income remaining constant, their real income and purchasing power decrease, leading to a corresponding reduction in their living standards. The fixed-income group includes those who receive welfare benefits, pensions, salaried employees, government officials, and individuals who rely on welfare and other transfer payments[1] to support their livelihoods. Conversely, those relying on variable incomes to sustain their lives (such as workers in expanding industries with strong union support or business owners receiving income from profits) benefit from inflation as their monetary incomes rise before the increase in prices and living costs. Inflation is also unfavorable for savers. As prices rise, the real value or purchasing power of the savings decreases. Similarly, assets such as insurance payouts, pensions, and fixed-value securities also lose their real value. Inflation can also lead to an income distribution between debtors and creditors. Inflation benefits debtors at the expense of creditors. For example, if person A borrows 10,000 yuan from person B and repays it after one year, and the price level doubles over this period of time, assuming both parties do not anticipate inflation, the 10,000 yuan repaid by A to B is worth only half of the value when borrowed. However, if both parties anticipate inflation, the aforementioned distribution effect will change. If the nominal interest rate[2] on the loan is 10% and the inflation rate is 20%, the real interest rate is –10%. The real interest rate is the difference between the nominal interest rate and the inflation rate, and whenever the inflation rate is higher than the nominal interest rate, the real interest rate becomes negative.

---

[1] transfer payments: one-way payments by the government to individuals without a good or service in return through social programs, such as welfare, student grants, and even Social Security.

[2] nominal interest rate: the interest rate before taking inflation into account.

Many economists believe that moderate demand-pull inflation can have expansionary effects on both output and employment. Suppose aggregate demand increases and a certain degree of demand-pull inflation occurs. Product prices outpace wages and other resource prices, leading to increased business profit. Higher profits stimulate companies to expand their production and reduce unemployment. By contrast, cost-push inflation can lead to reduced income or output, resulting in unemployment. If cost-push inflation occurs, the number of real products that can be purchased with the original total demand will decrease, leading to a decline in actual output and an increase in unemployment. This point is confirmed by the situation in the United States during the 1970s. At the end of 1973, the OPEC[1] doubled the price of oil, leading to cost-push inflation, and the price level rapidly increased from 1973 to 1975. Meanwhile, the unemployment rate in the United States rose from less than 5% in 1973 to 8.5% in 1975.

8.2 Unemployment

8.2.1 Unemployment and Its Classification

Market economies also suffer pain and damage from unemployment. Unemployment can be classified as **frictional**, structural, or cyclical unemployment. Frictional unemployment is short-term unemployment arising from the process of matching workers and jobs. Job search takes time, and there are always some workers who are frictionally unemployed when they are between jobs and in the process of searching for new ones. Structural unemployment arises from the **mismatch** between labor supply and demand. It is characterized by both unemployment and job vacancies. The unemployed may lack suitable skills or **reside** in locations where they cannot fill existing job vacancies. Cyclical unemployment occurs during economic downturns and recessions. When the reduction in total demand in the economy leads to a decrease in total output, workers who have lost their jobs experience cyclical unemployment.

Unemployment is also classified as voluntary and involuntary unemployment. Voluntary unemployment occurs when unemployed individuals are unwilling to accept the prevailing wage level, while involuntary unemployment arises

---

[1] OPEC: the Organization of the Petroleum Exporting Countries, an organization enabling the cooperation of leading oil-producing countries to influence the global oil market and maximize their profit. It was founded on 14 September 1960 in Baghdad.

when individuals are willing to work at the current wage rate but cannot find employment.

Unemployment is measured by the unemployment rate, which refers to the proportion of the labor force that is unemployed but actively seeking employment. As frictional unemployment is universal and inevitable, there is always a certain proportion of the population unemployed in any period of time, which is termed the natural rate of unemployment. It represents the unemployment rate when the labor market is in a state of supply and demand equilibrium, where neither inflation nor deflation occurs. If the labor market is stable, the number of people who find jobs must be equal to the number of people losing jobs. The natural unemployment rate depends on the quit rate❶ and the job-finding rate❷. The higher the quit rate, the higher the natural rate of unemployment; the higher the job-finding rate, the lower the natural rate of unemployment.

8.2.2　Impacts of Unemployment

Unemployment has both social and economic impacts. Unemployment threatens households' stability as social and economic units.

With no income or reduced income, families find it difficult to meet their needs and demands, thus causing damage to family relationships. High unemployment rates are often associated with drug abuse, high divorce rates, and high crime rates. Psychological studies have shown that the **trauma** caused by unemployment is comparable to the loss of a loved one or academic failure. An unemployed individual loses self-esteem and influence among the employed, faces the possibility of rejection by colleagues, and may experience a severe emotional blow, resulting in loss of self-respect and confidence.

The economic impact of unemployment can be understood through the concept of opportunity cost. When the unemployment rate increases, the products and services that could have been produced by unemployed workers are lost. From the perspective of output accounting, the total income loss of the unemployed is equal to production loss. Therefore, lost output is the main measure of cyclical unemployment loss, indicating that the economy is in a state of under-employment. In the 1960s, American economist Arthur Okun proposed the empirical relationship between unemployment and output during economic

---

❶　quit rate: the proportion of employed individuals losing their jobs.
❷　job-finding rate: the proportion of unemployed individuals finding jobs.

cycles, known as Okun's Law: For every 1 percentage point above the natural rate of unemployment, the actual GDP will be 2 percentage points below the potential GDP. According to Okun's Law, changes in the unemployment rate can be inferred or estimated based on changes in GDP, and vice versa. For example, if the actual unemployment rate is 8%, which is 2% above the natural rate of 6%, then the actual GDP will be approximately 4% lower than the potential GDP. An important conclusion of Okun's Law is that the actual GDP must grow at the same rate as the potential GDP to prevent an increase in the unemployment rate.

8.3 Economic Growth

8.3.1 Significance of Economic Growth

Economic growth refers to an increase in output. Output can be represented as the total output or output per capita. Considering that population growth offsets the increased total output, economic growth is better defined as an increase in output per capita. The extent of economic growth can be described by the growth rate. An economic growth rate is the percentage change in the value of total output or that of output per capita during a specific period of time, as compared to an earlier period. The economic growth rate is used to measure the comparative health of an economy over time. An increase in the economic growth rate is often seen as positive. As a fundamental basis for human welfare progress, the importance of economic growth is self-evident. There are significant differences in economic growth rates between countries, and countries with faster growth rates can achieve higher income levels over time. Even minor differences matter if sustained over a long period of time.

As economic and social development continues, the economic structure becomes more complex, and economic growth centered on indicators such as GDP growth can no longer truly reflect the implications and extent of economic and social development. Therefore, the concept of economic development was proposed. As a core concept of development economics, economic development is the high-quality qualitative and quantitative development of the economic and social structure of a country or region on the basis of economic growth. It is not merely about quantitative growth but encompasses innovations in economic and social structures, improvements in the quality of social life, and enhancements in input-output efficiency.

With rapid economic growth rates, China's real GDP per capita is now much higher than it was decades ago, and it is possible for the typical family in China to aspire to buy goods that have long been taken for granted by consumers in high-income countries. China believes that rapid economic growth rates and the improvement in people's well-being will only be attained through high-quality economic growth with the concept of "innovation, coordination, ecological conservation, openness, and sharing". An increase in the economic growth rate is seen as positive only when the output is maximized with the minimum input of productivity factors, which would otherwise be impossible without innovation. Coordination is key to addressing the imbalance of economic growth in different regions and sectors because they are integrated as a whole. People's well-being does not improve with an increase in economic growth at the cost of the environment. Only when ecology is well conserved will people live better lives. To make the economy more competitive and vigorous, China will adhere to the Policy of Opening-Up to the outside world and ensure everyone shares the benefits of economic growth, whose ultimate goal and sole reason is to enhance people's sense of gain.

8.3.2 Modern Economic Growth Theories

Since World War II, due to the implementation of Keynesian economic policies, coupled with the strong impetus of science and technology, the world economy has achieved nearly 20 years of peaceful development, and the gross national product of all countries has had varying degrees of sustained growth. At the same time, however, it has also generated a lot of urgent theoretical and practical problems, which has prompted some economists to focus their attention on the problem of economic growth. In this context, labor, capital, and technological progress are generally believed to be factors that drive economic growth.

In the late 1940s, the British economist R. F. Harrod and the American economist E. D. Domar, based on the theory of J. M. Keynes, proposed the Harrod-Domar growth model to analyze the conditions for stable and balanced growth of the economy over the long term and to illustrate the causal relationship between the process of growth of the national income of a country and the process of growth in the form of savings, investment, the amount of factor inputs and output, and so on.

According to the Harrod-Domar model, the savings rate represents total savings as a proportion of total national income; only two factors of production, labor and capital, are used in the production process. Harrod held that there is a proportional relationship between capital inputs and output (or national income), which is represented by the capital-output ratio (the amount of capital that must be invested to produce one unit of national income). When capital increases, output increases, and the increase in both is known as the marginal capital-output ratio, which is the amount of capital that should be added to each unit of output or income.

The Harrod-Domar model assumes that there is no depreciation and that all capital increases come from new investment; according to Keynes' theory of national income determination, the economy reaches equilibrium only when investment equals savings. The condition for equilibrium economic growth is shown to be that the rate of growth of national income must be equal to the ratio of the social saving rate to the capital-output ratio. Further, Harrod points out that the necessary condition for balanced growth with full employment is that only the three growth rates—population growth rate, guaranteed growth rate and natural growth rate—are equal.

However, although the Harrod-Domar model describes the path to long-term balanced economic growth, does this path really exist? This is the "existential problem" of the Harrod-Domar model. According to Harrod, since in real life the savings rate, the capital-output ratio and the labor force growth rate are independently determined by different factors, the three growth rates are equal only by chance, and in general it is difficult for the economy to grow in accordance with the equilibrium growth path of full employment.

Later, based on the Harrod-Domar model, the American economist Robert Merton Solow proposed the Solow model, a representative model of the neoclassical economic growth theory, in 1956, for which he won the 1987 Nobel Prize in Economics. From the 1960s to the mid-1980s, neoclassical growth theory was dominant in economic growth theory.

Since the Harrod-Domar model assumes that the three growth rates (savings rate, capital-output ratio, and labor force growth rate) often **diverge**, it is difficult to achieve equivalence. Thus, Solow called the extremely narrow path to equilibrium growth prescribed by the Harrod-Domar model the "sharp edge". The Solow model assumes that there are only two factors of production in the economy—capital and labor; that both factors of production are fully utilized to produce a homogeneous product; that labor grows at a constant rate, and that all savings are converted into investment, i.e., the rate of conversion of savings-investment is assumed to be 1; and that there is a diminishing marginal rate of return on investment, i.e., the returns to scale of investment are constant. The Solow model **amends** the production technology assumption of the Harrod-Domar model by adopting a neoclassical Cobb-Douglas production function in which capital and labor are substitutable, thus solving the problem that the economic growth rate and the population growth rate in the Harrod-Domar model are not spontaneously equal. According to the Solow model, in a simple two-sector economy with only residents and firms, the economy achieves equilibrium when investment equals savings.

The neoclassical growth model, represented by the Solow model, demonstrates a dynamic process of growth in which the national economy is stable over time and, when the economy deviates from its steady state, there exists some force that restores it to its long-run equilibrium, i.e., the economy can achieve a steady state of long-run equilibrium growth.

The steady state analysis of neoclassical growth theory suggests that rapid economic growth can be achieved, in the short run, by increasing capital per capita and output per capita at the steady state through increased savings, so that the capital stock grows faster than the labor force, which in turn causes output to grow faster until a new steady state is reached. Also, output can be increased by increasing labor productivity at constant capital per capita through technological progress.

8.4　The Business Cycle

8.4.1　The Business Cycle and Its Stages

The business cycle, also known as the economic cycle or trade cycle, refers to the phenomenon of periodic alternation between economic expansions and contractions, a cycle of ups and downs in economic activity, including fluctuations in national output, income, and employment.

These fluctuations are characterized by widespread expansions or contractions of major macroeconomic variables such as employment rates, price levels, and total output. The economic cycle occurs when real GDP rises or falls relative to the potential GDP.

Economic cycles are irregular, with no two cycles being exactly alike, and there is no precise formula for predicting the timing and duration of economic cycles. Economic cycles can be unpredictable as weather changes. The economic cycle can be divided into four stages: expansion, recession, depression, and recovery. In the expansion phase, the national economic activity is above the normal level, and the economy is in an expansionary state. During this period, there is a continuous increase in effective demand in society, products sell well, and wholesalers and retailers reduce their inventories and place orders with manufacturers. As a result, producers' profits increase significantly, leading to increased investment by manufacturers. This, in turn, leads to higher employment rates and better utilization of labor and other social resources. However, economic expansion will not last long because of the constraints on existing production facilities and capacity. The economy enters the recession stage when economic activity starts to decline from the peak of expansion with the **cessation** of consumption growth. Production declines with the decrease in investment. The effective demand and income levels also decrease. Furthermore, a substantial decline in demand occurs as unemployment rates rise. As a result, general commodity prices fall and some manufacturers begin to close due to sharp decreases in profits. Inventories increase and production contracts significantly. There is a prevailing sense of pessimism throughout society. After experiencing a recession, the economy enters the depression phase. The depression phase represents a continuation of the recession, and national economic activity is below the normal level. Enterprises lack confidence in the future and are unwilling to take new investment risks. Although both recession and depression involve a decline in economic activity, the economic activity level during a recession is still above the long-term average growth level of the economy, whereas the economic activity level during a depression is far below the long-term average level of economic activity.

The recovery phase refers to the period when the economy begins to rise from its lowest point. The worn-out technical equipment is upgraded. Production is promoted as investments increase. Employment, income, and consumption also start to increase. Thus, people will become more hopeful about the future. Risk investments that were previously unwillingly undertaken begin to appear. As demand increases, production continues to expand, and idle equipment, labor, and other production resources from the depression phase begin to be used. However, due to the effects of the depression phase, the social economy is in an adjustment stage and the pace of economic recovery will not be too fast. As economic recovery continues to improve, the pace of economic growth accelerates continuously until it reaches a certain level, entering the next period of prosperity. At this point, the entire economy completes one cycle and the next cycle starts.

8.4.2 Causes of the Business Cycle

Western economists have provided different explanations from various perspectives regarding the causes of economic cycles. They can be broadly categorized into **endogenous** and **exogenous** economic cycle theories. Endogenous economic cycle theory mainly seeks factors within the economic system that spontaneously generate economic cycle movements. This emphasizes that cyclical fluctuations are caused by factors within the economic system. Examples include changes in money supply, investment, consumption, and psychological factors. The exogenous economic cycle theory posits that the roots of economic cycles originate from factors external to the economic system. These external factors can be diverse and include technological innovations, population growth, resource discoveries, wars, revolutions, elections, immigration, and accidental events.

Economic cycles are not solely caused by purely endogenous or exogenous factors. Economic cycles often result from a combination of endogenous and exogenous factors. One of the most influential endogenous economic cycle theories is the **multiplier-accelerator** principle. This theory links the level of investment with the rate of change in national income, thus explaining the cyclical fluctuations in national income. According to Keynesian economists, economic cycles are primarily caused by fluctuations in total demand, with investment playing a critical role. In an economy, investment and consumption interact and adjust to each other. Investment is crucial in this self-regulating process, and economic cycles are primarily caused by changes in investment. An increase in investment through the multiplier effect[1] leads to a larger increase in GDP, which in turn leads to further increased investment through the accelerator effect. This combination results in an economic boom. The "multiplier" refers to the phenomenon where an increase (or decrease) in investment under certain conditions of marginal propensity to consume[2] can lead to a multiple-fold increase (or decrease) in national income and employment. The ratio of the

---

[1] multiplier effect: the proportional amount of increase, or decrease, in final income that results from an injection, or withdrawal, of capital.

[2] marginal propensity to consume (MPC): a measurement of the proportion of extra income that is spent on consumption.

increase in income to the increase in investment is known as an investment multiplier. The size of the investment multiplier is closely related to the **propensity** to consume: the higher the marginal propensity to consume, the larger the investment multiplier, and vice versa. The "accelerator coefficient" refers to the net investment needed to increase output by a certain amount. After GDP reaches a certain level where social demand and resources cannot increase further, the adjustment mechanism described by the multiplier principle causes a decrease in investment, which, through the multiplier effect, further reduces GDP. The joint action of these two processes leads to economic recession. After a certain period of recession, due to the upgrade of fixed assets such as machinery and equipment, investment increases again, leading to further growth in GDP and ushering in another period of prosperity.

In conclusion, economic cycles are a complex phenomenon. The multiplier-accelerator principle and real economic cycle theory are influential concepts used to explain the cyclical nature of economic activity.

Exercises

1 Short answer questions

Directions: *Answer the following questions in your own words or with sentences from the text.*

(1) What is inflation?

(2) What is frictional unemployment?

(3) How is unemployment measured?

(4) What is the business cycle?

2 Term explanation

Directions: *Explain the following terms in your own words or with sentences from the text.*

(1) CPI

(2) cyclical unemployment

(3) multiplier effect

(4) recession

❸ Banked cloze

Directions: *Fill in the blanks by selecting suitable words from the following box. You may not use any of the words more than once.*

A. demand	B. supply	C. inflation	D. employment	E. unemployment
F. declined	G. structurally	H. recession	I. competitors	J. inadequacies
K. finding	L. competing	M. competition	N. frictionally	O. cyclically

Lucent Technologies, known as the grandfather of high-technology firms, was founded in 1869. The company, originally the Western Electric Manufacturing Company, was purchased by the American Telephone and Telegraph Company (AT&T) in 1881 and renamed Bell Laboratories. Bell Labs became independent of AT&T in 1996 and took its current name, Lucent Technologies.

Lucent Technologies experienced a sharp decline in employment in the early 2000s. In 2000, Lucent employed 175,000 workers. It began laying off large numbers of workers in 2001. By 2005, Lucent employed only 31,500 workers. Was the unemployment caused by the layoffs at Lucent frictional unemployment, structural unemployment, or cyclical unemployment?

We can roughly categorize the (1) _____ at Lucent by considering the three basic reasons the layoffs occurred: the long-lived decline in the telecommunications products Lucent sells; the recession of 2001 that reduced the (2) _____ for Lucent's products, and the failure of Lucent managers to respond to rapid technological change in the industry. Each reason corresponds to a category of unemployment. Because the demand for the telecommunications products Lucent sells—particularly products used with fiber-optic cable networks—declined for a significant period, employment at Lucent and competing firms also (3) _____. Between late 2000 and mid-2002, employment in the telecommunications industry declined by more than 500,000. Certain categories of employees, such as optical engineers, had difficulty (4) _____ new jobs. They were (5) _____ unemployed because they were not able to find new jobs without learning new skills. Some of the decline in Lucent's sales was due to the (6) _____ rather than to long-term problems in the telecommunications industry. So some of the workers who lost their jobs at Lucent were (7) _____ unemployed. Finally, sales and employment declined more sharply at Lucent than at some (8) _____ firms because of mistakes made by Lucent's managers. Some workers who lost their jobs at Lucent were able to find new jobs at Lucent's (9) _____ after relatively brief job searches. These workers were (10) _____ unemployed.

4 Translation

Directions: *Translate the following paragraphs into Chinese or English.*

(1) China believes that rapid economic growth rates and the improvement in people's well-being will only be attained through high-quality economic growth with the concept of "innovation, coordination, ecological conservation, openness, and sharing". An increase in the economic growth rate is seen as positive only when the output is maximized with the minimum input of productivity factors, which would otherwise be impossible without innovation. Coordination is key to addressing the imbalance of economic growth in different regions and sectors because they are integrated as a whole. People's well-being does not improve with an increase in economic growth at the cost of the environment. Only when ecology is well conserved will people live better lives.

(2) 贯彻新发展理念是关系我国发展全局的一场深刻变革，不能简单以生产总值增长率论英雄（yardstick of success），必须实现创新成为第一动力、协调成为内生特点、绿色（eco-friendly growth）成为普遍形态、开放成为必由之路、共享（shared growth）成为根本目的的高质量发展，推动经济发展质量变革、效率变革、动力（impetus）变革。

5 Project

Title: Understanding the Economic Situation in China
Instructions:

Step 1: Choose a city in China and briefly describe its economic growth trends in the past decade.

Step 2: Investigate people's living aspirations in the chosen city and how their lives have been changing during this period.

Step 3: Explore the factors influencing the economic growth of the chosen city.

Step 4: Present your findings to the class. Explain the economic situation of the chosen city and how economic growth meets people's needs. Use examples from your research to illustrate your points.

Supplementary Reading

Scan the QR code to find out more about the unit.

Unit 9
Macroeconomic Policy

Learning Objectives

After studying this unit, you should be able to:

1) comprehend governments' economic roles, monetary and fiscal policies, objectives, types, and execution tools for macroeconomic policies;

2) use the words and phrases in this unit;

3) cultivate an awareness of the critical role of the Chinese government in shaping economies, foster informed and responsible citizenship, and understand the broader societal implications of economic policies.

Macroeconomic policy is a tool that policymakers use to assist them in regulating an economy. It plays a crucial role in managing and stabilizing the economy. Governments employ a combination of fiscal and monetary policies to address various economic challenges, such as inflation, unemployment, and economic inequality. This unit aims to explore the role of government in the economy, along with an in-depth analysis of monetary and fiscal policies.

9.1 The Role of Government in the Economy

In modern society, governments play three primary roles in the economy: market regulation, provision of public goods and services, and economic stabilization through macroeconomic policies. These roles are often **intertwined** and must be balanced to achieve optimal macroeconomic outcomes.

9.1.1 Market Regulation

As one of the key aspects of government intervention in the economy, market regulation refers to the rules imposed by governments to change the behavior of firms, correct market failure, promote competition, and remove anti-competitive behavior.

For example, governments can set the maximum price for monopolies mainly by two means. By using the RPI – X + K formula, governments force monopolies to charge prices below the profit-maximizing price. "RPI" stands for retail price index. "X" represents efficiency, and "K" is a constant term. Governments set a price below the inflation rate, forcing firms to become more efficient if they continue to make profits. This ensures that firms pass on efficiency gains to consumers.

However, owing to rapid improvements in technology, it is difficult to determine what X is. Governments have only **asymmetric** information, and their efforts may not be effective. K in RPI + K is capital investment. Governments allow firms to grow and make profits but force them to invest back in it.

Regulators can also set a price cap at P = MSC (marginal social cost). This ensures that monopolies are **allocatively** efficient. The price cap acts as a **proxy** for competition. Failure to act according to these price caps and regulations can result in huge fines that can affect firms' profits.

For example, Royal Mail, which provides mail and parcel delivery services to individuals and businesses across the United Kingdom, had a price cap on second-class stamps. The company increased the price above the price cap and was fined £1.5 million by Ofcom (Office of Communications, the regulatory authority for the communications industry in the United Kingdom).

However, it could be difficult for regulators to know where a firm's allocative efficient point is, due to asymmetric information. Additionally, inflation can reduce profits in the long run if the price does not adjust to inflation.

Instead of regulating prices, governments can control the profit maximization. Prices are set to allow firms to cover their operating costs and earn a "fair" rate of return, based on the capital employed.

The maximization of profit is used to prevent firms from setting too high a price, which encourages them to invest. However, firms could employ too much capital and allow it to **depreciate** so that governments can increase their rates of return. Additionally, firms do not earn more if their costs are reduced; thus they provide little incentive to reduce costs and improve efficiency.

Market regulations play a pivotal role in protecting consumers from unsafe products, unfair practices, and deceptive advertising. In addition, these regulations prevent monopolies and foster healthy competition, thereby enhancing market efficiency and benefiting consumers. Moreover, specific regulations, particularly those governing financial markets, reduce excessive risk-taking and contribute to overall economic stability. However, it is important to acknowledge the drawbacks of regulations, including the potential for excessive or poorly designed regulations to impose a heavy burden on businesses, especially small enterprises, ultimately impeding economic growth and innovation. Regulatory capture poses another challenge, as powerful interest groups can manipulate regulations for their own interests rather than for broader public welfare. Furthermore, market regulations can **inadvertently** lead to unintended consequences ranging from novel market distortions to **stifling** innovation.

9.1.2 Provision of Public Goods and Services

The provision of public goods and services is another essential role of government, which is justified for several reasons.

Public goods often suffer from market failure. Owing to their non-excludable and non-rivalrous nature, private markets may not provide them efficiently or at all. As individuals cannot be excluded from enjoying public goods, there is little incentive for private firms to invest in their production or maintenance.

Additionally, free-riding behavior can occur where individuals enjoy benefits without contributing to their provision. Government intervention is necessary to overcome these market failures and to ensure the provision of public goods.

Public goods contribute to social welfare by promoting equity and enhancing the well-being of both individuals and communities. Public goods such as education, healthcare, and social infrastructure ensure equal access to essential services and opportunities, regardless of an individual's ability to pay. They help **mitigate** disparities, promote social cohesion, and foster a more inclusive society.

Public goods often generate positive externalities and benefits that spill over to individuals or sectors, beyond those directly involved. For example, investments in education not only benefit individuals but also contribute to a more educated and skilled workforce, leading to economic growth and societal advancement. Government provision of public goods helps to capture these positive externalities and promotes overall social and economic development.

In addition to public goods, governments are responsible for providing public services that meet the needs of the population. These services include healthcare, education, transportation infrastructure, law enforcement, environmental protection, and social welfare programs.

Public services play a vital role in promoting societal well-being and in addressing collective needs. They ensure access to essential services that may not be adequately provided by the private sector. By providing public services, governments can help reduce inequalities, enhance the quality of life, protect public health and safety, and create an enabling environment for economic growth and development.

Governments encounter challenges in offering public goods and services, involving resource allocation decisions to optimize provision efficiency and effectiveness. This necessitates prioritizing needs, managing budgets, and maximizing utilization of limited resources. Additionally, public-private partnerships may be utilized to leverage private sector capabilities and market mechanisms for delivery. These collaborations maintain public control and accountability while benefiting from private-sector expertise and resources. Furthermore, governments need to ensure efficient delivery of public goods and services, minimize waste, and maintain accountability. **Transparency**, monitoring, and evaluation mechanisms are crucial to effective governance and public trust.

9.1.3 Economic Stabilization Through Macroeconomic Policies

Economic stabilization refers to the actions taken by the government to mitigate fluctuations in the business cycle, stabilize prices, and promote overall economic stability, which is an ongoing challenge, given the inherent volatility of market forces. Governments are responsible for ensuring the stability of their respective economies. They intervene to prevent severe economic fluctuations such as recession or depression through policy measures. This stabilization function often involves mitigating the impact of business cycles by employing appropriate monetary and fiscal policies.

Central to economic stabilization is the **adept** use of monetary policy. Central banks, often independent entities, play a pivotal role in adjusting interest rates and managing the money supply. In times of economic downturn, they may lower interest rates to encourage borrowing and spending, thus stimulating the economy. Conversely, during periods of overheating, interest rates may be raised to curb inflationary pressure.

Complementing monetary policy, fiscal policy becomes a counter-cyclical force in economic stabilization. Governments may deploy expansionary fiscal measures during downturns by injecting funds into the economy through increased spending or tax cuts. This stimulates demand and helps mitigate the depth of recession. Conversely, during periods of economic **exuberance**, contractionary fiscal policies are implemented to cool the economy and prevent inflation.

While economic stabilization policies are essential, they are not without challenges and trade-offs. Striking the right balance between inflation and unemployment, avoiding policy lags, and addressing the diverse impacts on different sectors of the economy require careful consideration. Governments continually **grapple** with these complexities in pursuit of macroeconomic stability.

In conclusion, as we navigate the intricate interplay between economic efficiency and stability, the role of the government becomes even more pronounced. Economic stabilization policies, alongside measures to enhance efficiency, form a comprehensive strategy to foster a resilient and flourishing economy.

9.2 Monetary Policy

Monetary policy plays a crucial role in shaping a country's economy by influencing key financial variables such as interest rates, money supply, and inflation. It serves as a vital tool for central banks to achieve macroeconomic objectives and maintain economic stability.

9.2.1 Monetary Policy and Its Functions

Monetary policy refers to the actions and measures implemented by a central bank or monetary authority to regulate and control the supply of money, credit, and interest rates in an economy. It encompasses a range of tools and strategies employed to achieve specific economic goals, primarily focusing on price stability, sustainable economic growth, and full employment.

The functions of monetary policy vary across countries and may be set by legislation or determined by the central bank, in line with government priorities.

One of the primary functions of monetary policy is to maintain price stability within the economy. Price stability refers to a low and stable inflation rate. Central banks strive to keep inflation in check❶ to preserve the purchasing power of money and provide a stable foundation for economic activities. When prices are relatively stable, individuals and businesses can make informed decisions regarding their spending, saving, and investment choices. Price stability fosters economic certainty, reduces uncertainty, and promotes long-term planning, which is essential for sustainable economic growth.

Another key function of monetary policy is fostering sustainable economic growth. Central banks aim to create an environment **conducive** to a robust and balanced economic expansion. Policymakers seek to encourage borrowing, investment, and consumption by influencing interest rates, credit availability, and overall monetary conditions. This in turn stimulates economic activity, leading to increased output, productivity, and job creation. Sustainable economic growth helps raise living standards, reduce poverty, and enhance overall welfare within a society.

Achieving and maintaining full employment is a crucial objective of monetary policy. Full employment implies that most individuals who are willing and able to work find suitable employment opportunities. Central banks

---

❶ keep inflation in check: to maintain a stable and moderate rate of inflation in an economy.

utilize monetary tools to influence aggregate demand, investment levels, and labor market dynamics to promote job creation and reduce unemployment. By maintaining a healthy level of economic activity, monetary policy aims to minimize involuntary unemployment and maximize employment opportunities, thereby fostering social stability and enhancing the well-being of individuals and communities.

In some countries, maintaining exchange rate stability is also the goal of monetary policy. A stable exchange rate provides certainty for international trade, investment, and capital flow. Central banks may employ various measures to manage exchange rate fluctuations, including interventions in foreign exchange markets and setting interest rates to attract or deter foreign investments. Exchange rate stability is particularly important for economies that rely heavily on international trade and are significantly exposed to external shocks.

9.2.2 Classification of Monetary Policy and Its Tools

There are two main types of monetary policy: contractionary and expansionary. Contractionary monetary policy is used to decrease the amount of money circulating throughout the economy, typically by raising interest rates and increasing bank reserve requirements. The government uses this method to avoid inflation. Expansionary monetary policy can increase the economy's money supply by decreasing interest rates, lowering reserve requirements for banks, and purchasing government securities by central banks. This policy helps to lower unemployment rates and stimulates business activities and consumer spending. The overall goal of this policy is to fuel economic growth, but it can also have adverse effects, occasionally leading to hyperinflation. Understanding these two types of monetary policy provides insights into the flexibility and **versatility** of central banks in managing their respective economies.

A contractionary policy reduces the rate of monetary expansion of a central bank. This macroeconomic tool is used to combat rising inflation. Contractionary policies strive to prevent potential capital market distortions. Distortions include high inflation from an expanding money supply, unreasonable asset prices, or crowding-out effects❶, where a **spike** in interest rates leads to a reduction in private investment spending such that it dampens

---

❶ crowding-out effects: economic theories which argue that rising public sector spending drives down or even eliminates private sector spending.

the initial increase in total investment spending. While the initial effect of contractionary policy is to reduce nominal gross domestic product, which is evaluated at current market prices, it often ultimately results in sustainable economic growth and smoother business cycles. It is typically employed when inflation rises above target levels and there is a need to cool down an overheating economy.

Expansionary monetary policy works by expanding the money supply faster than usual or by lowering short-term interest rates. It is enacted by central banks and comes about through open market operations, reserve requirements, and interest rates. It is typically employed during periods of low economic growth or high unemployment, or when there is a need to stimulate demand and investment.

In practice, central banks often employ a combination of these monetary policy measures, **tailoring** their approach to specific economic conditions and objectives. The choice of monetary policy depends on factors such as inflation levels, economic growth rates, labor market conditions, and the overall stability of the financial system. Central banks continually assess the effectiveness of their policies and adjust their approaches as necessary to support macroeconomic stability and achieve their goals.

Monetary policy is implemented using a variety of tools and instruments.

Open market operations (OMOs) are the most commonly used monetary policy tool. An OMO is an activity taken by a central bank to give (or take) liquidity in its currency to (or from) a bank or a group of banks. Central banks conduct OMOs by buying or selling government securities, typically bonds, in an open market. When the central bank buys government securities, it injects money into the economy, increasing money supply. Conversely, when the central bank sells government securities, it reduces the money supply.

The impact of OMOs on the economy is two-fold. First, it affects the level of reserves held by commercial banks and influences their lending capacity. Second, it influences interest rates. When the central bank buys government securities, it increases the demand for these securities, driving up their prices and lowering their yields (interest rates). Lower interest rates encourage borrowing and investment and stimulate economic activity.

The legal deposit reserve rate is a key tool in monetary policy and banking regulations. This rate represents the interest paid by a central bank to the reserves that commercial banks are required to hold. In many economies, commercial banks are obligated to maintain a certain percentage of their deposits as reserves, and the central bank determines the legal deposit reserve rate as interest compensation for holding these reserves. The rate influences the opportunity cost for banks, as it affects the return they receive to keep funds in reserve rather than lending them.

The legal deposit reserve rate plays a crucial role in shaping the behavior of commercial banks, impacting their decision to either hold reserves or extend loans to consumers and businesses. Adjustments by the central bank to this rate can have ripple effects on a country's money supply, inflation, and overall economic activity. It is an instrument through which central banks manage liquidity in the banking system and consequently influence broader economic conditions.

The rate of rediscount is a significant monetary policy tool employed by central banks to regulate the flow of money in the financial system. This rate represents the interest charged by the central bank when commercial banks borrow funds by discounting or selling **eligible** short-term financial instruments, such as bills of exchange or promissory notes[1].

Through the process of rediscounting, commercial banks can obtain liquidity from the central bank before the maturity of their short-term assets. The rate of rediscount directly influences the cost of this borrowing for commercial banks. Central banks use adjustments to the rate of rediscount as a means to control the money supply and credit conditions in the broader economy.

These tools of monetary policy are not used in isolation but are often implemented in combination to achieve desired macroeconomic outcomes. The selection and combination of tools depend on the prevailing economic conditions, policy objectives, and the central bank's assessment of the transmission mechanisms within the economy. Central banks continuously monitor and adjust their use of these tools to maintain macroeconomic stability, promote economic growth, and achieve their policy objectives.

9.2.3 Challenges of Monetary Policy

While monetary policy plays a crucial role in economic management, it is not without challenges. One of the significant challenges of monetary policy is the presence of time lags between policy actions and their impacts

---

[1] promissory notes: written and signed promises to repay a sum of money in exchange for a loan or other financing.

on the economy. Changes in interest rates or money supply take time to be transmitted through the financial system and influence economic activity. There may be delays in how individuals, businesses, and financial markets respond to monetary policy measures, making it difficult to achieve precise and timely outcomes.

Another challenge arises when interest rates approach or reach the zero lower bound (ZLB)❶. When interest rates are very low, reducing them further becomes difficult or ineffective in stimulating borrowing and investments. At the ZLB, conventional monetary policy tools may lose their **potency**, limiting the central bank's ability to stimulate the economy further. To address this challenge, central banks have explored unconventional monetary policy measures, such as quantitative easing❷ or forward guidance❸, as alternative tools to provide additional **stimulus** when interest rates are near zero.

The increasing complexity of financial systems poses challenges to monetary policy. Financial innovations, globalization, and interconnectedness have made it more difficult for central banks to fully understand and monitor the transmission mechanisms of their policy actions. Changes in financial conditions, such as asset price **bubbles** or excessive risk-taking, can have significant implications for the broader economy. Central banks must carefully monitor financial markets and institutions, assess potential risks, and respond swiftly to maintain their financial stability. Failure to address financial imbalances effectively can undermine the effectiveness of monetary policy and lead to economic instability.

9.3 Fiscal Policy

Fiscal policy is a crucial component of macroeconomic management employed by governments to influence the overall health and performance of an economy. Fiscal policy tries to **nudge** the economy in different ways through either expansionary or contractionary policies, which try to either increase

---

❶ zero lower bound: a macroeconomic problem that occurs when the short-term nominal interest rate is at or near zero, causing a liquidity trap and limiting the central bank's capacity to stimulate economic growth.

❷ quantitative easing: a form of monetary policy in which a central bank purchases securities from the open market to reduce interest rates and increase the money supply.

❸ forward guidance: the communication from a central bank about the state of the economy and the likely future course of monetary policy.

economic growth through taxes and spending or slow economic growth to cut inflation, respectively.

9.3.1 Fiscal Policy and Its Functions

Fiscal policy refers to the use of government spending and tax policies to influence economic conditions, especially macroeconomic ones. During a recession, the government may lower tax rates or increase spending to encourage demand and **spur** economic activity. Conversely, to combat inflation, it may raise tax rates or cut government spending to cool the economy. Fiscal policy is often utilized alongside monetary policy, which involves the regulation of the banking system, management of interest rates, and supply of money in circulation.

Fiscal policy functions are multifaceted and encompass a range of economic and social aspirations. Here, we explore the primary functions that governments aim to fulfill through the strategic use of fiscal policy.

One of the central functions of a fiscal policy is to stimulate and sustain economic growth. By strategically increasing government spending on crucial infrastructure projects, education, healthcare, and R&D, fiscal policy can create a conducive environment for economic expansion. Additionally, tax cuts or incentives can encourage private investment and consumer spending, further driving economic growth.

Fiscal policies also seek to maintain price stability and control inflation rates. During periods of rising prices and overheating economic conditions, the government can implement contractionary fiscal measures by reducing excessive spending and increasing taxes to cool the economy and prevent inflationary pressures.

Fiscal policies can be used to address income inequality by redistributing wealth and providing social support to less privileged segments of society. Progressive taxation, wherein higher-income individuals are taxed at higher rates, allows the government to collect more revenue from the **affluent** and allocate resources to welfare programs, healthcare, and education to uplift the disadvantaged population.

It is important to note that achieving these functions through fiscal policy requires careful planning, analysis, and consideration of the prevailing economic conditions. Moreover, fiscal policy operates in conjunction with other economic policies such as monetary policy, and should be tailored to the specific needs and challenges faced by each nation. When effectively implemented, fiscal policy serves as a potent instrument for governments to shape their economies, foster social welfare, and ensure long-term economic prosperity.

9.3.2 Classification of Fiscal Policy and Its Tools

Fiscal policies encompass various strategies employed by governments to manage economic conditions and achieve specific goals. The two primary types are contractionary and expansionary fiscal policies, each of which has distinct aims and tools.

Governments may implement contractionary fiscal policies during periods of economic overheating, high inflation, or unsustainable growth. These policies aim to:

Slow inflation. By reducing government spending or increasing taxes, contractionary fiscal policies decrease aggregate demand, curb inflationary pressure, and stabilize prices.

Guide economic growth. Maintaining a steady pace of economic growth is therefore crucial. Contractionary policies help prevent rapid economic expansion, which could lead to a subsequent recession, ensuring a sustainable business cycle.

Manage unemployment. While low unemployment is desirable, excessively low levels can disrupt the economic equilibrium. Contractionary fiscal policies prevent unemployment from falling below optimal levels, maintain stability, and avoid inflationary pressures.

Governments employ expansionary fiscal policies to counter economic contractions and prevent recessions. These policies aim to:

Increase aggregate demand. Through heightened government spending and tax cuts, expansionary fiscal policies inject money into the economy and stimulate consumer spending and investment.

Address economic downturn. During the recessions or contractionary phases of the business cycle, expansionary policies aim to boost economic activity and foster growth and employment.

Mitigate the multiplier effect. Despite short-term budget deficits, expansionary policies anticipate a long-term economic expansion. By catalyzing economic activity, they generate a multiplier effect, driving overall growth and offsetting initial deficits.

Fiscal policies employ various tools to achieve their objectives.

Governments can influence the direction of the economy by altering spending patterns. Increased spending on infrastructure, healthcare, education, and other sectors can boost aggregate demand and stimulate economic growth.

Transfer payments such as social security benefits, unemployment benefits, and welfare programs can directly impact income distribution and social welfare. Adjusting these payments can be a powerful tool to address poverty and inequality.

Certain aspects of the fiscal system, such as progressive taxation and unemployment benefits, act as automatic stabilizers. During economic downturns, they provide a **cushion** that automatically increases government spending and reduces tax revenue, which helps stabilize the aggregate demand.

Understanding the classification of fiscal policy and its accompanying tools is indispensable for policymakers and economists alike, offering crucial insights into the management of economic cycles and the pursuit of sustained prosperity.

9.3.3 Challenges of Fiscal Policy

Just like monetary policy, fiscal policy also faces challenges and criticism. One such challenge is the presence of time lags, in which the implementation of fiscal measures may experience delays before their actual effects are felt within the economy. These delays, stemming from legislative processes or the initiation of spending projects, can **impede** timely response to economic fluctuations. Additionally, fiscal policy decisions are often influenced by short-term political considerations, which might prioritize immediate political advantages over long-term economic objectives. This can result in **suboptimal** policies that undermine overall economic stability. Another concern is the possibility of crowding out, wherein increased government borrowing to fund deficits can drive interest rates and subsequently diminish private investments. This counterproductive effect could offset the positive outcomes of fiscal policy.

In practice, fiscal policy implementation requires careful consideration of the prevailing economic conditions, policy goals, and potential impacts. A successful fiscal policy framework involves a delicate balance between stimulating economic growth, controlling inflation, and ensuring fiscal sustainability. The effectiveness of fiscal policy also depends on other factors such as monetary policy, external trade dynamics, and global economic conditions. Policymakers must remain **vigilant** and adaptive to address the ever-changing economic challenges and strive for sustainable and inclusive growth.

Exercises

❶ Short answer questions

Directions: *Answer the following questions in your own words or with sentences from the text.*

(1) What are the three primary roles of the government in the economy, and how are they interconnected to achieve optimal macroeconomic outcomes?

(2) How do market regulations promote competition and protect consumers?

(3) Why is maintaining exchange rate stability considered important for some countries?

(4) What are the two main types of fiscal policies, and what are their purposes in the economy?

❷ Term explanation

Directions: *Explain the following terms in your own words or with sentences from the text.*

(1) market regulation

(2) price stability

(3) expansionary fiscal policy

(4) contractionary fiscal policy

❸ Banked cloze

Directions: *Fill in the blanks by selecting suitable words from the following box. You may not use any of the words more than once.*

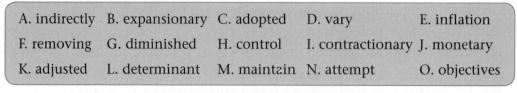

A. indirectly	B. expansionary	C. adopted	D. vary	E. inflation
F. removing	G. diminished	H. control	I. contractionary	J. monetary
K. adjusted	L. determinant	M. maintain	N. attempt	O. objectives

Monetary policy is policy (1) _____ by the monetary authority of a nation to affect monetary and other financial conditions to accomplish broader (2) _____ like high employment and price stability (normally interpreted as a low and stable rate of inflation). Further purposes of monetary policy may be to contribute to economic stability or to (3) _____ predictable exchange rates with other currencies. Today most central banks in developed countries conduct their monetary policy within a(n) (4) _____ targeting framework, whereas the monetary policies of most developing countries' central banks target a fixed exchange rate system. A third monetary policy strategy, targeting money supply, was widely followed during the 1980s, but has (5) _____ in popularity since then, although it is still the official strategy in a number of emerging economies.

The tools of monetary policy (6) _____ from central bank to central bank, depending on the country's stage of development, institutional structure, tradition, and political system. Interest rate targeting is generally the primary tool, obtained either directly by administratively changing the central bank's own interest rates or (7) _____ via open-market operations. Interest rates affect general economic activity and, consequently, employment and inflation via a number of different channels, collectively known as the monetary transmission mechanism, and are also an important (8) _____ of the exchange rate. Other policy tools include communication strategies such as forward guidance, and the setting of reserve requirements in some countries. Monetary policy is often referred to as being either (9) _____ (stimulating economic activity and consequently employment and inflation) or (10) _____ (dampening economic activity, hence decreasing employment and inflation).

How best to conduct monetary policy is an active and debated research area, drawing on fields such as monetary economics as well as other subfields within macroeconomics.

4 Translation

Directions: *Translate the following paragraphs into Chinese or English.*

(1) There are two main types of monetary policy: contractionary and expansionary. Contractionary monetary policy is used to decrease the amount of money circulating throughout the economy, typically by raising interest rates and increasing bank reserve requirements. The government uses this method to avoid inflation. An expansionary monetary policy can increase the economy's money supply by decreasing interest rates, lowering reserve requirements for banks, and purchasing government securities by central banks. This policy helps

to lower unemployment rates and stimulates business activities and consumer spending. The overall goal of this policy is to fuel economic growth, but it can also have adverse effects, occasionally leading to hyperinflation. Understanding these two types of monetary policy provides insights into the flexibility and versatility of central banks in managing their respective economies.

(2) 经济是一个国家发展的根本，也是一个国家兴旺（prosperity）的基础。自改革开放以来，中国经济逐步迈向现代化（modernization），并成功成为全球第二大经济体（the world's second largest economy）。然而，随着国际经济环境的不断变化和国内经济发展方式的调整，中国宏观经济面临着众多挑战。近年来，中国政府已采取一系列宏观经济政策措施，这些举措旨在解决当前经济发展中的问题，并确保中国经济持续稳健增长（sustained and steady growth）。在全球化的时代，中国继续坚定地与世界各国合作，共同应对全球性挑战，促进经济的共同繁荣。

5 Project

Title: Macroeconomic Marvels

Instructions:

Step 1: Begin by researching the fundamental concepts of macroeconomic policy, including fiscal and monetary policy, and their impact on the broader economy. Then engage in group discussions to share perspectives on the role of macroeconomic policy in addressing economic challenges and fostering sustainable economic development.

Step 2: Select a country or region and investigate recent macroeconomic policy initiatives. Analyze how these policies have influenced key economic indicators such as GDP growth, unemployment rates, and inflation.

Step 3: Based on your research and analysis, propose a set of macroeconomic policy recommendations for a hypothetical country facing specific economic challenges.

Step 4: Reflect on the learning experiences and insights gained throughout the project. Consider how macroeconomic policies shape the economic trajectory of a nation. Then conclude with setting goals for further exploration or research in the field of macroeconomic policy and its implications.

Unit 9 Macroeconomic Policy

Supplementary Reading

Scan the QR code to find out more about the unit.

Unit 10

International Economy

Learning Objectives

After studying this unit, you should be able to:

1) understand the concepts of absolute and comparative advantage, the development of economic globalization, and basic information about tariffs;

2) use the words and phrases in this unit;

3) apply what you have learned from this unit to the discussion of China's role in the development of the global economy.

To analyze the complex dynamics of the international economy, it is essential to understand the principles of absolute advantage, comparative advantage, and economic globalization. In addition to the above concepts, this unit also provides a brief introduction to tariffs and tariff effects.

10.1 Absolute Advantage and Comparative Advantage

Absolute advantage and comparative advantage are two important concepts in economics and international trade. They largely influence how and why nations and businesses devote resources to the production of goods and services.

10.1.1 Absolute Advantage

In the late 18th and early 19th centuries, Adam Smith and David Ricardo explored the basis of international trade as part of their efforts to make a case for free trade. Their writings were responses to the doctrine of **mercantilism** that prevailed at the time. Their classic theories swayed policymakers for the whole century, even though today we view them as only special cases of a more basic and more powerful theory of trade.

Adam Smith helped originate the concepts of absolute advantage and comparative advantage in his book *The Wealth of Nations*. Smith argued that countries should specialize in the goods they can produce most efficiently, and trade for any products they cannot produce. Specializing in the products that they each have an absolute advantage in, and then trading the products can make all countries better off, as long as they each have at least one product for which they hold an absolute advantage over other nations. The absolute advantage explains why it makes sense for individuals, businesses, and countries to trade with each other. Because each has advantages in producing certain goods and services, both entities can benefit from the exchange. This mutual gain from trade forms the basis of Smith's argument that specialization, division of labor, and subsequent trade lead to an overall increase in prosperity, from which all can benefit.

David Ricardo (1772–1823), a British economist, later built on Smith's concepts by more broadly introducing comparative advantage in his book *On the Principles of Political Economy and Taxation* in the early 19th century. According to Ricardo, nations can benefit from trading even if one of them has an absolute advantage in producing everything. In other words, countries must choose to diversify the goods and services they produce, which requires them to consider the opportunity costs.

Absolute advantage is the ability of an individual, company, region, or country to produce a greater quantity of a good or service with the same quantity of inputs per unit of time or to produce the same quantity of a good or service per unit of time using a lesser quantity of inputs than its competitors. An absolute advantage can be accomplished by creating a good or service at a lower absolute cost per unit using a smaller number of inputs, or by a more efficient process.

This analysis helps countries avoid producing goods and services that would yield little to no demand, ultimately leading to losses. A country's absolute advantage (or disadvantage) in a particular industry can play an important role in the type of product it chooses to produce. Some of the factors that can lead an entity to an absolute advantage include lower labor costs, greater access to (natural) resources, and a larger pool of available capital.

For example, if Japan and Italy can both produce automobiles, but Italy can produce sports cars of a higher quality and at a faster rate with greater profit, then Italy is said to have an absolute advantage in that particular industry. On the other hand, Japan may be better served to devote limited resources and labor to other types of vehicles (such as electric cars) or other industries. This may help the country enjoy an absolute advantage over trying to compete with Italy's efficiency.

10.1.2 Comparative Advantage

Comparative advantage describes a situation in which an individual, business, or country can produce a good or service at a lower opportunity cost than another producer. A comparative advantage is used to explain why companies, countries, or individuals can benefit from trade. While this usually illustrates the benefits of trade, some contemporary economists now acknowledge that focusing only on comparative advantages can result in the **exploitation** and depletion of a country's resources.

The key to understanding comparative advantage is a solid grasp of the opportunity costs. Opportunity costs represent the potential benefits that an individual, investor, or business may miss when choosing one alternative over another. As opportunity costs are unseen by definition, they can be easily overlooked. Understanding the potential missed opportunities when a business or individual chooses one investment over another allows for better decision-making.

Suppose there are two countries, Country A and Country B, that both produce wine and cheese. However, the production of wine requires more labor than cheese, whereas the production of cheese requires more land than wine.

Country A has abundant labor but limited land resources, while Country B has abundant land but limited labor resources. By specializing in the production of goods in which they have a comparative advantage (wine for Country A and cheese for Country B), both countries can increase their productivity and output.

As a result, Country A can produce more wine using its abundant labor resources, whereas Country B can produce more cheese using its abundant land resources. Both countries have the option to trade with each other, allowing them to consume a wider variety of goods than they could produce on their own.

By doing so, Country A can import cheese from Country B and enjoy more diverse meals, whereas Country B can import wine from Country A and enjoy more varied beverage options. This mutually beneficial exchange of goods leads to increased efficiency, higher levels of consumption, and overall economic growth in both countries.

David Ricardo famously showed how England and Portugal both benefit by specializing and trading according to their comparative advantages. Portugal was able to make wine at a low cost, while England was able to cheaply manufacture cloth. Ricardo predicted that each country would eventually recognize these facts and stop attempting to make a product that was more costly to generate.

Indeed, as time went on, England stopped producing wine and Portugal stopped manufacturing cloth. Both countries saw that it was to their advantage to stop their efforts at producing these items at home and, instead, to trade with each other to acquire them.

10.1.3 Comparative Advantage and International Trade

The principle of comparative advantage states that countries should specialize in producing goods and services with a relative efficiency advantage over other countries. By specializing in the production of goods and services in which it has a comparative advantage, a country can increase its overall productivity and output, leading to higher levels of economic growth and prosperity.

There are several reasons why a comparative advantage leads to increased trade between countries. First, specialization allows countries to produce more goods and services in which they have a comparative advantage, leading to higher levels of productivity and output. Second, trade allows countries to consume a wider variety of goods and services than they can produce on their own, leading to higher levels of consumer satisfaction. Third, trade can lead to increased competition between firms, which can drive prices down and improve the quality of goods and services.

However, there are potential drawbacks to international trade. For example, some workers in industries that have lost out to foreign competition may experience job losses and reduced wages. Additionally, trade can lead to environmental degradation if countries do not enforce strict pollution and resource use regulations. Finally, trade can exacerbate income inequality within countries if its benefits are not evenly distributed among all members of society.

Despite these potential drawbacks, a comparative advantage remains a powerful tool for promoting international trade and economic growth. By allowing countries to specialize in producing goods and services that have a comparative advantage, trade can lead to increased productivity, higher levels of consumption, and improved standards of living for people around the world.

10.2 International Economy and Globalization

Economic globalization is a process by which countries integrate their economies through the exchange of goods, services, capital, and technology. This process has been facilitated by advancements in communication and transportation technologies as well as the liberalization of trade policies.

10.2.1 Economic Interdependence

A concept that came about in the 19th and early 20th centuries, economic interdependence is when people rely on others to provide the goods and services required to support their lives or for convenience.

Because many countries are unable to acquire goods due to a lack of particular skills or knowledge, "labor specialization" becomes key to this reliance. It can be a complicated system that involves businesses, people, and other societal factors. Labor is often separated in such a way that most people work towards providing services or resources for other individuals/companies. People seldom work directly to source for themselves a certain good or service.

Often, advanced economies trust other nations for goods and services that are not made nationwide (in their own country), again reinforcing dependency. As a populace develops, it can either advance further to create its own required goods within its own borders, or it will continue to seek commodities and raw materials further **afield**. Countries such as the U.K. and the U.S. rely on other nations for manufactured goods, such as clothing, electronics, and even food.

However, it is not just the manufacturing of goods that forms a reliance. Certain countries are the only ones that produce a needed product, such as oil or rice. Therefore, a heavier burden is placed on these nations to meet the demand.

Economic interdependence leads to economic growth. This **affiliation** allows specialist industries to thrive. Success can lead to job and wage/salary increases and an overall improvement in wealth and lifestyle.

Therefore, it is reasonable that consumption by countries with stronger economies and governments, as well as advanced technology, can drive economic growth considerably. Consequently, when interdependence blossoms, so do trade networks, which are key to the flow of goods. Note that when organizations, including the World Bank and the IMF, increased the level of international trade and worldwide investment, it increased global economic interdependence.

From this worldwide trading comes globalization. Globalization involves the goods and services as well as the economic resources of another country's capital, technology, and data. While the mixing and interdependence between the economies of different countries **amplify** global connections, they also increase growth in international trade, ideas, and culture. Likewise, they bring into question the burden of environmental impacts such as global warming, over exploitation of water resources, and air pollution.

10.2.2 Evolution of Globalization

Globalization is a revolution which in terms of scope and significance is comparable to the Industrial Revolution, but whereas the Industrial Revolution took place over a century ago, today's global revolution is taking place under our very eyes. Globalization is not new. Roman coins circulated throughout the empire 2,000 years ago, and the Chinese currency was used in China even earlier. More recently, the world has experienced three periods of rapid globalization, 1870–1914, 1945–1980, and 1980 to the present.

Globalization in 1870–1914 resulted from the Industrial Revolution in

Europe and the opening up of new, resource-rich but **sparsely** populated lands in North America, South America, Australia, New Zealand, and South Africa. These lands received millions of immigrants and vast amounts of foreign investment, principally from England, to open up new land for food and raw material production. These so-called regions of recent settlement grew rapidly during this period by exporting increasing amounts of food and raw materials to Europe, in exchange for manufactured goods. This period of modern globalization came to an end with the breakout of World War I in 1914.

The second period of rapid globalization began at the end of World War II in 1945 and continued until around 1980. During this time, international trade experienced a significant increase due to the removal of heavy trade protection measures that had been implemented during the Great Depression in the United States in 1929 and World War II.

However, what sets today's globalization revolution (since 1980) apart from previous periods is its speed, depth, and immediacy. This is largely due to tremendous advancements in telecommunications and transportation, as well as the elimination of most restrictions on international capital flows across national boundaries. As a result, most countries around the world have been able to participate in this process of globalization, making it much more **pervasive** and dramatic than in earlier periods. Despite the financial and economic crisis of 2008–2009, which was the deepest postwar crisis to date, globalization has continued to advance at a rapid pace. While the crisis did temporarily slow down the march of globalization, it did not halt its progress entirely. In fact, many experts believe that globalization will continue to be a major force shaping the world economy and society for years to come.

As with all revolutions, however, today's globalization brings many benefits and advantages but also has some disadvantages or harmful side effects. These disadvantages and negative aspects of globalization have given rise to a rethinking of the age-old belief in free trade and a strong antiglobalization movement, which blames globalization for many human and environmental problems worldwide. Nevertheless, globalization is important because it increases efficiency in the production of material things; it is inevitable because we cannot hide or run away from it. However, we would like globalization to be sustainable and humanizing and, ultimately, "fair". This requires a profound change in global governance. Such is the challenge facing humanity today.

10.3 Tariffs

10.3.1 Definition of Tariff

A tariff is a tax **levied** on imported or exported goods by a country's government. It is a form of trade barrier designed to restrict the flow of goods across borders or to raise revenue.

There are various types of tariffs. Each type has a unique purpose and effect on trade dynamics, highlighting the intricate ways in which countries manage their economic relationships globally.

Ad valorem tariffs: Ad valorem tariffs are charged as a percentage of the value of imported or exported goods. This type of tariff is flexible because it adapts to the value of the goods; if the price of the product changes, the tariff amount also changes. For example, a government may impose a 15% ad valorem tariff on smartphones, which means the tax will be 15% of the smartphone's price.

Specific tariffs: Specific tariffs are flat rates that do not fluctuate with the value of goods. They are set at a fixed amount per unit of good, regardless of the market price. For instance, there might be a $2 tariff on every pair of shoes imported into a country.

Compound tariffs: A compound tariff combines both ad valorem and specific tariffs. It calculates a tax based on the percentage of the value and adds a fixed amount per unit. This dual method can provide a stable source of revenue for governments while retaining flexibility.

Preferential tariffs: These are tariffs with reduced rates applied to goods from certain countries that have preferential trade agreements with importing countries. For example, goods from a country within a free-trade area may receive a lower tariff rate than those from non-member countries.

Revenue tariffs: Revenue tariffs are imposed primarily to generate income for the government rather than to protect domestic industries. These tariffs are usually set at rates that do not discourage trade but are high enough to collect significant revenue.

Protective tariffs: Protective tariffs aim to **shield** domestic industries from foreign competition. By imposing high tariffs on similar foreign goods, these tariffs make imported products more expensive, thereby protecting local producers from external market forces.

Retaliatory tariffs: When one country feels that another country has unfairly raised tariffs, it might respond with retaliatory tariffs. These are essentially "in kind" tariffs that match or exceed the level of the original tariffs in an attempt to pressure the offending country to reduce its tariffs.

Prohibitive tariffs: Prohibitive tariffs are extremely high tariffs that effectively ban the import of certain goods by making them too expensive to be viable in the domestic market. Although rare, they can completely shut down the import of particular goods.

Anti-dumping duties: These tariffs aim at **counteracting** the practice of dumping, in which a company exports a product to a foreign country at a price below the cost of production or the price in the home market. Anti-dumping duties are designed to protect domestic industries from being undercut by unfairly priced imports.

Countervailing duties: Countervailing duties offset any subsidies that foreign governments provide to exporters, leveling the playing field for domestic producers who do not receive similar government support.

10.3.2 The Economic Effects of Tariffs

The tariff effect refers to changes that occur in the marketplace as a direct result of the imposition or alteration of tariff rates. These effects can be both immediate and long-term, and affect different stakeholders in unique ways.

Immediate Effects

Price increases: The direct effect of a tariff is an increase in the price of imported goods. The added cost can be passed on to consumers, making these products less competitive with domestically produced goods.

Reduced imports: Higher prices may discourage some consumers from purchasing affected goods, leading to reduced imports. This can benefit domestic producers, who face less competition from foreign rivals.

Trade diversion: Importers might seek alternative suppliers in countries not subject to tariffs, causing trade to divert to those nations.

Revenue generation: Governments collect revenue from tariffs, which can be used for various public expenditures or to protect domestic industries.

Long-Term Effects

Domestic industry protection: By making imported goods more expensive, tariffs can shield domestic industries from foreign competition, potentially allowing them to grow and become more competitive internationally.

Retaliation: Tariffs can lead to retaliatory measures by other countries, resulting in a trade war in which multiple nations impose tariffs on each other's goods, ultimately disrupting global trade flows.

Supply chain disruption: Over time, tariffs may cause companies to restructure their supply chains to avoid tariffed goods, leading to shifts in production locations and trade partnerships.

Consumer habit changes: As prices rise, consumers may adjust their consumption habits, look for alternatives, or reduce their spending on affected goods.

Industry consolidation: Domestic industries that benefit from tariff protection may experience consolidation as they gain market share, and smaller competitors struggle to compete.

10.3.3 The Welfare Effects of Tariffs

As a form of trade policy tariffs, have long been a subject of economic debate because of their potential impact on the welfare of different stakeholders within an economy. A tariff aims to shield domestic industries from foreign competition, raise government revenue, and negotiate trade **concession**s from other countries. By making imported products more expensive, tariffs can alter the market dynamics and affect the economic welfare of consumers and producers.

Consumer Surplus

Consumer surplus is the difference between what consumers are willing to pay for a good or service and the actual price they pay. This represents the additional benefit that consumers receive above the market price. When tariffs are imposed, they increase the price of imported goods, leading to a reduction in consumer surplus, as consumers have to pay closer to their maximum willingness to pay than before the tariff is applied.

The following are the impacts on the consumer surplus:

Higher prices: With the addition of a tariff, the retail prices of imported goods increase, reducing the amount that consumers are willing to purchase at the new higher price.

Reduced consumption: Some consumers may opt out of purchasing the good altogether if the price rises beyond their willingness to pay, leading to a decrease in consumption and thus a reduction in consumer surplus.

Limited substitutes: If substitute goods are not readily available or are more expensive, consumers may be forced to buy now-tariffed goods at a higher price, further diminishing their surplus.

Producer Surplus

On the other hand, producer surplus is the difference between the market price of a product and the minimum price at which producers are willing to sell it. This surplus represents the extra profit that producers earn above the cost of production. Tariffs can increase producer surpluses by allowing domestic firms to charge more for their products and capture a larger share of the domestic market.

The following are the impacts on the producer surplus:

Increased market price: Domestic producers can sell their products at a higher price because of the reduced competition from cheaper imports, increasing their surplus.

Greater production: With the price floor set by the tariff, domestic firms may find it profitable to increase production levels to meet the demand previously served by imports.

Market dominance: Tariffs can create a more favorable market environment for domestic producers, enabling them to gain or maintain dominance in their home markets.

Exercises

❶ Short answer questions

Directions: *Answer the following questions in your own words or with sentences from the text.*

(1) What are the differences between absolute advantage and comparative advantage?

(2) Can you provide another example of economic interdependence?

(3) According to this unit, what are the three periods of globalization that the world has experienced?

(4) What are the effects of tariffs?

财经基础英语
Basic English for Economics and Finance

2 Term explanation

Directions: *Explain the following terms in your own words or with sentences from the text.*

(1) absolute advantage

(2) comparative advantage

(3) economic globalization

(4) tariff

3 Banked cloze

Directions: *Fill in the blanks by selecting suitable words from the following box. You may not use any of the words more than once.*

A. across	B. license	C. common	D. expense	E. occurs
F. innovation	G. negatively	H. prosper	I. effective	J. such
K. happen	L. more	M. limiting	N. ensure	O. conserve

Why doesn't the world have open trading between countries? When there is free trade, why do some countries remain poor while others (1) _____? While free trade has been touted as a solution to many of the world's economic problems, it is not always (2) _____ in practice due to various factors. One of the most significant challenges is the phenomenon of rent-seeking, which (3) _____ when certain groups within a country lobby the government to protect their interests and prevent competition from foreign countries or industries.

Rent-seeking can take many forms, such as subsidies, tax breaks, and restrictions on imports or exports. By (4) _____ competition and protecting their own profits, these groups may be able to maintain their relative advantages over time, even if this comes at the (5) _____ of consumers or other stakeholders. For example, American shoe producers may understand and agree with the free-trade argument but also know that their narrow interests would be (6) _____ impacted by cheaper foreign shoes. As a result, they may lobby for special tax breaks for their products or outright bans on foreign footwear.

Another factor that can undermine the benefits of free trade is intellectual property rights (IPR) which shape comparative advantage. IPR systems are designed to encourage (7) _____ and creativity by protecting the rights of inventors and creators. However, excessive or restrictive use of IPR can also stifle competition and limit the flow of ideas and knowledge (8) _____ borders. For example, a country with a strong IPR system may refuse to (9) _____ its technology to foreign firms, preventing them from benefiting from comparative advantages in scale or cost savings.

While comparative advantage is an important concept in understanding global economic dynamics, it is not always sufficient on its own to (10) _____ open and fair trade between countries.

4 Translation

Directions: *Translate the following paragraphs into Chinese or English.*

(1) An international economic organization is established by two or more national governments or civil society groups through certain agreements to achieve common economic goals, with permanent organizational structures and economic functions. International economic organizations facilitate cooperation and coordination among countries in the global economy.

(2) 世界各国要坚持真正的多边主义（multilateralism），坚持拆墙而不筑墙、开放而不隔绝、融合而不脱钩（decoupling），推动构建开放型世界经济，推动经济全球化朝着更加开放、包容、普惠、平衡、共赢的方向发展，让世界经济活力充分迸发出来。

5 Project

Title: China's Rise and Its Impact on the Global Economy

Instructions:

Step 1: Clearly define the purpose of the research. The objectives of the study are to analyze the economic indicators that demonstrate China's rise, investigate the factors contributing to this rise, examine the global implications of China's rise, and suggest potential strategies for other countries.

Step 2: Start by examining existing research and data related to China's rise and its impact on the global economy. This could include studies of China's economic growth over the past few decades, an analysis of the factors that have contributed to this growth (such as government policies and investment in infrastructure), and an examination of the impact of China's rise on other economies around the world.

Step 3: Once you have collected all the necessary data, organize it in a way that allows for easy analysis. Such data as GDP growth, inflation rates, trade balance, FDI flows, technological advancements, etc. are necessary. In addition, it would be important to collect data on the global economic impact of China's rise, such as changes in trade patterns, shifts in production networks, etc. Then create graphs and charts to visualize trends and patterns. You will need to analyze the data to answer the research questions.

Step 4: After analyzing the data, write up your findings in a clear and concise manner. Make sure to explain what you have found and how it relates to your research objectives. Also, be sure to include any limitations of your study.

Step 5: Share your research findings by giving a presentation in class.

Supplementary Reading

Scan the QR code to find out more about the unit.

Unit 11

Money and Interest Rates

Learning Objectives

After studying this unit, you should be able to:

1) understand the development of money and the concept of interest rates;
2) use the words and phrases in this unit;
3) discuss money issues in China with the knowledge acquired.

In the grand narrative of human civilization, money is an **evolutionary** instrument that is crucial to the advancement of economic systems. The origin and development of money, its usefulness and intrinsic nature, the concept of value, and the role of the monetary system are all fundamental topics within the **realm** of economics that **merit** a comprehensive understanding. Interest rates are the lifeblood of financial markets and influence decision-making at all economic levels, from individual households to global financial institutions. This unit delves into the origin and development of money, the nature and function of interest rates, the factors influencing their change, and their impact on the economy.

11.1 Money

11.1.1 Definition of Money

Money is a product of the long-term development of commodity production and exchange. In the era of the commodity economy, it is easy to know what money is; however, it is not easy to give an accurate definition of money because it requires an essential understanding of the nature of money.

Karl Marx's systematic study of monetary theory began in the 1840s. In the study of the development history of the value form, Marx proposed the labor theory of value, which revealed the essence of money. He defined money as a commodity separated from the commodity world and fixed as a universal equivalent which could reflect certain production relations. It is the product of human labor, the unity of value, and the use value. Money is the material used to present and measure the value of all commodities and has the ability to exchange with all other commodities as a general means of exchange.

As a universal equivalent, money is just a **superficial** phenomenon when it is presented in gold and silver or some kind of value symbol. At the same time, it also reflects the relationship between commodity producers, and social relations between people through equivalent exchange, which is called social production relations.

Monetary **denomination** theory defines money as a technical tool that is easy to exchange, a symbol of value in exchange for wealth, a unit of calculation of ideas, and a ticket. The monetary function theory holds that money is generally accepted by the public to pay for goods and services. The monetary quantity theory denies the intrinsic value of money itself and suggests that the value of money is determined by the quantity of money supply. Modern monetary quantity theory regards money as an important tool for the state to regulate and manage its economy.

In general, money is defined as a widely accepted means of payment by economists. Essentially, money is anything that can be easily used to buy goods and services.

11.1.2 Origins of Money

The origins of money are deeply rooted in the prehistoric barter system[1], in which goods are directly exchanged for other goods without a standard unit of account. This practice facilitated simple transactions, but it had its limitations, as it required a double **coincidence** of wants, meaning that both parties had to have something that the other wanted, which made trade difficult and inefficient. As societies became more complex, the need for a more efficient medium of exchange was felt, marking the birth of money. People began to use commodities such as cattle, grains, and shells as a medium of exchange. These commodities had intrinsic value and were widely accepted as a means of payment.

The development of money continued with the introduction of coins made from precious metals. Coins were easy to carry, recognizable, and could be easily divided into smaller units. Over time, precious metals such as gold and silver emerged as the preferred medium of exchange because of their durability, divisibility, and scarcity. The use of paper money followed, which was initially backed by precious metals but eventually became fiat money[2], meaning that it was backed by the government rather than a physical commodity. Money's evolution is a **testament** to human innovation, ranging from the use of shells and **beads** and cattle to precious metals such as gold and silver. With the dawn of the digital age, society has embraced digital currencies, **cryptocurrencies**, and electronic payment systems, demonstrating the continuing evolution of money.

In economics, there is an economic principle named Gresham's Law positing

---

[1] barter system: a system of exchange that was prevalent centuries ago, before the introduction of the monetary system. In this arrangement, goods and services are traded for goods and services. This means that the parties exchange each other's commodities directly without any mediation of money based on equivalent estimates of price and goods.

[2] fiat money: a government-issued currency that does not have intrinsic value and is not backed by a physical commodity such as gold. It has been used for centuries, but its use has become increasingly common in the modern world. Most countries use fiat currencies. The U.S. dollar is a fiat currency, and so are the euro, British pound, and Japanese yen, to name a few.

that in a system where two types of commodity money circulate as legal tender with equal face values, the more valuable currency, termed "good money", tends to be **hoarded** and withdrawn from circulation, while the less valuable currency, termed "bad money", remains in circulation. This principle is **succinctly** summarized as "bad money drives out good". To illustrate, consider two coins both denominated as one penny but differing in composition, one being silver and the other copper. Individuals will retain the silver coins, preferring to transact with the copper ones. Consequently, the "good" money (silver) is gradually withdrawn from circulation due to hoarding, leaving only the "bad money" (copper) in use.

As defined by the Financial Times glossary, Gresham's Law suggests that if individuals have the option to use an alternative currency with equal nominal value but higher real value (due to increased metal content or stronger purchasing power abroad), they will persist in using the established currency and hoard the alternative, effectively removing it from circulation.

11.1.3　Function and Nature of Money

The function of money refers to its inherent function. In the metallic monetary system, scholars have no **substantive** differences in their understanding of the functions of money due to the intrinsic value of money itself. Marx identified five functions of typical currency: value scale, means of circulation, means of payment, store of value, and world currency. With the emergence and circulation of credit money which has no intrinsic value, it is generally believed that money, in its essence, serves three main functions: as a medium of exchange, a unit of account, and a store of value.

The most important function of money is the medium of exchange to facilitate transactions. Without money, all transactions would have to be conducted by a barter, which involves the direct exchange of one good or service for another. The difficulty with a barter system is that to obtain a particular good or service from a supplier, one must possess a good or service of equal value, which the supplier also desires. In other words, in a barter system, exchange can occur only if there is a double coincidence of wants between the two transacting parties. However, the likelihood of a double coincidence of wants is small and makes the exchange of goods and services rather difficult. Money effectively eliminates the double coincidence of wants problem by serving as a medium of exchange that is accepted in all transactions by all parties regardless of whether they desire each other's goods and services. It solves this problem by allowing people to buy and sell goods and services using a common medium that everyone accepts, thereby enhancing the efficiency of market exchanges.

Money provides a common measure of value that allows people to compare the prices and values of various goods and services. Without money, people would have to use relative prices based on barter ratios, which could be confusing and inconsistent. Knowing the value or price of a good in terms of money enables both the supplier and the purchaser of the good to make decisions about how much of the good to supply and how much to purchase. Money simplifies economic calculations and accounting by providing a standard unit that can be used to express prices and values.

To be a medium of exchange, money must hold value over time; that is, it must be a store of value. If money could not be stored for some period of time and remain valuable in exchange, it would not solve the double coincidence of wants problem and therefore would not be adopted as a medium of exchange. As a store of value, money is not unique; many other stores of value exist, such as land, works of art, and even baseball cards❶ and stamps. Money may not even be the best store of value, because it depreciates with inflation. However, money is more liquid than most other stores of value because as a medium of exchange, it is readily accepted everywhere. Furthermore, money is an easily transported store of value that is available in a number of convenient denominations. Thus, money enables people to save and accumulate wealth over time by retaining its purchasing power. Without money, people would have to store their wealth in the form of goods or services, which might **deteriorate** or lose value over time. Money preserves its value because it is durable, divisible, portable, and scarce.

According to Marx, money is not only a physical or digital object but also a social institution that depends on human behavior and expectations. Money is based on trust and confidence; it works because people trust the issuer and the system that supports it. Money is also subject to social norms and conventions; it works because people follow certain rules and customs regarding how to use it. The nature of money pertains to its physical form and the trust that individuals place in it. Money has evolved from being commodity money (e.g., gold and silver), which has intrinsic value, to being fiat money, which carries no inherent

---

❶ A baseball card is a trading card with a picture of a baseball player and information about his playing record; each individual baseball card is assigned a unique value depending on its attributes such as edition number, design, player, and rarity. In America, baseball cards have monetary value depending on how good the player is.

value. Fiat money is supported by the confidence and trust that individuals and businesses place in the issuer. The belief that it will be accepted by others in exchange for goods and services gives it its value.

The value of money refers to the amount of goods and services that one unit of money can buy. Unlike commodities, which have inherent value based on their utility, the value of money is largely symbolic and subjective and is determined by two factors: the supply and demand for money. It is based on people's perceptions of and their confidence in the stability of the economy. The value of money is **inversely** proportional to general price levels. Thus, when inflation occurs, the purchasing power of money decreases, and vice versa.

11.1.4 The Monetary System

The monetary system is the set of institutions, rules, and procedures that govern the creation, distribution, and use of money in an economy. It consists of four main components: the issuer, money supply, payment system, and monetary policy. The issuer is an entity that has the authority and responsibility to issue and regulate money in an economy. It can be a government, a central bank, a private bank, or a **decentralized** network. The issuer determines the type and form of money, the amount and growth rate of the money supply, the legal tender[1] status, acceptance of money, and so on. Money supply is the total amount of money available in an economy at a given time. It can be classified into different categories based on its liquidity, which is the ease and speed with which it can be converted into cash or other forms of money. The most common categories are M0 (cash), M1 (cash plus demand deposits[2]), M2 (M1 plus savings deposits[3] and other short-term instruments) and M3 (M2 plus long-term instruments). The payment system is a network of mechanisms and channels that enables people to transfer money from one person or entity to another. It can be physical or electronic, centralized or decentralized, public or private, and so on. A payment system facilitates trade and exchange, reduces transaction costs and risks, and increases efficiency and convenience. Monetary policy is the set of actions and strategies that the issuer uses to influence the supply

---

[1] legal tender: any form of payment recognized by a government, used to pay debts or financial obligations, such as tax payments.

[2] demand deposit: a type of deposit that lets you withdraw your money—at any time, for any reason—without having to notify your bank.

[3] savings deposits: bank deposits usually of an individual or a nonprofit organization drawing regular interest and payable on 30 days' notice.

and demand of money, interest rate, exchange rate, and other macroeconomic variables. Monetary policy can be expansionary or contractionary, depending on whether it increases or decreases the money supply. Monetary policy affects economic growth, inflation, unemployment, trade balances, and so on.

The modern monetary system is a framework within which money is created, circulated, and managed in an economy. Central banks play a pivotal role in this system by managing money supply and interest rates to ensure price stability and trust in the currency. They **implement** monetary policies, such as open market operations, reserve requirements, and changes in the discount rate, to control the money supply. Banks and financial institutions play an integral role by accepting deposits and providing loans, thereby influencing the quantity of money in the economy.

Furthermore, the **advent** of the digital age has **heralded** significant changes in the monetary system. Cryptocurrencies such as Bitcoin, decentralized and operating on block chain technology, challenge traditional notions of monetary control and offer an alternative medium of exchange, unit of account, and store of value. Understanding the multifaceted nature and value of money, along with the monetary system's role, is crucial for comprehending the dynamics of the modern economy. As humans **traverse** into the future, the concept and usage of money will continue to evolve, reflecting the ever-changing landscape of human society.

11.2 Interest Rates

11.2.1 Definition of Interest Rates

Generally, interest can be defined as the price paid for using borrowed money, or alternatively, the return earned on lent money. The interest rate is typically expressed as a percentage of the principal, or the original amount of money borrowed or invested, for a specified period, usually one year. This concept is pivotal to the functioning of any modern economy, as it serves as an incentive for saving and investing and a **deterrent** for unnecessary borrowing.

The function of interest is two-fold: compensating for the lender's opportunity cost and accounting for the risk associated with lending. The opportunity cost reflects the return that the lender forgoes by choosing to lend money instead of investing elsewhere. The risk is that the borrower may default and the lender may lose the principal. Thus, interest serves as the "price" that encourages individuals and businesses to save and invest, stimulating the flow of money within the economy.

Marx's interest theory includes three points. First, only when there is a division of labor, especially the separation of borrowing capitalists and lending capitalists, will a debtor-creditor relationship and interest be generated. Second, interest comes from surplus value, and is a special form of profit transformation. Third, the borrowing capitalist must pay interest to the lending capitalist, who sells the temporary right to use the money capital, which can bring surplus value.

11.2.2 Types of Interest Rates and Influential Factors

There are several categories of interest rates, including nominal interest rate, real interest rate, and effective interest rate.

The nominal interest rate is the stated interest rate of a bond or loan, which signifies the actual monetary price borrowers pay lenders to use their money. Nominal interest rates refer to interest rates unadjusted for inflation. In other words, it is the stated or quoted interest rate on a loan or investment without considering the impact of inflation or deflation over time. Nominal interest rate is typically expressed on an annual basis and represents the percentage of the loan amount or investment principal that must be paid as interest during a specific period.

The real interest rate is an interest rate that has been adjusted to remove the effects of inflation, which gives investors a more accurate measure of their buying power after they **redeem** their positions. The real interest rate is crucial for making informed financial decisions, especially in the context of investments and loans. When assessing investment opportunities or evaluating the cost of borrowing, it is essential to consider the real interest rate to understand the true economic impact and how inflation may affect the return on investment or actual cost of borrowing. A positive real interest rate implies that the lender's purchasing power increases, whereas a negative real interest rate implies a decrease.

Effective interest rate considers the **compounding** of interest and represents the true cost or reward for borrowing or lending money. Effective interest rate is a crucial term in finance, as it helps compare various financial products that calculate interest on a compounding basis. These financial products can be lines of credit[1], loans, or investment instruments such as certificates of deposit.

---

[1] line of credit: an amount of credit extended to a borrower.

Changes in interest rates are influenced by several elements that fluctuate based on the interaction of supply and demand for funds in the loanable funds market. The main factors affecting the supply and demand of funds in the market are as follows:

Inflation rate: A higher inflation rate reduces the real value of money and erodes the purchasing power of lenders, who demand a higher nominal interest rate to compensate for their loss. Conversely, a lower inflation rate increases the real value of money and enhances the purchasing power of lenders, who accept a lower nominal interest rate as a reward.

Economic growth: Higher economic growth increases the demand for funds for investment and consumption purposes, which pushes up the market interest rate. Conversely, lower economic growth decreases the demand for funds for investment and consumption purposes, which reduces the market interest rate.

Fiscal policy: Higher government spending or lower taxation increases the budget deficit and public debt, which increases the demand for funds from the government sector and pushes up the market interest rate. Conversely, lower government spending or higher taxation decreases the budget deficit and public debt, which decreases the demand for funds from the government sector which reduces the market interest rate.

Monetary policy: A higher policy interest rate increases the cost of borrowing and reduces the availability of credit in the economy, which decreases the supply of funds from the banking sector and increases the market interest rate. Conversely, a lower policy interest rate decreases the cost of borrowing and increases the availability of credit in the economy, which increases the supply of funds from the banking sector and reduces the market interest rate.

Furthermore, global economic conditions affect domestic interest rates. In an interconnected world, investors seek the best return for their capital, and international interest rates can influence these rates in a domestic economy. Finally, the government's borrowing requirements influence interest rates. High government borrowing can lead to higher interest rates if it is perceived as increasing the risk of inflation.

The impact of interest rates on the economy is both pervasive and multifaceted. Interest rates influence individuals' decisions to save, borrow, or spend. Higher interest rates make borrowing expensive, encourage savings, and discourage consumption and investment. Conversely, lower interest rates encourage borrowing and spending, thus stimulating economic activity. On a larger scale, interest rates affect financial market performance. When interest rates are low, investors tend to invest more in the stock market for better returns, driving stock prices up. Conversely, higher interest rates can lead to a sell-off in the stock market.

Interest rates also affect inflation and exchange rates. Central banks often adjust their interest rates to control inflation. When inflation is high, central banks may raise interest rates to reduce money supply. Conversely, during deflation or low inflation, interest rates may be lowered to increase the money supply and stimulate spending. Interest rates can also influence the exchange rate, as higher interest rates attract foreign capital, leading to appreciation of the domestic currency, and vice versa.

In conclusion, interest rates are a vital aspect of the economic framework that profoundly impact individual behavior and macroeconomic conditions. Understanding their nature, categories, factors influencing them, and their effects on the economy is crucial for comprehending the financial aspects of economics.

Exercises

❶ Short answer questions

Directions: *Answer the following questions in your own words or with sentences from the text.*

(1) What problems in the exchanges have been resolved with the emergence of money?

(2) What are the components of the monetary system?

(3) Can you list some major factors that influence changes in interest rates?

(4) What impact can interest rates have on the economy?

2 Term explanation

Directions: *Explain the following terms in your own words or with sentences from the text.*

(1) Gresham's law

(2) value of money

(3) nominal interest rate

(4) real interest rate

3 Banked cloze

Directions: *Fill in the blanks by selecting suitable words from the following box. You may not use any of the words more than once.*

A. macroeconomic	B. changing	C. history	D. determined	E. facilitating
F. involve	G. standardized	H. integral	I. monetary	J. cover
K. encompasses	L. origins	M. necessary	N. boosting	O. maintaining

Money is a product of the long-term development of commodity production and exchange. The concept of money (1) _____ its role as a widely accepted means of payment, (2) _____ transactions for goods and services. While modern transactions often (3) _____ checks or debit cards, money's (4) _____ trace back to the primitive barter system, which lacked a(n) (5) _____ measure of value. Over time, precious metals such as gold and silver emerged as the preferred medium of exchange because of their durability, divisibility, and scarcity. With the dawn of the digital age, society has embraced digital currencies, cryptocurrencies, and electronic payment systems, demonstrating the continuing evolution of money.

With the emergence and circulation of credit money which has no intrinsic value, it is generally believed that money, in its essence, serves three main functions: as a medium of exchange, a unit of account, and a store of value. Its evolution from commodity money to fiat money has impacted its nature and value. Money's value is (6) _____ by supply, demand, and people's confidence in the economy. It plays a vital role in (7) _____ economic stability.

Interest rates are a vital aspect of the economic framework that profoundly impact individual behavior and macroeconomic conditions. The impact of interest rates on the economy is both pervasive and multifaceted. It can be defined as the price paid for using borrowed money, or alternatively, the return earned on lent money. Interest rates are (8) _____ to economies, influencing savings, borrowing, spending, and financial markets. The interest rate is typically expressed as a percentage of the principal, or the original amount of money borrowed or invested, for a specified period, usually one year. Different types of interest rates (nominal, real, and effective) account for inflation and compounding. Factors like (9) _____ policy, inflation, global conditions, and government borrowing impact interest rates. They affect individual behavior and (10) _____ conditions, including inflation, exchange rates, and financial market performance.

4 Translation

Directions: *Translate the following paragraphs into Chinese or English.*

(1) Changes in interest rates are influenced by several elements that fluctuate based on the interaction of supply and demand for funds in the loanable funds market. Key factors include monetary policy, inflation expectations, global economic conditions, and government borrowing. Central banks use interest rates as a monetary policy tool, altering them to manage economic stability. Lowering interest rates stimulates borrowing and spending, which can boost economic activity. In contrast, raising interest rates can cool down an overheated economy. Inflation expectations, often affected by economic prospects, can also influence interest rates. If businesses and consumers expect high inflation, interest rates may increase to compensate for the anticipated decrease in purchasing power.

(2) 马克思从劳动价值论（the labor theory of value）出发，认为货币是充当一般等价物的特殊商品，它是由偶然的（accidental）、扩大的、一般的价值形态发展演变而来的。另外一些经济学家从交易成本出发，认为货币能够被普遍接受，是因为它是为了克服物物交换的困难而形成的，并且为不断降低交易成本而发展演进。

5 Project

Title: Money Matters: Exploring the Impact of Interest Rates on the Economy
Instructions:

Step 1: You will conduct research on the role of interest rates in the economy. You should explore how central banks set interest rates, the impact of interest rates on borrowing and lending behavior, and the effect of interest rate changes on economic indicators such as inflation, employment, and GDP.

Step 2: You will select a real-world example or case where changes in interest rates have had a significant impact on economic outcomes. Examples could include the Federal Reserve's response to the 2008 financial crisis, the effects of negative interest rates in certain countries, or the impact of low interest rates on housing markets.

Step 3: Based on your research and case studies, you will analyze the implications of different interest rate scenarios on various stakeholders in the economy, such as consumers, businesses, banks, and government entities. They should consider both short-term and long-term effects.

Step 4: You will prepare a presentation summarizing your findings and analysis. Each presentation should include a discussion of the chosen case, the role of interest rates in the scenario, and the broader economic implications. Visual aids, such as graphs or charts, should be utilized to enhance understanding.

Step 5: After all presentations are complete, you will engage in a group discussion to compare and contrast the different cases and analyses. They should consider similarities and differences in the effects of interest rate changes.

Supplementary Reading

Scan the QR code to find out more about the unit.

Unit 12

Financial Institutions and Financial Markets

Learning Objectives

After studying this unit, you should be able to:

1) understand the definitions, functions, and types of financial institutions and financial markets;
2) use the words and phrases in this unit;
3) discuss the functions of important international financial institutions with the knowledge acquired.

Financial institutions and financial markets are integral components of modern economies, playing a crucial role in the allocation of funds, risk management, and economic growth. This unit centers on the functions, types, and significance of these institutions and markets.

12.1 Financial Institutions

Financial institutions can be narrowly defined as **intermediaries** in financial activities. These entities serve as intermediaries in transactions between parties lacking funds and those with extra funds in the field of indirect financing. They are specialized institutions engaged in monetary and credit activities, mainly referring to banks and other financial institutions involved in deposit and lending services. This category of financial institutions has close ties to currency issuance and credit creation, primarily including central banks and commercial banks.

Financial institutions, in a broad sense, refer to all entities engaged in financial activities, including financial institutions in the field of direct financing, indirect financing, and various institutions providing financial services. The primary role of financial institutions in the field of direct financing is to act as intermediaries between investors and fundraisers, acting as brokers for buying and selling securities. Sometimes, they also participate in securities trading themselves, such as securities firms and investment banks.

There are numerous types of financial institutions, and these diverse institutions together form the overall financial system. Based on whether they belong to the banking system, financial institutions can be classified into banking institutions and non-banking institutions.

12.1.1 Banking Institutions

Banking institutions are primarily engaged in accepting deposits and conducting fund transfer and settlement operations. They have the function of credit creation, and their **liabilities** can serve as means of exchange and payment. Their asset operations mainly involve short-term lending, thus operating on the basis of deposit liabilities.

The system of banking institutions can be further classified. Based on their roles and functions within the banking system, there are central banks, commercial banks, specialized banks, and policy banks.

Central Bank and Similar Financial Institutions

The central bank is a type of bank that emerged from the development of the banking industry in Western countries, separated from commercial banks. Its role and functions have been strengthened as countries increasingly intervene in economic and social affairs. As a special financial institution representing government control over financial activities, the central bank holds a unique position in the social and economic life of each country. It serves as the core and dominant element of the financial institution system, representing leadership and management of the entire financial system internally, maintaining the safe operation of the financial system, implementing macro-financial regulation, and serving as the highest authority in national monetary finance. Externally, it symbolizes a country's monetary sovereignty. Today, nearly all countries or regions worldwide have central banks or similar financial institutions.

The People's Bank of China (PBC) serves as the central bank of China, responsible for formulating and conducting monetary policies, preventing and dissolving financial risks, and maintaining financial stability under the leadership of the State Council. Besides PBC, there are two other national institutions: the National Administration of Financial Regulation (NAFR), which was founded in May 2023 on the basis of the China Banking and Insurance Regulatory Commission, and the China Securities Regulatory Commission (CSRC). The three are responsible for overseeing, regulating, and managing the activities of financial institutions in the financial markets in accordance with national laws and regulations.

The National Administration of Financial Regulation (NAFR) is responsible for supervising and managing banks, insurance companies, financial asset management companies, and other deposit-taking financial institutions. Its goal is to maintain the legal and stable operation of the banking and insurance industries and to protect the rights and interests of financial consumers.

Commercial Banks and Specialized Banks

Commercial banks are the earliest modern banking institutions. They are profit-oriented and engage in various credit transactions, including demand deposits. By handling transfer and settlement operations, commercial banks facilitate the majority of monetary circulation in the national economy and contribute to the creation of deposit money.

In Western countries, commercial banks, due to their numerous branches, widespread business penetration, and significant asset proportions, have become the backbone of the financial institution system, holding an irreplaceable position.

Specialized banks specialize in specific business areas and provide specialized financial services. They cater to the needs of specific industries or sectors within the economy. Based on the characteristics of service **recipient**s and the use of credit funds, specialized banks can be categorized as development banks, investment banks, savings banks, export-import banks, and housing credit banks, among others.

Development banks are established to meet the long-term funding needs of economic development projects. Their loans typically support projects with a developmental focus, requiring large amounts of capital and having long-term investment horizons. These banks are often government-founded and operated to support national **infrastructure** development, such as energy, transportation, and raw material projects.

Investment banks specialize in providing securities financing and long-term credit services to industrial and commercial enterprises. Unlike commercial banks, investment banks primarily raise funds by issuing their own stocks and bonds. Their main activities include direct investment in stocks and bonds of industrial and commercial enterprises, providing medium- and long-term loans, underwriting stocks and bonds issuance for enterprises, participating in corporate establishment and restructuring, underwriting government and foreign government bonds, and offering investment and financial advisory services.

Savings banks specialize in managing savings deposits from small and medium-sized depositors. They pool idle funds from consumers and invest them in production and circulation fields. Savings banks offer consumer credit and other types of loans, including housing mortgage loans for residents and loans to municipal institutions. Their funds are often invested in real estate mortgage loans, government bonds, and corporate stocks and bonds, with excess funds❶ deposited in commercial banks or other financial institutions.

Export-import banks specialize in providing international financial services for foreign trade and non-trade settlements, as well as credit services. They are established to promote a country's import and export business, enhance international financial cooperation, attract international capital, and gather international information. Export-import banks are generally government financial institutions, such as the Export-Import Bank of the United States and

---

❶ excess funds: funds that are remaining after paying taxes, costs, and all expenses of a tax sale made by the tax commissioner.

the Japan Bank for International Cooperation.

Housing credit banks provide financing services specifically for residential property purchases. These institutions support the development of housing markets and provide funding options for residents to buy homes. Examples include the U.S. Federal Home Loan Banks system and the Japan Housing Finance Agency.

Apart from the specialized banks mentioned above, different countries often establish specialized banks based on their economic development and specific financial needs. These can include agricultural banks, industrial and commercial banks, real estate banks, and various other specialized banks catering to specific sectors.

Policy Banks and Similar Financial Institutions

The policy banks mainly refer to the financial institutions initiated and guaranteed by the government to carry out policy-related financing activities in specific sectors, implementing and aligning with government socioeconomic policies.

China Eximbank, established in 1994, is a policy bank under the direct leadership of the State Council. It focuses on providing financial services to expand China's exports and imports, promote overseas contracting and investment by Chinese enterprises, and support international economic and trade cooperation.

Founded in 1994, the Agricultural Development Bank of China (ADBC) is the only policy bank dedicated to supporting the development of agriculture and rural areas in China. It provides financing services to rural and agricultural sectors, as well as support for rural development and agricultural production.

China Development Bank was established in 1994 and restructured into a state-owned joint-stock company in 2008. It is dedicated to supporting China's national development strategies by providing funding for key infrastructure projects, industrial development, and technological innovation.

Financial asset management companies were established in 1999 to handle the non-performing loans transferred from major state-owned banks, such as China Industrial and Commercial Bank (ICBC), China Agricultural Bank (ABC), Bank of China (BOC), and China Construction Bank (CCB). These companies aim to manage and dispose of these **distressed** assets, contributing to the stability of the financial system.

12.1.2 Non-banking Financial Institutions

Non-banking financial institutions are institutions that offer various banking services but do not have banking licenses. They cannot take deposits from the public as regular banks do. This difference means that they do not follow the same rules as traditional banks, which gives them more flexibility to try new things in the financial world. These institutions can either stand on their own or belong to larger financial groups. They offer services such as giving loans, exchanging currencies, helping with retirement plans, and dealing with money markets and business mergers. Examples include insurance companies, contractual-savings institutions, and other non-banking institutions.

In China, non-banking financial institutions include insurance companies, trust and investment firms, securities firms, financial leasing companies, finance companies, and foreign-funded financial institutions.

The following section introduces foreign non-banking financial institutions.

Insurance Companies

Insurance companies handle different types of risks in situations such as death, illness, property damage, and other potential losses. They promise financial protection if any of these events lead to losses. There are two main types of insurance companies: those that deal with life insurance and those that provide general insurance. General insurance usually covers shorter periods, whereas life insurance is a longer commitment that ends when an insured person passes away. Both types of insurance are available to all. Because insurance companies need a lot of information to assess the risk in each case, they are good at efficiently using information.

General insurance has two main types: market and social insurance. Social insurance safeguards against income loss due to unexpected events such as unemployment, disability, illness, or natural disasters. These risks are hard to predict, and people may not share all the important details with the insurer, which can lead to moral hazards. Consequently, private insurance companies often do not offer social insurance. Governments typically fill this gap in the insurance industry. Social insurance is more common in developed Western societies, where **close-knit** family networks and community support are not as prevalent.

Contractual Savings Institutions

Contractual savings institutions (also known as institutional investors) offer individuals the opportunity to invest in collective investment groups while acting as fiduciaries rather than principals. These groups, known as collective investment vehicles (CIVs), pool the resources of individuals and companies to invest in stocks, bonds, and **derivatives**. However, individuals hold ownership of the CIV itself, not of their specific investments. The most common examples are mutual funds and private pension plans.

Mutual funds come in two main types: open-end and closed-end funds. Open-end funds allow the public to buy new shares whenever they want to make new investments. Shareholders can sell their shares to funds at their net asset value. By contrast, closed-end funds issue a set number of shares in an initial public offering (IPO), and shareholders can sell their shares on a stock exchange to cash in on their asset value.

Pension funds, which are a type of mutual funds, restrict investors from accessing their investments until a predetermined date. In response to this limitation, pension funds receive significant tax benefits. These funds encourage people to save a portion of their current income during retirement.

Hedge funds gather capital from investors who are officially recognized or approved to invest in a wide array of assets. They often use intricate strategies to achieve substantial returns. Notable hedge fund examples include Bridgewater Associates[1] and Renaissance Technologies[2].

Market makers are broker-dealer firms that offer both buying and selling prices for the assets they hold in stock. These assets include stocks, government and corporate bonds, derivatives, and foreign currencies. When they receive an order, the market maker sells swiftly from their inventory or buys it to balance the decrease in inventory. The profit for market makers comes from the difference between their buying and selling prices, known as the bid-offer spread. By doing so, market makers enhance the ease of trading assets in their possession.

Non-banking financial institutions play a complementary role along with banks in offering financial services to individuals and businesses. They introduce healthy competition to the landscape of financial services, challenging

---

[1] Bridgewater Associates: an American investment management firm founded by Ray Dalio in 1975. The firm serves institutional clients including pension funds, endowments, foundations, foreign governments, and central banks.

[2] Renaissance Technologies: an American hedge fund based in East Setauket, New York, on Long Island, which specializes in systematic trading using quantitative models derived from mathematical and statistical analysis.

traditional banks. While banks often provide a bundled set of financial services, non-banking financial institutions unbundle these services and customize their offerings for specific groups.

12.2 Financial Markets

After an introduction to financial institutions as intermediaries in the financial world, our exploration turns to financial markets. Financial markets can be classified into several categories based on various criteria. One common classification is based on the traded assets, resulting in distinctions between money markets and capital markets. Another classification is based on the maturity of the financial instruments, leading to primary markets and secondary markets.

12.2.1 Money Markets and Capital Markets

Money Markets

Money markets are the places where short-term debt investments are bought and sold. They are fast-moving marketplaces for loans and savings and possess a variety of instruments for people to trade. These instruments include cash, cash equivalent securities, and high-credit-rating, debt-based securities with a short-term maturity.

Money market funds can be seen as baskets of short-term investments that big companies and banks use to lend and borrow money. Common people can invest in them too.

Money market accounts are a special type of savings account with some features not found in regular savings accounts. They usually give better interest than regular savings accounts. It is considered a safe investment, although it is generally more useful in the short term than as a long-term investment.

The financial instruments commonly associated with the money market include certificates of deposit (CDs), commercial paper, banker's acceptances, and repo (repurchase agreement).

There are several pros and cons of money market investments. Most money market securities are considered extremely low-risk. They are also very liquid, meaning that they can readily be exchanged for cash at short notice.

Their returns are modest, so significant profits are unlikely. They also might not beat rising prices, and sometimes there are fees that cut into your earnings.

Some might not have full protection, and there is a small chance some borrowers might not pay back.

So, the money market is like a **hub** for quick trades involving short-term loans and savings. It is safe but not very profitable.

Capital Markets

In contrast to money markets, capital markets are expansive financial ecosystems where long-term securities are bought and sold. These markets are where buyers and sellers engage in the trade of financial securities.

Key participants in capital markets include individual and institutional investors, issuers (companies and governments), investment banks, and various regulatory bodies.

Securities in capital markets vary widely, ranging from common stocks that represent ownership in a company to bonds that signify debt agreements. Additionally, derivatives such as options and futures are actively traded, providing investors with tools for risk management and speculation.

At their core, capital markets facilitate the flow of long-term capital from investors to businesses and governments seeking funds for substantial projects or operations. Unlike money markets, which focus on short-term debt, capital markets are concerned with the issuance and trading of securities that have a more extended investment horizon.

While capital markets offer the potential for higher returns compared with money markets, they come with increased risks. The value of securities in capital markets can fluctuate based on market conditions, economic factors, and company performance. Investors in capital markets assume a certain level of risk in exchange for the prospect of capital appreciation and dividends.

12.2.2 Primary Markets and Secondary Markets

Primary Markets

When a company publicly sells new stocks or bonds for the first time, such as in an initial public offering (IPO), it does so in the primary capital market. This market is sometimes called the new issues market. When investors purchase securities on the primary capital market, the company that offers the securities hires an underwriting firm to review it and create a **prospectus** outlining the price and other details of the securities to be issued.

All issues on the primary market are subject to strict regulation. Companies must file statements with the Securities and Exchange Commission (SEC) and other securities agencies and must wait until their filings are approved before they can go public.

Small investors are often unable to buy securities on the primary market because the company and its investment bankers want to sell all of the available securities in a short period of time to meet the required volume, and they must focus on marketing the sale to large investors who can buy more securities at once.

Secondary Markets

The secondary markets include **venues** overseen by a regulatory body like the SEC where these previously issued securities are traded between investors. Issuing companies do not have a part in the secondary market. The New York Stock Exchange (NYSE) and Nasdaq are examples of secondary markets.

The secondary market has two different categories: the **auction** market and the dealer market. The auction market is home to the open **vocalization** system where buyers and sellers **congregate** in one location and announce the prices at which they are willing to buy and sell their securities. The NYSE is one such example. In dealer markets, though, people trade through electronic networks. Most small investors trade through dealer markets.

The capital market features various securities, including stocks (equities), bonds, and derivatives.

Exercises

❶ Short answer questions

Directions: *Answer the following questions in your own words or with sentences from the text.*

(1) What is the basic function of the central bank?

(2) What is the major difference between commercial banks and policy banks? Can you give an example?

(3) Can you illustrate the advantages and disadvantages of money market investments?

(4) Can you explain the composition of the secondary financial market?

❷ Term explanation

Directions: *Explain the following terms in your own words or with sentences from the text.*

(1) financial institution

(2) specialized bank

(3) non-banking financial institution

(4) money market

❸ Banked cloze

Directions: *Fill in the blanks by selecting suitable words from the following box. You may not use any of the words more than once.*

A. scale	B. operations	C. appreciation	D. approval	E. infrastructure
F. organizations	G. intermediaries	H. derivatives	I. within	J. collectively
K. worldwide	L. instruments	M. regulations	N. cash	O. nationwide

Financial institutions, money and capital markets, and international financial organizations (1) _____ form the intricate fabric of the global financial landscape, shaping economies, driving growth, and fostering cooperation on a global (2) _____.

Financial institutions, ranging from banks to investment firms, serve as (3) _____, connecting individuals and entities with surplus funds to those in need of money. They facilitate economic activities, provide essential services, and manage risks, contributing to the efficient allocation of capital.

The money market, a vital subset of financial markets, deals with short-term liquidity needs. Instruments like certificates of deposit, commercial paper, and repurchase agreements facilitate short-term borrowing and lending, supporting day-to-day financial (4) _____. Financial institutions play a central role by borrowing and lending (5) _____ this market, ensuring the smooth flow of funds and maintaining financial stability.

Capital markets, on the other hand, facilitate the trade of long-term securities. Stocks, bonds, and (6) _____ enable investors to allocate their funds for capital (7) _____ and income generation. Financial institutions participate as intermediaries, assisting in underwriting securities, executing trades, and managing investment portfolios.

International financial (8) _____ add another layer to this intricate landscape. The World Bank, the Bank for International Settlements, and the Asian Development Bank are just a few examples. These organizations play critical roles in supporting economic development, financial stability, and cooperation at both the global and regional levels, with each having its specific focus and mission.

The Asian Infrastructure Investment Bank (AIIB), among other things, further exemplifies international financial organizations' role. AIIB, founded to support (9) _____ development, enhances connectivity and economic integration in the Asian region.

In short, these elements shape a dynamic and interconnected financial landscape that influences economies (10) _____.

4 Translation

Directions: *Translate the following paragraphs into Chinese or English.*

(1) Insurance companies handle different types of risks that come with situations such as death, illness, property damage, and other potential losses. They promise financial protection if any of these events lead to losses. There are two main types of insurance companies: those that deal with life insurance and those that provide general insurance. General insurance usually covers shorter periods, whereas life insurance is a longer commitment that ends when an insured person passes away. Both types of insurance are available to all.

(2) 中国证监会成立于1992年10月，为国务院直属部级政府机构（a ministry-level government agency）。2006年，中国证监会获批受《中华人民共和国公务员法》管辖（be governed under）。中国证监会根据法律、法规和国务院授予的权力（mandate）运作，是中国监管和保护全国证券期货市场（futures markets）的中央机构（central agency）。其任务是维护公平、公正和透明的证券和期货市场，预防系统性风险，保护投资者，促进两个市场健康发展。

5 Project

Title: How to Maximize the Returns of My New Year's Money

Instructions: Imagine there has been and will be an annual gift for you of

10,000 yuan for the Chinese New Year. Previously, this money was managed by your parents. Now you are 20 years old, so they feel that you have become an adult and want you to handle this money on your own, but you do not need to use this money for your living expenses.

Step 1: Have a group discussion on the pros and cons of keeping the money in a bank's current account, and those of using the money to purchase bonds and other alternatives.

Step 2: Do an investigation on the specific returns and risks of various investment tools available on the market.

Step 3: Make a PPT presentation to illustrate your way to maximize the returns of your "New Year's money".

Supplementary Reading

Scan the QR code to find out more about the unit.

Unit 13

International Payments

Learning Objectives

After studying this unit, you should be able to:

1) understand the concepts of foreign exchange, foreign exchange rates, and balance of payments;
2) use the words and phrases in this unit;
3) apply the acquired knowledge to the analysis of cases of international payments.

In the era of global economic **connectivity**, the international balance of payments is a crucial concept for anyone seeking to comprehend the intricate world of finance as it serves as a comprehensive record of a country's economic transactions with the rest of the world. This unit delves into two important components: foreign exchange and exchange rates, which influence trade, investment, global economic stability, and the international balance of payments.

13.1 Foreign Exchange and Exchange Rate

13.1.1 Foreign Exchange

Foreign exchange, often referred to as forex or FX, is the conversion of a country's currency into another. Firms and organizations require foreign exchange to purchase goods from abroad. It facilitates international trade and investment by providing a mechanism for converting one currency into another, thereby influencing the competitiveness of nations in the global economy. Understanding foreign exchange is fundamental to comprehend the dynamics of the international balance of payments.

In a broad sense, the following can be taken as foreign exchange: foreign currency (banknotes and coins); foreign securities (government bonds, treasury bills, corporate bonds, stocks, coupons, etc.); foreign currency payment documents (bills, bank certificates of deposit, certificates of postal savings, bank cards, etc.); and Special Drawing Rights (SDR)❶ and other foreign exchange funds (life insurance money abroad and remuneration, **royalties**, and patent transfer fees of domestic residents abroad).

The foreign exchange market comprises various participants, each with distinct roles. At the core of the market are various national currencies, each representing the economic standing and monetary policies of its respective country. Central banks and other government institutions hold foreign exchange reserves, including foreign currencies and other assets. These reserves serve as **buffers** to stabilize the domestic currency and manage the balance of payments. Commercial banks and financial institutions actively participate in the market by acting as intermediaries for businesses, investors, and governments involved

---

❶ Special Drawing Right (SDR): an interest-bearing international reserve asset created by the IMF in 1969 to supplement other reserve assets of member countries. The SDR is based on a basket of international currencies comprising the U.S. dollar, Japanese yen, euro, pound sterling, and Chinese CNY. It is not a currency, nor a claim on the IMF, but is potentially a claim on freely usable currencies of IMF members.

in cross-border transactions. Corporations engage in forex transactions for international trade, and the main function of forex derivatives, such as forex futures (exchange-traded currency derivative contracts obligating the buyer and seller to transact at a set price and predetermined time), is to hedge against currency risk, whereas institutional investors and speculators seek profit opportunities. Foreign exchange transactions can be categorized as follows based on their nature and purpose:

Spot transactions: Spot transactions involve the immediate exchange of currencies at the current market rate. This is the most common type of foreign exchange transaction and is often used for day-to-day trade.

Forward transactions: In forward transactions, two parties agree to exchange currencies at a future date and a predetermined exchange rate. This allows businesses to hedge against future exchange rate fluctuations.

Derivatives: Derivative instruments, such as currency futures and options, are financial contracts whose value is derived from the underlying foreign exchange rates. These instruments are used for hedging and speculation purposes.

13.1.2 Exchange Rate

The exchange rate is the rate at which one currency can be exchanged for another. It represents the value of one currency in terms of another currency. Exchange rates are crucial in international trade because people can compare the prices of goods and services in different countries. For instance, if a Chinese consumer has to choose between a Lincoln Navigator for 77,000 U.S. dollars from America and a Toyota Land Cruiser for 9,500,000 Japanese yen from Japan, he would use exchange rates to translate foreign prices into the domestic currency terms. Once the money prices of the two models of the vehicle are expressed in terms of the same currency, the consumer can make a decision.

Exchange rates are quoted using two primary methods. In a direct quotation, domestic currency is expressed in terms of a fixed amount of foreign currency. For example, 1 USD = 7.1614 CNY. An indirect quotation expresses foreign currency in terms of a fixed amount of domestic currency, just as 1 CNY = 0.1396 USD. The choice of quotation method depends on the conventions and preferences in different regions.

Changes in exchange rates are referred to as appreciation or depreciation. Take RMB as an example. An appreciation of the CNY against the U.S. dollar is a rise in the CNY's price in terms of dollars, whereas a depreciation of the CNY against the U.S. dollar is a fall in the dollar price of CNY.

Exchange rate systems can be broadly classified into three categories:

Floating Exchange Rates

Under this system, currency values are determined mainly by market forces, with supply and demand in the foreign exchange market setting rates. Thus, the relative prices of currencies are determined by purchases and sales among businesses and individuals. Most major currencies, including the U.S. dollar and euro, operate under floating exchange rates. The value of the U.S. dollar is determined by market forces in the foreign exchange market. It needs to be specifically pointed out that most countries employing a floating exchange rate system are subject to intervention by their central banks or national governments. For instance, the Federal Reserve, the central bank of America, occasionally intervenes in the currency markets to stabilize the dollar or achieve specific policy objectives. The flexibility of the floating exchange rate system allows these countries to adjust to their economic conditions and external shocks.

In theory, under a floating exchange rate system, exchange rates should be determined solely by the supply and demand in the foreign exchange market. However, because of the close relationship between a country's exchange rate fluctuations and its economic trade and capital movements, even with the implementation of a floating exchange rate system, central banks cannot completely **relinquish** control over exchange rates. Central banks may still intervene or adjust exchange rates when necessary, creating the managed floating exchange rate system.

Fixed Exchange Rates

In a fixed exchange rate system, governments or central banks set the value of their currency relative to a reference currency or basket of currencies. This system requires intervention to maintain a fixed rate. For instance, The Bretton Woods System, referring to the post-World War II international monetary system, is centered around the U.S. dollar. From July 1–22, 1944, representatives from 44 countries, including the U.S., the Soviet Union, China, and France, gathered at the Mount Washington Hotel in Bretton Woods, New Hampshire, U.S.A. During the United Nations Monetary and Financial Conference, they adopted documents such as the "Final Act of the United Nations Monetary and Financial Conference", the "Articles of Agreement of the International Monetary Fund", and the "Articles of Agreement of the International Bank for Reconstruction and Development", collectively known as the Bretton Woods System. The General

Agreement on Tariffs and Trade (GATT), as a supplement to the 1944 Bretton Woods Conference, constituted a multilateral economic system focusing on foreign exchange liberalization, capital liberalization, and trade liberalization, forming the core of the capitalist **bloc**. The establishment of the Bretton Woods System facilitated the recovery and development of the post-war capitalist world economy. However, due to frequent crises, including the U.S. dollar crisis and economic troubles in the United States, along with inherent contradictions within the system, it was declared terminated by the Nixon administration on August 15, 1971. Since the beginning of World War II, the United States has emerged as the world's strongest economic power, holding a significant portion of the global gold reserves. In the Bretton Woods Agreement, the U.S. officially replaced gold with the dollar (known as the gold standard), setting the exchange rate at $35 per ounce of gold. This arrangement allowed foreign governments and central banks to exchange their dollars for gold within certain limits. The Bretton Woods System established a fixed exchange rate regime linking international currencies to the U.S. dollar, which, in turn, was tied to gold.

As history unfolded, the fixed exchange rate system began to show signs of **strain**. By the late 1950s and the 1960s, the U.S. experienced a growing trade deficit, leading to a significant outflow of gold. On August 15, 1971, President Nixon announced the devaluation of the U.S. dollar and its **suspension** from being convertible to gold, resulting in the collapse of the Bretton Woods System. This event, known as the "Nixon Shock", marked the end of the gold standard.

Despite the **demise** of the Bretton Woods System, the U.S. dollar remained a key global currency. To prevent the disruption of the international financial order, the U.S. engaged in a series of bilateral and multilateral meetings with major industrialized nations. In December 1971, the Smithsonian Agreement was reached among ten countries, adjusting the gold exchange rate to $38 per ounce and allowing greater flexibility in currency fluctuations. However, in 1972, the United Kingdom abandoned its obligation to maintain a fixed exchange rate for the pound, causing instability in the Smithsonian Agreement. By February 1973, the U.S. experienced a second devaluation of the dollar, prompting Japan to announce the implementation of a floating exchange rate for the yen. In March of the same year, European countries and other major capitalist nations, including West Germany, France, Belgium, the Netherlands, Luxembourg, and Denmark, withdrew from the fixed exchange rate system. At this point, for major countries, the international financial system effectively transitioned into a floating exchange rate regime, leading to the complete **dissolution** of the fixed exchange rate system.

Even so, the U.S. dollar continued to demonstrate its importance and power in the world. The post-war economic boom, driven by the increased demand for war materials, positioned the U.S. with 70% of the world's gold reserves. As the U.S. dollar became the primary international medium of exchange, it played a dominant role in global trade. This shift facilitated extensive investments by American capitalists worldwide in the post-war era.

Managed Exchange Rates

In a managed system, exchange rates are influenced by a combination of market forces and government intervention. This system allows for flexibility while preventing excessive volatility. For example, in 2005, the People's Bank of China issued an announcement entitled "Notice on Improving the Reform of the RMB Exchange Rate Formation Mechanism", declaring the adoption of a managed floating exchange rate system based on market supply and demand, referencing a basket of currencies for adjustments. Starting on July 21, 2005, the Renminbi was no longer **pegged** solely to the U.S. dollar, establishing a more flexible exchange rate mechanism for the Chinese currency.

Several factors influence exchange rates:

Interest rates: Differences in interest rates between countries can influence the demand for their currencies. Higher interest rates often attract foreign investors seeking better returns, leading to currency appreciation.

Inflation rates: Countries with lower inflation rates tend to appreciate their currency value. Lower inflation preserves the purchasing power of a currency, making it more attractive to investors.

Economic indicators: Various economic indicators, such as GDP growth, employment rates, and trade balances, impact investor confidence and influence the strength of a country's currency.

Political stability and economic performance: Political stability and positive economic performance enhance investor confidence, attract foreign capital, and potentially lead to a stronger currency.

Government debt: Countries with lower levels of government debt are perceived as more fiscally responsible, which can contribute to currency appreciation.

We have to be aware that international exchange markets feature high competitiveness by nature since large quantities of sellers and buyers meet here to form one worldwide market and they possess up-to-the-minute information about the exchange rates between any two currencies.

13.2 International Balance of Payments

In the complex world of international finance, the concept of the balance of payments (BOP) serves as a crucial framework for understanding a nation's economic interactions with the rest of the world. As we delve into this intricate topic, we explore the fundamental components of the international balance of payments, the factors contributing to imbalances, and the mechanisms through which nations adjust to restore equilibrium.

13.2.1 Definition of International Balance of Payments

The international balance of payments is a comprehensive accounting system or a summary statement that records all the transactions of the residents of a country with the residents of the rest of the world over a specific period. The term "residents" refers to individuals, businesses, and government agencies that make the country in question their legal **domicile**, but the overseas branches or **subsidiaries** of those businesses or agencies are not included. Tourists, workers working temporarily overseas, government diplomats, and military personnel are considered residents of the country where they possess citizenship.

At its core, the balance of payments is statistical and **captures** the flow of money and assets between a nation and other countries, shedding light on the **intricacies** of international trade, finance, and investments. Please note that millions of transactions of the residents of a nation with residents of all other nations cannot appear individually in the balance of payments, which aggregates all merchandise trade into a few major categories. The balance of payments will provide detailed information about the demand and supply of a country's currency, keep the government informed of the country's international position in international economic competition, and help the country in the formulation of monetary, fiscal, and trade policies.

When arranging international transactions into a BOP account, each transaction must be entered as **credit** or **debit**. A credit transaction refers to one resulting in the receipt of payments from foreigners. These items are recorded with a positive sign (+). Conversely, a debit transaction leads to payment to foreigners, and such items are recorded with a negative sign (–). Normally, transactions such as merchandise exports, transportation and travel receipts, income received from investments abroad, and aid received from foreign governments are credits, while merchandise imports, transportation and travel expenditure, income paid on the investments of foreigners, and aid given by the government are debits. Although we classify transactions into credit or debit, every international transaction has both credit and debit sides.

The structure of the BOP consists of two main subaccounts: the current account and the capital and financial account. The current account encompasses the exchange of goods, services, income, and **unilateral** transfers, which do not create liability. It reflects a nation's trade balance, capturing the value of exports and imports, and considers earnings from foreign investments and **remittances**. Complementing the current account, the capital and financial account delves into cross-border capital movement. If a transaction creates a liability, such as selling a bond to another country, it is counted in the capital and financial account.

When a country exports an item, it is a current account transaction and effectively imports foreign capital because that item is paid for with a capital account transaction. Anything that occurs in one account is offset by the opposite in the other. For example, if the current account increases by $100, the capital and financial account must decrease by the same amount. In other words, an entry in the current account is offset by an entry in the capital and financial account.

13.2.2 Imbalance of International Payments

In the real world, international payments are not always harmonious. Imbalances can emerge, posing challenges to economic stability and raising questions about sustainability.

In the current account, trade imbalances occur when a nation consistently imports more goods and services than it exports or vice versa. For instance, the U.K. often experiences a current account deficit due to its reliance on imports of goods, particularly consumer electronics, cars, and clothing from countries such as China and Germany. This deficit often worsens during economic expansion when domestic demand for imported goods increases. The current account deficit suggests that the country is dependent on foreign capital to finance its imports, leaving it **vulnerable** to external impacts such as changes in foreign investor sentiment or interest rates. It can also apply downward pressure on the value of the pound sterling. On the other hand, the U.S. recently became a net petroleum exporter for the first time in 70 years and experienced its first monthly trade surplus in petroleum since 1949. As a significant producer of petroleum, the exports of petroleum generate foreign exchange income in the U.S. This surplus can help offset other imbalances in the current account, such as deficits in the trade of goods and services.

While they are essential for economic development, capital inflows can, nevertheless, become a source of imbalance in an economy. The following example from Australia illustrates such an imbalance in capital and financial accounts. Australia is known for its significant foreign investment inflows, particularly from Japan, China, and the U.S., all of which seek natural resources and real estate opportunities. These investments are often directed towards mining projects, property development, and other natural-resource-based areas of the economy. Such inflows of foreign capital can, however, have the effect of putting upward pressure on the exchange value of the Australian dollar as demand of Australian assets then increases relative to supply. The resulting revaluation can make Australian exports less competitive in global markets, though, at the same time, these inflows can also support the domestic economy by providing capital for investment and growth.

The causes of imbalance in international payments in different countries or regions have special characteristics. Generally, the causes are divided into four categories: **contingency**, cyclical, monetary, and structural. Contingency imbalance is a phenomenon of unbalanced payments caused by accidental reasons. The consequences of accidental imbalance are **reversible**. Cyclic imbalances are mainly due to the fact that countries are at different stages of the economic cycle, resulting in an imbalance in international payments. For example, in a short period, countries and regions with weak economies will have correspondingly less demand for supply, and when supply exceeds demand, they will stimulate exports accordingly. In such cases, trade surpluses are more likely to be generated and countries with which international imports and exports take place are more **susceptible** to trade deficits. On the premise that other influencing factors remain unchanged, countries or regions with fast economic growth have enormous import demand, which is more likely to cause trade deficits, and vice versa. Monetary imbalance is caused by factors in money supply and demand. Assuming that all other conditions remain constant, an oversupply of money will lead to price rises in the country, which will affect exports and reduce total exports, but will correspondingly stimulate imports and cause trade deficits. A structural imbalance results from a country's economic structure. This is usually due to the lack of innovation in a country's economic structure, which cannot keep pace with economic changes in the new era; or the insufficient diversification of its industrial structure; or the inelasticity of its income in response to export demand or price in response to import demand.

The negative influence of an imbalance in payments on a country's economy includes the following aspects. First, balance-of-payments surpluses are prone to inflationary pressure, which has an impact on a country's economic growth, or can even have a serious impact on the country's social stability. Second, the balance-of-payments surplus puts upward pressure on a country's currency. Normally, when a country's foreign exchange reserves gradually increase with a balance of payments surplus, it brings about a continuous appreciation of its currency. Finally, the balance-of-payments surplus is the main factor causing contradictions in **bidding** between countries. Therefore, if a country has a trade surplus, it will inevitably cause a trade deficit in its trading counterparts, thus causing dissatisfaction among them and leading to international conflict.

When there is an absence of an adequate balance of payments adjustment mechanism, an imbalance of international payments is taken as a sign of a need for a change in economic policy, as well as an actual or potential threat to the existing exchange system.

13.2.3 Adjustment of the Imbalance of Payments

Recognizing the inevitability of imbalances, the international economic system has devised mechanisms to facilitate adjustments and restore equilibrium.

Exchange rates play a pivotal role in the adjustment process. In the early 1930s, the Great Depression took hold, and the global economy was in **tatters**. The U.K. found itself with a large trade deficit, and the government decided to devalue the pound sterling to make British exports more competitive in the global market. By devaluing the pound, the British government made the currency cheaper than other currencies. This made British goods and services more affordable to foreign buyers, thus increasing demand and exports. The devaluation of the pound sterling successfully boosted British exports and narrowed the trade deficit. It also stimulated the domestic economy, which was struggling due to the Depression.

In addition, governments and central banks can **deploy** fiscal and monetary policies to influence the international balance of payments. In the **aftermath** of the Great Recession of 2008, the U.S. government implemented a series of fiscal stimulus measures to boost the economy and reverse the downturn. The

U.S. government responded to the recession by passing stimulus packages that provided fiscal stimulus, such as tax cuts, infrastructure spending, and other forms of government spending. The goal was to increase the aggregate demand and encourage economic growth. The U.S. stimulus package had mixed effects on the balance of payments. On the one hand, increased government spending led to higher imports of goods and services, contributing to a trade deficit. On the other hand, the stimulus package also supported domestic production and exports, which helped narrow the trade deficit in some cases. Additionally, the package boosted aggregate demand that supported U.S. exports to other countries, thus influencing the international balance of payments in favor of the U.S.

In conclusion, the international balance of payments serves as a compass for navigating the intricate web of global economic relations. Understanding its components, factors contributing to imbalances, and mechanisms for adjustment is crucial for comprehending the dynamics of international finance.

Exercises

❶ Short answer questions

Directions: *Answer the following questions in your own words or with sentences from the text.*

(1) What factors influence the exchange rate?

(2) How can one appropriately cite the exchange rate?

(3) What is the significance of balance of payments?

(4) How does a country adjust the imbalance of payments?

❷ Term explanation

Directions: *Explain the following terms in your own words or with sentences from the text.*

(1) foreign exchange

(2) exchange rate

(3) spot transaction

(4) international balance of payments

财经基础英语
Basic English for Economics and Finance

❸ Banked cloze

Directions: *Fill in the blanks by selecting suitable words from the following box. You may not use any of the words more than once.*

A. avoid	B. received	C. up	D. In addition	E. forward
F. improving	G. imposing	H. fluctuations	I. sustainable	J. for
K. promoting	L. important	M. using	N. interrelated	O. international

Foreign exchange reserves are foreign currency and other assets held by a country that can be used for (1) _____ payments. They can be used to resist external financial risks and market fluctuations, maintain exchange rate stability and promote international trade and investment. (2) _____, foreign exchange reserves can provide sufficient liquidity to support the operation of the domestic financial system. Foreign exchange reserves of countries play an important role in the balance of payments. On the one hand, they can help the countries maintain a relatively stable exchange rate and avoid excessive currency (3) _____. This helps promote international trade and investment and provides a reliable investment climate. On the other hand, foreign exchange reserves also need to be carefully managed to (4) _____ adverse impact on the value of reserve assets. The foreign exchange policy and foreign exchange reserve management have also (5) _____ world attention. Countries in the world manage the foreign exchange market in a number of ways, including adjusting exchange rates, (6) _____ capital controls, etc. At the same time, many countries have also taken an active part in international financial cooperation and strengthened currency swaps（互换）with other countries and regions to promote a stable and (7) _____ international financial system. In short, foreign exchange and balance of payments are (8) _____ elements in the international economy which cannot be ignored. They are (9) _____ and collectively affect a country's economic situation and development prospects. By properly managing and (10) _____ its foreign exchange reserves, countries will be able to better tackle external risks and promote steady economic growth.

❹ Translation

Directions: *Translate the following paragraphs into Chinese or English.*

(1) The international balance of payments is a comprehensive accounting

system or a summary statement that records all the transactions of the residents of a country with the residents of the rest of the world over a specific period. The term "residents" refers to individuals, businesses, and government agencies that make the country in question their legal domicile, but the overseas branches or subsidiaries of those businesses or agencies are not included. Tourists, workers working temporarily overseas, government diplomats, and military personnel are considered residents of the country where they possess citizenship.

(2) 2023年一季度，我国国际收支保持基本平衡。其中，经常账户顺差820亿美元，与同期国内生产总值之比为2.0%；双向跨境资金流动保持合理有序。我国制造业加快转型升级（transformation and upgrading），产业链及供应链保持稳定，新的贸易增长点涌现。面对复杂的外部环境，我国坚持着力推动高质量发展，经济发展呈现回升向好态势（upturn to a positive trend），为我国国际收支基本平衡提供根本支撑。

5 Project

Instructions: Read the following chart of China's investment in ASEAN countries during 2016–2020 and write an essay with no more than 250 words. Your essay should be composed of three parts:

Part I. Describe the chart of China's investment in ASEAN countries during 2016–2020.

Part II. Your opinion on China's investment in ASEAN countries.

Part III. Summary of your points.

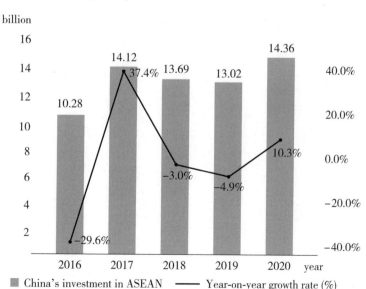

Supplementary Reading

Scan the QR code to find out more about the unit.

Unit 14

Financial Risk, Crisis, and Supervision

Learning Objectives

After studying this unit, you should be able to:

1) understand the concepts of financial risk, financial crisis, financial supervision, and the functions of the financial regulation system;
2) use the words and phrases in this unit;
3) understand the cases of financial risks, crises, and supervision.

In finance, risk is an inherent and unavoidable aspect that affects individuals, businesses, and governments in decision-making. Financial crises are pivotal events reshaping the economic landscape, invoking a sense of economic **turmoil** and instability, and reflecting moments in history when the very fabric of financial systems is strained to its limits. This unit provides an overview of financial risks and crises, and explores financial supervision and regulation for a robust financial system.

14.1 Financial Risk

Financial risk includes financial market risk, financial product risk, and financial institution risk. The consequences of risks in financial institutions often have extensive impacts. Risks that arise in specific financial transactions within a financial institution may pose a threat to the institution's survival. A crisis stemming from the mismanagement of a specific financial institution may threaten the sound operation of the entire financial system. Once systemic risk occurs and the financial system malfunctions, it will inevitably lead to a disorder of the entire economy in society and even **trigger** serious political crises.

14.1.1 Overview of Financial Risk

In the dynamic realm of finance, individuals and entities are exposed to various uncertainties that can adversely affect their financial well-being. These uncertainties stem from factors such as market fluctuations, economic downturns, and operational challenges.

Financial risks are **omnipresent**, and their inevitability is deeply rooted in the nature of financial markets. The challenge lies in understanding, quantifying, and managing these risks effectively to ensure sustainable financial health. Understanding the characteristics of financial risks is fundamental to devising risk management strategies.

Financial risk exhibits several key features:

Uncertainty: Financial risks encompass factors such as the unpredictability of influencing elements, uncertainty regarding the timing of occurrence, and the indeterminate nature of risk magnitudes. The challenges posed by these uncertainties make it difficult to predict outcomes for future events.

Variability: Financial risks stem from the variability in market conditions, interest rates, exchange rates, and other economic factors that impact the value of financial instruments.

Correlation: Risks in financial markets are usually interrelated and the occurrence of an event may trigger a chain reaction, expanding the scope and impact of risks. For example, the bankruptcy of a company may lead to default risks for other companies that have business deals.

Potential for gain or loss: Every financial risk presents an opportunity for gain and the possibility of loss. The delicate balance between risk and rewards makes financial decisions challenging.

Time sensitivity: The impact of financial risks often evolves, and their consequences may not be immediately apparent. Timely and vigilant risk management is crucial.

Financial markets face financial risk owing to various macroeconomic forces, changes in the market interest rate, and the possibility of default by sectors or large corporations. Individuals face financial risk when they make decisions that may **jeopardize** their income or their ability to pay a debt they have assumed. Financial risks are **ubiquitous** and come in many shapes and sizes, affecting nearly everyone. Everyone should be aware of the presence of financial risk. Knowing the dangers and protecting oneself will not eliminate the risks, but can mitigate their harm and reduce the chances of a negative outcome.

Financial risk can be classified based on its nature and origin. The most commonly recognized classifications, according to the latest data, include market risk, credit risk, operational risk, and liquidity risk.

Market risk: This type of risk arises from changes in market variables such as interest rates, exchange rates, and commodity prices. Investors and businesses are exposed to the resulting return or risk of changes in income or asset values because of the unpredictable nature of these variables.

Credit risk: Credit risk, also known as default risk, **emanates** from the possibility of a borrower failing to meet their financial obligations. Lenders, investors, and financial institutions face credit risk when extending loans or investing in securities.

Operational risk: Operational risk stems from internal processes, systems, and human error within an organization. It includes the risks associated with technology failures, fraud, and inadequate internal controls.

Liquidity risk: Liquidity risk arises when an entity encounters difficulties in buying or selling financial instruments without significantly affecting its market price. This risk is particularly **pertinent** during economic downturns and financial crises.

Financial risk can be triggered by both internal and external factors. The internal factors include poor financial management, inadequate internal controls, and strategic missteps. For instance, a company with excessive leverage may face heightened financial risks during economic downturns. External factors, such as **geopolitical** events, economic downturns, and natural disasters, can significantly impact financial markets. The interconnectedness of the global economy implies that events in one part of the world can have far-reaching consequences.

Financial risk, in itself, is not inherently good or bad but only exists to different degrees. Of course, "risk" by its very nature has a negative connotation, and financial risk is no exception. Risk can spread from one business to affect an entire sector, market, or even the world. Risk can stem from uncontrollable external sources or forces, and it is often difficult to overcome.

While it is not a positive attribute, understanding the possibility of financial risk can lead to better, more informed business or investment decisions. Assessing the degree of financial risk associated with a security or asset helps determine or set the value of the investment. The risk is the flip side of the reward. One could argue that no progress or growth can occur, be it in a business or **portfolio**, without assuming some risk. Finally, while financial risk usually cannot be controlled, exposure to it can be limited or managed.

14.1.2　Management of Financial Risk

Financial risk management measures and controls the risks and rewards of profit-oriented and non-profit organizations. With the development of financial integration and economic globalization, financial risks are becoming increasingly complex and diverse, highlighting the growing importance of financial risk management.

The management of financial risk requires the following steps:

Risk identification and assessment: The first step in managing financial risks is to identify and assess them. This involves a thorough analysis of the various risks that an individual or entity is exposed to. Quantitative and qualitative methods, such as risk models and scenario analysis, can be employed to assess the severity of the potential risks.

Diversification: Diversification is a fundamental risk management strategy that involves the spread of investments across different assets and sectors. This helps reduce the impact of adverse events in any single area and minimizes the overall portfolio risk.

Hedging strategies: Financial instruments, such as derivatives, can be employed to hedge against specific risks. For example, businesses can use futures contracts to hedge against currency fluctuations, thus reducing the impact of exchange rate risk.

Insurance and risk transfer: Insurance serves as a risk transfer mechanism, allowing individuals and businesses to transfer a portion of their financial risk to insurance providers. This is particularly relevant for mitigating operational and liability risks.

Stress testing and scenario analysis: Conducting stress tests and scenario analyses helps assess the resilience of financial decisions under adverse conditions. This enables individuals and entities to identify vulnerabilities and develop contingency plans.

14.2 Financial Crisis

The impact of the financial crisis on the global economy is profound, manifested primarily in widespread economic recessions, bank failures, and the collapse of asset values. Enhancing awareness of financial crises is of utmost importance.

14.2.1 Overview of Financial Crisis

A financial crisis can be broadly defined as a sudden and severe disruption to the normal functioning of financial markets and institutions, leading to widespread economic distress. Financial crises not only harm the financial system within an economy but also often **escalate** into a crisis for the entire economy, leading to output decline, increased unemployment, and severe economic recession, and sometimes even causing serious political crises such as social unrest and government changes. Financial crises are not isolated incidents, but rather complex phenomena with multifaceted causes and manifestations. A financial crisis is a specific phase of economic development with the following distinctive features:

Transient nature: Financial crises are typically temporary. While their impact may endure, the actual outbreak and severity of the crisis tend to be short-lived.

Supercyclical characteristics: Financial crises often surpass regular fluctuations in the economic cycle. They can occur even during times of relative economic health.

Potential and far-reaching consequences: Financial crises have profound effects on the entire economy, leading to reduced output, heightened unemployment, and a severe economic recession. Some crises extend beyond borders, triggering global **repercussions** and instability in the financial system.

Multifactor complexity: Financial crises are often the result of multiple factors working together, including market failures, credit bubbles, regulatory deficiencies, and the accumulation of risks.

The causes of financial crises encompass a complex interplay of various factors that contribute to disruptions in the economic and financial systems. Financial crises, which tend to accompany the boom phase of the economic cycle, are often seen as a **self-inflicted** self-correction of the **dysfunctions** of the economic system, in particular a "**liquidation**" of market failures. When a crisis occurs, all or some of the financial indicators, such as short-term interest rates, asset prices, the number of business bankruptcies, financial institution failures, etc., produce a very sharp deterioration and distress in financial institutions and industries, with a significant impact on economic fundamentals. Crisis has been one of the most dominant research topics in economics since its birth, and the causes of financial crisis outbreaks are the primary research questions. According to the IMF (1998), there are four main types of financial crisis with corresponding outbreak triggers.

The first is the banking crisis. If a bank fails to repay its debts as scheduled, this may jeopardize the bank's credit, and if the problem gradually escalates and spreads, it may evolve into a crisis of the entire banking system. The causes of banking crises include monetary policy failures, endogenous instability in the financial system, accumulation of risks of financial overexpansion, financial panics, and moral hazard, which do not work singularly but are intertwined. For example, the 1990s Nordic financial crisis was a typical banking crisis caused by the removal of lending restrictions in 1985, leading to intense inter-bank competition, excessive credit issuance, and gradual accumulation of risks.

Secondly, there is a currency crisis. When a currency's exchange rate and its system fail to reflect economic fundamentals and reform is seriously lagging, it is easy to encounter the speculation of international speculative capital, which may have sustained and substantial depreciation, and monetary authorities are forced to rescue or even give up the original exchange rate system, which finally results in a currency crisis. The most typical currency crises are the East Asian financial crisis and the 1992 crisis of the British pound and the Italian lira. The root causes of currency crises include conflicts between the internal and external equilibria of the economy, multiple objectives of policies, and moral hazard.

Thirdly, there is a debt crisis, which mostly occurs in developing countries. There are serious disruptions in the balance-of-payments system of an economy, loss of national credit, and so on because of the inability of **sovereign** and/or private debt to repay the external debt owed on time. Debt crises can be caused by overindebtedness, the downward effect of asset prices, changes in the economic cycle, and large capital inflows. The Latin American debt crisis that erupted in the early 1980s was typical of this type of crisis.

Finally, there is a systemic financial crisis. Serious problems arise in all major financial areas of an economy, with currency exchange rate disruptions, financial institution bankruptcies, and real economic disasters occurring one after another or simultaneously. So far, the Great Depression, the East Asian financial crisis, and the American **subprime** crisis can all be considered systemic financial crises. The reasons for such crises may be multifaceted, like in the case of the subprime crisis, which was a thorough liquidation of loose monetary policy, non-prudent home mortgages, excessive financial innovation, and inadequate financial regulation.

In fact, there are other types of financial crises in addition to the above categories, such as the 1987 U.S. stock market crash and the 1992 Japanese stock market bubble.

After financial globalization, the causes of various crises have become increasingly complex and diversified, and the boundaries of crises have become increasingly blurred. For example, the East Asian financial crisis of 1997 can be attributed to the impact of financial globalization, not only currency problems and subprime mortgages.

14.2.2 Impacts of Financial Crisis

Each major impact of the financial crisis has not only led to a large number of bankruptcies of financial institutions but has also had a huge impact on the financial sector and even the real economy as a result of the undermining of financial stability. However, on the other hand, each financial crisis has brought about a greater or lesser correction to the financial market and the financial system, which is favorable to financial development in a certain sense.

Financial crises are very destructive, the **brunt** of which is the massive bankruptcy of financial institutions and the creation of a large number of bad debts. Taking the Great Depression as an example, in 1930–1933, the proportion of bank failures each year was 5.6%, 10.5%, 7.8%, and 12.9%, respectively. By the end of 1933, the number of banks sticking to their business was only more than half of what it was in 1929, and the number of banks in the United States had been reduced from 25,000 to less than 15,000.

More importantly, the financial crisis was destructive in that it undermined the money-lending function of financial markets. 1930–1933 was the most difficult and chaotic phase of the financial system in the history of the U.S. Bank failures reached a peak in March 1933, **crippling** the banking system, with defaults and bankruptcies of such magnitude as to affect virtually all borrowers except the federal government, so that financial institutions and investors were vulnerable to a loss of refinancing functions. This caused the overall liquidity of the market to shrink dramatically (i.e., a sudden credit halt), creating a liquidity crisis that affected the financial system's financing function and reduced the efficiency of capital allocation.

In addition, the outbreak of a financial crisis affects financial stability. After the outbreak of the financial crisis, the market begins to experience serious loan shyness and a **credit crunch**, especially the collapse of large financial institutions, bringing significant confidence problems. The money supply and capital allocation are, to some extent, detached from the control of the central bank and increasingly subject to the domination of internal factors of the economic system, such as changes in the money multiplier[1]. This seriously weakens the central bank's ability to control the money supply and the extent of its control. Thus, a financial crisis will create great uncertainty in financial markets, dealing a great blow to financial stability.

Finally, a financial crisis can trigger a recession. Following the outbreak of a banking crisis, fears of a **run** lead to massive early withdrawals of deposits by depositors, forcing governments to raise reserve ratios, and banks to increase their liquid assets. When the financial sector as a whole becomes much less efficient in delivering services and the real cost of intermediation rises sharply, borrowers find credit expensive and difficult to obtain, and the credit crunch evolves into a contraction of aggregate demand and ultimately into a recession.

---

[1] money multiplier: the ratio of the money supply to the monetary base, or the amount of money produced by one unit of the monetary base. Its size determines the ability of the money supply to expand.

Beyond the economic realm, financial crises often have social and political repercussions, which can exacerbate income inequality, as the burden of economic downturns falls disproportionately on lower-income households. Job losses, wage **stagnation**, and asset price declines contribute to widening the income gap. Social and economic dislocations caused by financial crises can contribute to political instability and social unrest. The costs of addressing a financial crisis, including **bailouts** and stimulus measures, often result in increased government debt. In turn, this may lead to fiscal challenges, **austerity** measures, and long-term economic consequences. Financial crises erode public trust in financial institutions, regulatory bodies, and government authorities. Rebuilding this trust requires considerable time and effort.

Of course, any crisis is designed for both danger and opportunity; only the magnitude of danger and opportunity varies in degree. Generally, after a financial crisis, the government will correct the failures of the financial market and system, and at the same time strengthen the relevant financial regulation, improve the financial system and legal framework, and lay a more solid foundation for further development of the financial market and financial system.

14.3 Financial Supervision

Financial supervision plays a vital role in promoting economic growth, protecting consumers, and maintaining trust and confidence in the financial sector. Financial supervision helps mitigate systemic risks and prevent financial crises. By imposing prudential requirements on financial institutions such as capital adequacy ratios and liquidity standards, regulators aim to ensure that banks and other financial entities have sufficient buffers to absorb losses and withstand adverse shocks. This helps maintain the stability of the financial system and prevents **contagion** of financial distress.

14.3.1 Definition of Financial Supervision

Financial supervision refers to regulatory oversight and monitoring of financial institutions and markets to ensure their stability, integrity, and compliance with established rules and regulations. The primary purpose of financial supervision is to maintain the soundness of the financial system, protect the interests of consumers, and prevent systemic risks that could lead to financial crises.

Financial supervision is comprised of various components, each serving a specific purpose to ensure the stability and integrity of the financial system. Prudential regulation focuses on setting standards for the financial soundness of institutions. This includes the requirements related to capital adequacy, risk management, and liquidity. Market conduct oversight involves monitoring and regulating the behavior of market participants to ensure fair and ethical practices, prevent market manipulation, and protect consumers. Macroprudential supervision assesses and addresses systemic risks that can affect the financial system. It involves monitoring trends, such as excessive credit growth, and implementing measures to mitigate systemic vulnerabilities. Financial supervisors establish rules to protect consumers from abusive practices, misleading information, and unfair treatment. This includes ensuring the clear disclosure of terms and conditions for financial products. Oversight of critical financial infrastructure such as payment systems and **clearinghouses** is essential for maintaining the smooth functioning of financial markets.

14.3.2 Financial Regulation System

The financial regulation system refers to the comprehensive set of institutions and organizational structures through which a country oversees and manages financial institutions and markets so as to govern the behavior and operations of financial institutions and markets. The objective is to create a stable, fair, and transparent financial environment that fosters economic growth while mitigating risk.

Financial regulation is crucial for maintaining the stability of the financial system by preventing excessive risk-taking and ensuring the financial soundness of institutions. Clear and robust financial regulations enhance investor confidence by providing a framework that ensures fair dealings, transparent information, and protection from **fraudulent** activities. Regulations are designed to protect consumers from unfair practices, ensuring that financial products and services are offered transparently, with clear terms and conditions, as well as to prevent market abuse, insider trading, and other activities that could compromise the integrity of financial markets.

Broadly speaking, the financial regulation system encompasses regulatory objectives, scope, principles, methods, establishment of regulatory entities, and **delineation** of regulatory authority. Specifically, it involves the establishment and allocation of authority for regulatory entities. Countries generally categorize their financial regulatory systems into three types:

The unitary multilateral financial regulatory system, where regulatory authority is centralized at the national level with multiple agencies jointly responsible.

The dual multilateral financial regulatory system, where both central and local authorities have regulatory power over financial institutions or services, with different agencies overseeing distinct aspects.

The centralized unilateral financial regulatory system, where a single regulatory agency at the national level exercises financial regulatory authority.

Different countries establish or adjust their financial regulatory systems based on their own national conditions.

The United States employs a regulatory framework that involves multiple regulatory agencies, each with specific **mandates** and responsibilities. The key regulatory bodies include the Federal Reserve, Securities and Exchange Commission, Commodity Futures Trading Commission, Office of the Comptroller of the Currency, Federal Deposit Insurance Corporation, and the Consumer Financial Protection Bureau. The U.S. regulatory system is characterized by a principles-based approach that emphasizes market discipline and flexibility. Regulatory authorities collaborate to address the diverse needs of the financial sector while maintaining the overall system integrity.

In recent years, China's financial regulatory system has undergone significant reforms to address the challenges of a rapidly growing and complex financial sector. Key regulatory bodies include the People's Bank of China, the National Financial Regulatory Administration, the China Securities Regulatory Commission, and the State Administration of Foreign Exchange. Regulatory authorities work collaboratively to address emerging challenges and align the financial sector with broader economic development goals.

Exercises

1 Short answer questions

Directions: *Answer the following questions in your own words or with sentences from the text.*

(1) What are the features of financial risks?

(2) What are the features of financial crises?

(3) What are the main types of financial crises and their corresponding outbreak triggers?

(4) What are the purposes of financial supervision?

2 Term explanation

Directions: *Explain the following terms in your own words or with sentences from the text.*

(1) financial risk

(2) financial crisis

(3) financial supervision

(4) financial regulation system

3 Banked cloze

Directions: *Fill in the blanks by selecting suitable words from the following box. You may not use any of the words more than once.*

A. fluctuate	B. accurate	C. defaults	D. individual	E. financial
F. authorities	G. establish	H. various	I. contribute	J. assessment
K. privacy	L. monitoring	M. formulating	N. long-term	O. sustainable

Financial markets are exposed to financial risks due to (1) _____ macroeconomic forces, changes in market interest rates, and the possibility of sector or large company defaults. Volatility or equity risk may cause the price of a stock to (2) _____ suddenly. Volatility reflects stakeholders' confidence that market returns will match the actual valuation of (3) _____ assets and the market as a whole, while also introducing uncertainty about the fair value of market assets. Both (4) _____ and risks arising from changes in market interest rates may lead to a decline in the asset quality of financial institutions and even trigger systemic financial risks. In order to cope with these risks, financial institutions need to establish a sound risk management framework, including measures in risk assessment, risk (5) _____, and risk control.

Regulatory (6) _____ regulate the operation of financial markets, protect the rights and interests of investors, and reduce the occurrence of financial risks by (7) _____ and implementing relevant laws and policies. Among them, the formulation and implementation of green finance standards also contribute to the realization of (8) _____ development goals and promote the development of green finance products and services. The application of fintech brings new opportunities and challenges to financial risk management. On the one hand, fintech can provide more efficient and (9) _____ risk assessment and monitoring tools to help financial institutions better manage risks. On the other hand, the application of fintech may also bring new risks, such as information security risks and data (10) _____ risks.

4 Translation

Directions: *Translate the following paragraphs into Chinese or English.*

(1) Following the outbreak of a banking crisis, fears of a run lead to massive early withdrawals of deposits by depositors, forcing governments to raise reserve ratios, and banks to increase their liquid assets. When the financial sector as a whole becomes much less efficient in delivering services and the real cost of intermediation rises sharply, borrowers find credit expensive and difficult to obtain, and the credit crunch evolves into a contraction of aggregate demand and ultimately into a recession.

(2) 我国政府时刻发挥着监管金融市场的重要作用。近期，中国金融监管机构对维持粮食稳产保供（stable food production and supply）提出了具体的要求。要求加快农村信用社（rural credit cooperative）改革，强化风险防范化解，增强"三农"（agriculture, rural areas, and farmers）金融服务能力，为全面推进乡村振兴（rural revitalization）、加快建设农业强国（agricultural power）提供更强有力的金融支撑。

5 Project

Title: Enhancing Financial Resilience Along the Belt and Road Initiative—Navigating Financial Risks, Crisis Management, and Supervision

Instructions: Explore the financial dynamics of China's Belt and Road Initiative (BRI) initiated in 2013. Emphasize key milestones, financial risks, and crisis management. You can follow the following steps:

Step 1: Historical context of BRI (2013 onwards). Highlight BRI milestones and align with China's Reform and Opening-Up.

Step 2: Financial risks and crisis management in BRI. Identify risks, analyze historical crises, and evaluate government responses and financial supervision.

Step 3: Macro-level indicators. Introduce essential economic indicators for BRI countries, showcasing performance and challenges.

Step 4: Share insights, fostering a class discussion on navigating financial complexities in China's Belt and Road Initiative.

Supplementary Reading

Scan the QR code to find out more about the unit.

References

Bade, R. & Parkin, M. 2021. *Foundations of Microeconomics* (8th ed.). Beijing: China Renmin University Press.

Baldwin, R. 2016. The great convergence: Information technology and the new globalization. Cambridge: The Belknap of Harvard University Press.

Boulding, K. E., Kleinsorge, P. L. & Pen, J. 2023. Wage and salary. Retrieved Sept. 23, 2023 from Britannica website.

Carbaugh, R. J. 2022. *International economics* (17th ed). Beijing: China Renmin University Press.

Demekas, D. & Grippa, P. 2022. Walking a tightrope: Financial regulation, climate change, and the transition to a low-carbon economy. *Journal of Financial Regulation*, 8(2), 203–229.

Fernando, J. 2023. Opportunity cost: Definition, calculation formula, and examples. Retrieved Aug. 08, 2023 from Investopedia website.

Hayes, A. All about fiscal policy: What it is, why it matters, and examples. Retrieved Aug. 16, 2023 from Investopedia website.

Heilbroner, R. L. & Boettke, P. J. 2023. Economic system. Retrieved Aug. 10, 2023 from Britannica website.

Hubbard, G. R. & Obrien, A. P. 2016. *Microeconomics*. Beijing: China Machine Press.

Hubbard, G. R. & Obrien, A. P. 2022. *Microeconomics* (5th ed.). Beijing: China Machine Press.

Kaufman, G. 2001. The U. S. *Financial Systems: Money, Markets and Institutions*. Beijing: Economic Science Press.

Langdana, F. 2009. *Macroeconomic Policy: Demystifying Monetary and Fiscal Policy* (2nd ed.). Berlin: Springer.

Mankiw, N. G. 1998. *Principles of Economics*. Beijing: China Machine Press.

Mankiw, N. G. 2020. *Macroeconomics* (10th ed.). Beijing: China Renmin University Press.

Mankiw, N. G. 2022. *Essentials of Economics*. Beijing: Peking University Press.

Paul, R.; Krugman, E. 2021. International Economics: Theory and Policy. Beijing: Tsinghua University Press.

Reiss, J. Public goods. Retrieved July. 28, 2023 from *Stanford Encyclopedia of Philosophy website*.

Salvatore, D. 2019. *Introduction to international economics* (3rd ed.). Beijing: Tsinghua University Press.

Samuelson, P. & Nordhaus, W. 2012. *Macroeconomics* (19th ed,). Beijing: Posts and Telecom Press.

Taylor, J. B. & Weerapana, A. 2012. *Principles of Macroeconomics* (6th ed.). Beijing: China Renmin University Press.

Tuovila, A. Normal profit: Definition, formula to calculate, example. Retrieved Aug. 20, 2023 from Investopedia website.

Walsh, C. E. 2017. *Monetary Theory and Policy* (4th ed.). Cambridge: MIT Press.

陈孟熙，郭建青．2017．经济学说史教程（第 4 版）．北京：中国人民大学出版．

程霖．2023．从传统到现代：近代以来中国经济思想的变迁路径．经济思想史学刊，（1）：3-45．

冯伟．2019．微观经济学讲义．北京：北京大学出版社．

高鸿业．2010．西方经济学（宏观部分）．北京：中国人民大学出版社．

国彦兵．2020．经济学原理．北京：机械工业出版社．

韩可卫，冯兵．2014．微观经济学．北京：中国人民大学出版社．

何玉长编译．2006．牛津英汉双解经济学词典．上海：上海外语教育出版社．

教育部高教司组编．2014．西方经济学（微观部分·第 6 版）．北京：中国人民大学出版社．

李健．2016．微观经济学．北京：人民邮电出版社．

李晓红．2015．财经英语．北京：清华大学出版社．

刘辉煌．2015．微观经济学．北京：中国人民大学出版社．

刘玉平，储峥．2019．金融学．上海：立信会计出版社．

刘忠泽，赵丛．2010．经济学简明教程．北京：北京大学出版社．

卢照坤，徐娜．2014．微观经济学．天津：南开大学出版社．

References

骆志芳，许世琴．2013．金融学．北京：科学出版社．

宋利芳，张勇先，高宏存．2012．经济学专业英语教程（第3版）．北京：中国人民大学出版社．

谭淑霞．2015．微观经济学．北京：清华大学出版社．

王学文．2005．国际商务英语．北京：中国人民大学出版社．

杨玉生，杨戈．2015．经济思想史．北京：中国人民大学出版社．

张靖，张铁军．2021．金融英语教程（第3版）．北京：中国金融出版社．

赵晓雷．2022．中国经济思想史．大连：东北财经大学出版社．

朱孟楠．1999．国际金融学．厦门：厦门大学出版社．

Glossary

Unit 1

dismal	*adj.*	凄凉的；惨淡的；阴沉的
allocate	*v.*	划……给，分配……给
distribution	*n.*	（商品）经销，分销
alternative	*n.*	可供选择的事物
publication	*n.*	书刊等的出版、发行；出版物
agent	*n.*	原动力，动因（指对事态起重要作用的人、事物）
monopoly	*n.*	垄断；被垄断的商品（或服务）
aggregate	*adj.*	总数的；合计的
sector	*n.*	领域；行业
mechanism	*n.*	机制；方法
depletion	*n.*	损耗，耗尽
hypothesis	*n.*	假设
variable	*n.*	可变性；可变因素
intersect	*v.*	相交，交叉
toolkit	*n.*	工具箱
optimize	*v.*	使最优化
prioritize	*v.*	按重要性排列
incentive	*n.*	激励；刺激；鼓励
solar panel		太阳能电池板
interplay	*n.*	相互影响（或作用）
pharmaceutical	*adj.*	制药的

225

surplus	n.	过剩，剩余
revenue	n.	财政收入；收益
marginal	adj.	（主要指成本或收益）（与）微小（单位）变化有关的，由微小（单位）变化引起的
outweigh	v.	超过
fiscal	adj.	财政（尤指税收）的
recession	n.	经济衰退，经济萎缩
delineate	v.	（详细地）描述，描画；解释
leverage	v.	最大限度地利用，最优化使用
stimulate	v.	促使，促进；激发
vitality	n.	生命力；活力；热情
intervene	v.	插手，干预
prefix	n.	前缀
constraint	n.	限制
maximization	n.	最大化；极大化
equilibrium	n.	平衡
convert	v.	（使）转变
incur	v.	带来（成本、花费等）
oligopoly	n.	寡头垄断
excludable	adj.	不包括的；排他的
asymmetry	n.	不对称；不对等
subsidy	n.	补贴
devise	v.	发明；设计；想出
intricate	adj.	错综复杂的
tangible	adj.	有形的
counterpart	n.	相应的人或物
erode	v.	侵蚀
metric	n.	计量体系；衡量标准
denote	v.	预示，象征

contraction	n.	收缩
trough	n.	低潮
transaction	n.	（一笔）交易，业务，买卖
downturn	n.	（商业经济的）衰退，下降；衰退期
posit	v.	假设；认定；认为……为实
scenario	n.	（艺术或文学作品中的）场景
anticipate	v.	预期
pivotal	adj.	关键性的；核心的
panoramic	adj.	全景式的
dynamics	n.	动力
holistic	adj.	整体的
paradigm	n.	典范；范例；样式
formulation	n.	制订
validate	v.	证实；确认；确证
empirical	adj.	以实验（或经验）为依据的
verify	v.	核实
refrain	v.	克制；避免
justify	v.	证明……正确
ethical	adj.	道德的
prescriptive	adj.	指定的；规定的
degradation	n.	毁坏，恶化（过程）
robust	adj.	强劲的；稳健的

Unit 2

socioeconomic	adj.	与社会经济相关的
hinge on		取决于，依赖于
cater to		迎合；满足……的需求
alteration	n.	改变；变化

eradicate	v.	根除；消灭；杜绝
contemplate	v.	深思熟虑，苦思冥想
ideologist	n.	思想家；思想理论家
pursuit	n.	追求；寻找
disregard	v.	不予理睬；忽视
speculation	n.	推测，推断
manipulation	n.	（暗中）控制，操纵；影响
integrity	n.	诚实，正直
consent	n.	同意，允许
resonate	v.	产生共鸣；发出回响；回荡
feudalism	n.	封建制度；封建主义
regime	n.	组织方法；管理体制
absolute	adj.	绝对的；完全的；全部的
property	n.	所有物；财产；财物
courtier	n.	（尤指旧时的）侍臣，侍从，廷臣
entitlement	n.	（拥有某物或做某事的）权利，资格
manor	n.	庄园；宅第
primitive	adj.	原始的；远古的
fabric	n.	社会、组织或系统的基本结构
reciprocity	n.	互惠，互换
proponent	n.	倡导者，支持者，拥护者
ratiocination	n.	推理；推论
commentary	n.	注释；解释；评注；评论
subsequent	adj.	随后的；后来的；之后的；接后的
expenditure	n.	花费；消费；费用；开支
momentous	adj.	关键的；重要的；重大的
emergence	n.	起始；起源
immature	adj.	（行为）不成熟的，不够老练的，幼稚的

frugality	n.	（对金钱、食物等）节约的，节俭的
mirror	v.	反映；映照
enfeoffment	n.	领地授予；赐以封地
disintegration	n.	碎裂；解体；分裂
feudal	adj.	封建（制度）的
transformation	n.	（彻底的）变化，转变；改革
flourish	v.	繁荣，昌盛
invariably	adv.	始终如一地；一贯地
pertain	v.	存在，适用
persevering	adj.	坚韧不拔的；不屈不挠的
embrace	v.	欣然接受，乐意采纳（思想、建议等）；信奉（宗教、信仰等）
indispensable	adj.	不可或缺的；必不可少的
commoner	n.	平民
populace	n.	平民百姓；民众
detach	v.	（使）分开，脱离
valiant	adj.	英勇的；勇敢的，果敢的；坚定的
interventionism	n.	政府干预（政策）
impoverished	adj.	赤贫的；不名一文的
epitomize	v.	成为……的典范（或典型）
momentum	n.	推进力；动力；势头
spontaneously	adv.	自发地；非筹划安排地
veneration	n.	尊敬；崇拜

Unit 3

unveil	v.	（首次）展示，介绍，推出；将……公之于众
navigate	v.	找到正确方法（对付困难复杂的情况）
expertise	n.	专门知识，专门技能，专长
negatively	adv.	负向地
numerical	adj.	数字的；用数字表示的
antibiotic	n.	抗菌素；抗生素（如青霉素）
vertical	adj.	竖的；垂直的；直立的
horizontal	adj.	水平的；与地面平行的；横的
conversely	adv.	相反地；反过来
substitute	n.	代替者；代替物；替代品
complement	n.	补充物；互补品
gas-guzzling	adj.	耗油量大的
streamline	v.	精简使（系统、机构等）效率更高；（尤指）使增产节约
lead time	n.	从投产至完成生产相隔的时间；订货交付时间
inventory	n.	存货，库存
disrupt	v.	扰乱；使中断；打乱
optimal	adj.	最佳的；最适宜的
coordinate	n.	坐标
deviate	v.	背离；偏离；违背
halt	n.	停止；中止；暂停
unitary	adj.	单一的；形成单一个体的
diabetes	n.	糖尿病；多尿症
proportionally	adv.	成比例地；相称地

Unit 4

extract	v.	提取；获得
perceive	v.	认为；察觉
premise	n.	前提；假定
cumulative	adj.	累计的
albeit	conj.	尽管
self-interested	adj.	自利的
attainable	adj.	可获得的；可实现的
incentivize	v.	激励；刺激
coexist	v.	共存
fluctuate	v.	波动；变动
solicit	v.	征求；索求
subtract	v.	减去，删去；扣除
graphically	adv.	以图表形式
array	n.	大量；大群
explicit	adj.	显性的
implicit	adj.	隐性的
forgo	v.	放弃
mathematically	adv.	在数学上
inflow	n.	（资金、商品等的）流入
multiply	v.	乘；（成倍）增加
equation	n.	方程；等式
deduct	v.	减去
conjunction	n.	（引起某种结果的事物等的）结合，同时发生
entity	n.	实体
dominate	v.	控制；占优势
function	n.	函数

facilitate	v.	促进，促使；使便利
benchmark	n.	基准
metrics	n.	度量值；度量
incremental	adj.	增量的；增加的
dictum	n.	格言；名言

Unit 5

categorization	n.	分类；类别
virtual	adj.	虚拟的
differentiation	n.	区别，区分
hindrance	n.	障碍；阻碍
homogeneous	adj.	由同类事物组成的；同质的
predetermine	v.	预先决定；事先安排
surpass	v.	超过
exacerbate	v.	使加剧；使恶化；使加重
shutdown	n.	停业；停工
viable	adj.	可实施的，切实可行的
eliminate	v.	消除
spectrum	n.	范围；领域
exert	v.	施加；运用
compel	v.	强迫，胁迫；使不得不
deter	v.	制止；阻止
patent	n.	专利；专利权
entrant	n.	新加入者
align	v.	（使）一致
signify	v.	表示；意味着
discrimination	n.	歧视；区别
multitude	n.	众多

intrinsic	*adj.*	固有的；内在的
offset	*v.*	抵消；弥补；补偿
liquidity	*n.*	资产流动性，流通性
volatility	*n.*	波动性
proactive	*adj.*	积极主动的
prosecutor	*n.*	检察官；公诉人
conviction	*n.*	定罪
conspire	*v.*	共谋
leniency	*n.*	宽大处理
exempt	*adj.*	获豁免；免除（责任、付款等）
payoff	*n.*	收益；回报
matrix	*n.*	矩阵
tabular	*adj.*	表格的
opponent	*n.*	对手
ultimately	*adv.*	最终；最后
aptly	*adv.*	适当地
emission	*n.*	排放
divergence	*n.*	分歧
rectify	*v.*	纠正
internalize	*v.*	使……内化
grazing	*n.*	牧场；草场
free-rider	*n.*	搭便车者

Unit 6

entrepreneurship	*n.*	企业家精神；企业家（身份、行为）
maximal	*adj.*	最大的；最高的
complementarity	*n.*	互补性；补充；补足
piecework	*n.*	计件工作

barista	n.	咖啡馆服务员
demographic	adj.	人口的；人口统计的
legislation	n.	法规；法律
remunerate	v.	酬劳；付酬给
disposable	adj.	可动用的；可自由支配的
monopsony	n.	买方垄断
distort	v.	使变形；扭曲；使失真
dampen	v.	抑制，控制，减弱（感情、反应等）
depreciation	n.	（尤指财产因损耗而造成的）折旧贬值；（财产因时间而造成的）折旧
idle	adj.	闲置的
heterogeneity	n.	差异化
accessibility	n.	可接近性，易使用性
proximity	n.	（时间或空间）接近，邻近，靠近
amenity	n.	生活福利设施；便利设施

Unit 7

integral	adj.	必需的；不可或缺的
nominal	adj.	名义上的；有名无实的
proportional	adj.	相称的；成比例的；均衡的
intangible	adj.	无形的（指没有实体存在的资本性资产）
lever	n.	杠杆
assessment	n.	看法；评估
projection	n.	预测；推断；设想
intermediate	adj.	（两地、两物、两种状态等）之间的，中间的

Unit 8

complexity	n.	复杂性；难懂

galloping	*adj.*	迅速增加（或蔓延）的
velocity	*n.*	速度
plunge	*v.*	（价格、温度等）暴跌，骤降
unrest	*n.*	动荡
spiral	*n.*	螺旋形；螺旋形之物
detrimental	*adj.*	有害的；不利的
debtor	*n.*	债务人；借方
creditor	*n.*	债权人；贷方
frictional	*adj.*	摩擦的；由摩擦产生的
cyclical	*adj.*	周期的
mismatch	*n.*	错配；搭配不当
reside	*v.*	居住在；定居于
trauma	*n.*	精神创伤
diverge	*v.*	分歧，相异
amend	*v.*	修正，修订（法律文件，声明等）
cessation	*n.*	停止；中断
endogenous	*adj.*	内源性的；内生的
exogenous	*adj.*	外源性的；外生的
multiplier	*n.*	乘数
propensity	*n.*	（行为方面的）倾向；习性
coefficient	*n.*	系数

Unit 9

intertwine	*v.*	紧密相连
asymmetric	*adj.*	不对称的；不对等的
allocatively	*adv.*	以分配的方式；以分配为基础
proxy	*n.*	代表；代替物；代理人；受托人
depreciate	*v.*	贬值；跌价

inadvertently	adv.	无意地；不经意地
stifle	v.	压制
mitigate	v.	减轻，缓和
transparency	n.	透明，透明性
adept	adj.	熟练的，擅长的
exuberance	n.	快乐有活力的行为
grapple	v.	努力解决（问题）
conducive	adj.	使容易（或有可能）发生的
versatility	n.	多功能性；多才多艺；用途广泛
spike	n.	猛增，急升
tailor	v.	迎合，使适应；专门制作
eligible	adj.	符合条件的；有资格的
potency	n.	影响力；支配力；效力
stimulus	n.	促进因素；激励因素；刺激物
bubble	n.	泡沫（很可能持续不长的好景或好运）
nudge	v.	（朝某个方向）轻推，渐渐推动
spur	v.	促进，加速，刺激（某事发生）
affluent	adj.	富裕的
cushion	n.	起保护（或缓冲）作用的事物
impede	v.	妨碍，阻碍
suboptimal	adj.	次最优的；最适度下的；未达最佳标准的
vigilant	adj.	警觉的；警惕的；警戒的；谨慎的

Unit 10

mercantilism	n.	重商主义；商业主义
exploitation	n.	利用；开发；开采
afield	adv.	远离家乡；去远处；在远方
affiliation	n.	隶属；从属

amplify	v.	增强（声音等）；放大
sparsely	adv.	稀疏地；零星地
pervasive	adj.	遍布的；充斥各处的；弥漫的
levy	v.	征收；征（税）
shield	v.	保护某人或某物（免遭危险、伤害或不快）
retaliatory	adj.	报复性的；以牙还牙的
counteract	v.	抵制；抵消；抵抗
countervailing	adj.	抗衡的；抵消的
concession	n.	（尤指由政府或雇主给予的）特许权，优惠

Unit 11

evolutionary	adj.	进化的；演变的
realm	n.	（活动、兴趣、思想的）领域
merit	v.	值得；应受
superficial	adj.	表面的，外面的；粗略的；肤浅的；浅薄的
denomination	n.	面额，面值；计价
coincidence	n.	巧合；同时发生；相符
testament	n.	证据；证明
bead	n.	中间有孔的小珠子
cryptocurrency	n.	加密电子货币
hoard	v.	贮藏；囤积
succinctly	adv.	简洁地；简便地
substantive	adj.	有实质性的；重大的
deteriorate	v.	变坏；恶化；退化
inversely	adv.	相反地；倒转地
decentralize	v.	使分散；分权；去中心化
implement	v.	实施；贯彻；执行
advent	n.	出现；到来

herald	v.	预示
traverse	v.	穿过，越过
deterrent	n.	遏制；威慑
redeem	v.	赎回
compounding	n.	复利计算
appreciation	n.	升值

Unit 12

intermediary	n.	中间人；调解人
liability	n.	欠债，债务
recipient	n.	接受方
infrastructure	n.	基础设施
distressed	adj.	烦恼的；忧虑的；苦恼的
hazard	n.	危险，危害
close-knit	adj.	关系紧密的；紧密团结的；组织严密的
fiduciary	n.	受信托者，受托人
derivative	n.	衍生物，派生物
hub	n.	中心；枢纽
prospectus	n.	（企业的）招股简章，募股章程
venue	n.	（公共事件的）发生场所，举行地点；会场
auction	n.	拍卖
vocalization	n.	说话，发声
congregate	v.	聚集，集合

Unit 13

connectivity	n.	连接（度）；联结（度）
royalty	n.	版税
buffer	n.	缓冲物；起缓冲作用的人

relinquish	v.	（尤指不情愿地）放弃，交出（权力、职位等）
bloc	n.	集团，阵营
strain	n.	重负，压力
suspension	n.	暂缓；推迟
demise	n.	终止；失效；倒闭
dissolution	n.	（商业协议的）终止
peg	v.	使工资、价格等固定于某水平
domicile	n.	（尤指正式或法律意义的）住处，住所，定居地
subsidiary	n.	附属公司；子公司
capture	v.	（用文字图片）准确记录（或表达）
intricacy	n.	错综复杂的事物（或细节）
credit	n.	（付入银行账户的）存款金额，贷记
debit	n.	借项
unilateral	adj.	单方的
remittance	n.	汇款金额
vulnerable	adj.	（身体上或感情上）脆弱的，易受……伤害的
contingency	n.	可能发生的事；偶发（或不测、意外）事件
reversible	adj.	可逆的；可恢复原状的
susceptible	adj.	易受影响的；敏感的；过敏的
bidding	n.	（尤指拍卖中的）出价，喊价
tatter	n.	碎片
deploy	v.	有效利用；调动
aftermath	n.	（战争、事故、不快事情的）后果，创伤

Unit 14

turmoil	n.	动乱；骚动；混乱
trigger	v.	发动；引起；触发
omnipresent	adj.	无所不在的；遍及各处的

财经基础英语
Basic English for Economics and Finance

variability	n.	可变性；易变性；反复不定
jeopardize	v.	冒……的危险；危害
ubiquitous	adj.	普遍存在的，无所不在的
emanate	v.	产生；表示；显示
pertinent	adj.	有关的；适当的；相宜的
geopolitical	adj.	地缘政治学的
portfolio	n.	（个人或机构）投资组合
escalate	v.	（使）逐步扩大；不断恶化，加剧
transient	adj.	短暂的；转瞬即逝的
repercussion	n.	（间接的）影响，反响，恶果
self-inflicted	adj.	自己造成的；加于自身的
dysfunction	n.	功能失调
liquidation	n.	清算
sovereign	adj.	有主权的；完全独立的
subprime	adj.	（贷款）次级的
brunt	n.	主要压力；影响最大的部分
cripple	v.	严重毁坏（或损害）
crunch	n.	（突发的）不足，短缺；（尤指）缺钱
run	n.	（到银行）挤兑，挤提
stagnation	n.	停滞；不发展；不进步
bailout	n.	紧急财政援助
austerity	n.	（经济的）紧缩；严格节制消费
contagion	n.	（不良事物的快速）传播，蔓延，扩散
clearinghouse	n.	（银行之间的）结算所
fraudulent	adj.	欺骗的，欺诈的
delineation	n.	（详细的）描述，解释
mandate	n.	（政府或组织邓选举而获得的）授权

Terms

A

absolute advantage	绝对优势
accelerator	加数模型
accounting profit	会计利润
ad valorem tariff	从价关税
aggregate demand	总需求
aggregate supply	总供给
anti-dumping duty	反倾销税
appreciation	货币升值
asset price	资产价格
average cost	平均成本
average product	平均产量

B

balance of payments	国际收支平衡
bank reserve	银行储备金
banking system	银行体系
bankruptcy	破产
barrier to entry	进入壁垒
base year	基年
bid-offer spread	买卖价差

bond	债券
break-even	不盈不亏的
break-even point	盈亏平衡点
budget constraint	预算约束
business cycle	商业周期
business process reengineering	业务流程重组

C

capital	资本
capital adequacy	适量资本
capital inflow	资本流动
coefficient	系数
command economy	计划经济
commodity exchange	商品交易
comparative advantage	相对优势
compounding	复利
compound tariff	复合关税
consumer behavior	消费者行为
consumer equilibrium	消费者均衡
consumer price index (CPI)	消费者价格指数
consumer surplus	消费者剩余
consumption	消费
cost	成本
cost-benefit analysis	成本－收益分析
countervailing duty	反补贴税
credit crunch	信贷紧缩
creditor	债权人；贷方
cross elasticity of demand	需求交叉弹性

crowding-out effect	挤出效应
cryptocurrency	加密电子货币
cyclical unemployment	周期性失业

D

debt crisis	债务危机
debtor	债务人；借方
default	拖欠，不履行债务；违约
deficit	赤字
deflation	通货紧缩
demand	需求
demand curve	需求曲线
demand schedule	需求表
deposit	存款
depreciation	折旧；贬值
devaluation	货币贬值
development economics	发展经济学
diminishing marginal utility	边际效用递减
diminishing returns	报酬递减；收益递减
distribution	经销；分销
division of labor	分工
dominant equilibrium	占优均衡
dominant strategy	优势战略；占优策略
duopoly	双头垄断

E

econometrics	计量经济学
economic growth	经济增长

economic interdependence	经济相互依存
economic profit	经济利润
economies of scale	规模经济
elasticity of demand	需求弹性
entrepreneur	企业家
environmental economics	环境经济学
equilibrium	均衡
equilibrium price	均衡价格
exchange rate	汇率；兑换比率
explicit cost	显性成本
externality	外部性

F

factor market	生产要素市场
fiduciary	信托的；信用的
financial innovation	金融创新
financial market	金融市场
financial sector	金融机构
financial statement	财务报表
fiscal policy	财政政策
fixed cost	固定成本
fixed exchange rate	固定汇率
floating exchange rate	浮动汇率
fluctuation	波动
foreign exchange	外汇
forward guidance	前瞻性指引
freedom of entry	进入自由
freedom of exit	退出自由

frictional unemployment	摩擦性失业
fundamentals	基本因素
futures	期货

G

game theory	博弈论
gross domestic product (GDP)	国内生产总值
GDP deflator	国内生产总值缩减指数
GDP per capita	人均国内生产总值
globalization	全球化
gross national product (GNP)	国民生产总值

H

hedge funds	对冲基金；避险基金
hyperinflation	恶性通货膨胀

I

imperfect competition	不完全竞争
implicit cost	隐性成本
income effect	收入效应
income elasticity of demand	需求收入弹性
income inequality	收入不平等
indifference curve	无差异曲线
inferior good	低档货
inflation	通货膨胀
inflation rate	通货膨胀率
information asymmetry	信息不对称

insurance premium	保费
interest rate	利率
intermediary	中间人
international balance of payments	国际收支平衡
international economics	国际经济学
inventory	存货；存货价值
involuntary unemployment	非自愿失业

L

labor	劳动，人工
land	土地
lender	贷款人
liability	债务，负债
liquid assets	流动资产
liquidity	（资产的）流动性；（资产的）折现
loss	亏损

M

macroeconomics	宏观经济学
marginal cost	边际成本
marginal product	边际产量
marginal propensity to consume (MPC)	边际消费倾向
marginal revenue	边际收入
marginal revenue product	边际收入产品
marginal utility	边际效用
market	市场
market economy	市场经济

market equilibrium	市场均衡
market failure	市场失灵
market power	市场支配力
market price	市场价格
market structure	市场结构
merger	合并
microeconomics	微观经济学
minimum wage	最低工资
mixed economy	混合经济
monetarism	货币主义
monetary economics	货币经济学
monetary imbalance	货币失衡
monetary policy	货币政策
monetary system	货币体系
money supply	货币供给
monopolistic competition	垄断竞争
monopoly	垄断
moral hazard	道德风险
mortgage	（尤指购房的）按揭，抵押贷款
multiplier	乘数
multiplier effect	乘数效应

N

national income	国民收入
natural monopoly	自然垄断
natural rate of unemployment	自然失业率
network effect	网络效应
non-performing	（经济运转上）不良的

normal good	普通商品
normal profit	正常利润
normative economics	规范经济学

O

oligopoly	寡头卖方垄断
open market operations (OMOS)	公开市场业务
opportunity cost	机会成本
option	期权
out-of-pocket expenses	现付费用
ownership	所有权

P

Pareto optimality/efficiency	帕累托最优状态 / 效率
pay off table/matrix	支付矩阵
perfect competition	完全竞争
Pigouvian taxation	庇古税
position	头寸
positive economics	实证经济学
preferential tariff	优惠关税
premium	保险费
price discrimination	价格歧视
price elasticity of demand	需求价格弹性
price elasticity of supply	供给价格弹性
price maker	价格制定者
price taker	价格接受者
principal	本金
prisoner's dilemma	囚徒困境

private cost	私人成本
process innovation	生产工艺革新
producer price index (PPI)	生产者价格指数
producer surplus	生产者剩余
product innovation	产品革新
production	生产
production factor	生产要素
production function	生产函数
profit	利润
profit maximization	利润最大化
prohibitive tariff	禁止性关税
promissory note	期票
property right	产权
protective tariff	保护性关税
public goods	公共品
purchasing power	购买力
purchasing power parity	购买力平价

Q

quantitative easing	量化宽松
quantity demanded	需求量
quantity supplied	供给量

R

real GDP	实际国内生产总值
regulatory capture	接管
rediscount	再贴现
rent	租金

reserve ratio	准备金率
reserve requirements	储备金要求
retaliatory tariff	报复性关税
returns to scale	与生产规模成比例的收益
revenue	收入
revenue tariff	收入关税

S

scarcity	稀缺
shutdown point	停产点
social cost	社会成本
Special Drawing (SDR)	特别提款权
specific tariff	特定关税
speculation	投机
spillover effects	溢出效应
steady state	稳定状态；稳态
stock market	股票市场
structural unemployment	结构性失业
substitution effect	替代效应
supply	供给
supply curve	供给曲线
supply schedule	供给表
supply-side economics	供给侧经济学
surplus value	剩余价值

T

tariff	关税
the AD-AS model	总需求与总供给模型

OPEC	石油输出国组织
total cost	总成本
total product	总产量
total utility	总效用
transfer payment	转移支付

U

uncertainty	不确定性
underwriting	承保，（保险）认购
unemployment	失业
utility	效用

V

variable cost	可变成本
voluntary unemployment	自愿失业

W

wage rate	小时工资率

Z

zero lower bound	零利率下限

教师服务

感谢您选用清华大学出版社的教材！为了更好地服务教学，我们为授课教师提供本学科重点教材信息及样书，请您扫码获取。

▶▶ 最新书目

扫码获取 2024 **外语类**重点教材信息

▶▶ 样书赠送

教师扫码即可获取样书